William Playfair

The History of Jacobinism - Its Crimes, Cruelties and Perfidies

Vol. I

William Playfair

The History of Jacobinism - Its Crimes, Cruelties and Perfidies
Vol. I

ISBN/EAN: 9783337073503

Printed in Europe, USA, Canada, Australia, Japan

Cover: Foto ©ninafisch / pixelio.de

More available books at **www.hansebooks.com**

HISTORY

OF

JACOBINISM.

THE

HISTORY OF JACOBINISM,

Its CRIMES, CRUELTIES and PERFIDIES:

COMPRISING

AN INQUIRY

Into the Manner of Diſſeminating, under the Appearance of

PHILOSOPHY AND VIRTUE,

PRINCIPLES

WHICH ARE EQUALLY SUBVERSIVE OF

ORDER, VIRTUE, RELIGION,
LIBERTY AND HAPPINESS.

BY WILLIAM PLAYFAIR.

With an Appendix,

BY PETER PORCUPINE,

Containing a Hiſtory of the American Jacobins, commonly
denominated Democrats.

VOL. I.

" Hiſtory, who keeps a durable record of all our acts, and exer-
" ciſes her awful cenſure over *all ſorts of ſovereigns*, will not forget
" theſe events."

BURKE.

PHILADELPHIA:
PRINTED FOR WILLIAM COBBETT, NORTH SECOND
STREET, OPPOSITE CHRIST CHURCH.
1796.

PUBLIC.

SINCE the following work has been in the prefs, a publication on the French revolution has appeared from the pen of Dr. Moore, in the Dedication of which, addreffed to his Grace the Duke of Devonfhire, the author contrives to procure a fort of teftimony of his impartiality. Had this declaration of impartiality come directly from the author himfelf, it would have been un-neceffary to have noticed it; but this praife, he fays, came from a near connection of his Grace, whom he met with in a foreign country.

It is evident, that the elegant and accom-plifhed Duchefs is meant to be underftood as be-ing the perfon to whom this allufion is made; and the world at large may be apt to think, that the fpecies of impartiality to which the Doctor lays claim, on account of the compliment paid

to

to him, was that praiseworthy impartiality which, in cases of doubt or uncertainty, suspends opinion.

The learned Doctor gives the world to understand, through the medium of a dedication to his Grace, that his first work on the revolution of France, was such a production, that democrats thought him an aristocrat, and aristocrats called him a democrat.

Upon this the Doctor makes his own commentary, and in doing so is exceedingly favourable to himself, by insinuating that candour and impartiality are always liable to this hard fate.

With respect to the opinion of aristocrats, respecting the Doctor's democracy, it would be wrong and absurd to dispute it, because there are no grounds for going upon in doing so; and as for the opinion of democrats, there are so many different classes of them, that it would be strange indeed, if some of those classes should not find the Doctor too much of an aristocrat. Brissot and Petion, and even Hebert (who murdered the amiable friend of the Duchess of Devonshire, the man who murdered the Princess of Lamballe) were all accused of favouring royalty; so that it is not impossible that the Doctor might be suspected by such persons of being too much attached to government and order.

I should think it improper to take any notice of this Dedication, were it not in very legible characters a declaration, that all those persons

who

who shew themselves decided in their opinion with regard to the revolution, *are guided by partiality and prejudice.*

Whether it was a banter, or a compliment, which the relation of his Grace meant to bestow on the Doctor, I cannot pretend to determine; but I confess I am inclined to think, that it was not intended as a compliment. I am just as much at a loss to know with what intention he has retorted the equivoque upon the Duke, by claiming his patronage in a dedication, in which he plainly says, that he cannot decide between the murderers and their victims, between order and anarchy, between crime and misfortune.

The judge who condemns may be as impartial as the judge who acquits, but the judge who, with full evidence before him, forms no opinion at all, puts up a singular sort of claim to impartiality. When Robertson spoke of the cruelties of the Spaniards in Mexico, and Gibbon of the crimes of Roman emperors, they condemned, like men, actions which disgraced mankind. They did more still, they condemned the governments that permitted such iniquities, and they spoke with indignation of that love of gold, and that corruption of manners, which led to such disgraceful excesses. Like Addison, they thought that to be neutral in such a cause was a crime, and they would have joined in saying, with the austere and virtuous Roman,

I should have blush'd, if Cato's house had stood
Aloof, or flourish'd in a civil war,

The

The Doctor, ambitious perhaps of beginning a
new career in hiftory, means to feparate caufes
and effects, for he takes care, while he makes the
facrifice to decency, of condemning the maffacres,
not to hint at the firft caufes of thofe exceffes, although that is one of the profeffed objects of his
publication.   This conduct may appear to fome
to be like that of the French heroes themfelves,
who, though they difapprove of individual acts of
cruelty, never fhew any difapprobation of the
principles and opinions which led to them.

As the Doctor did not, probably, intend to
give the world merely what is to be found in the
Gazettes, he fhould have endeavoured to fhew
whether *there is*, *or is not*, any connection between the principles by which the revolutionifts
are guided, and the crimes which they have committed; it would have been a very great fatisfaction to know the opinion of an *impartial writer*
on this important fubject, and to know whether
the principle of revolt, as laid down in the Rights
of Man, *had*, *or had not*, any connection with the
facred revolts which brought a virtuous king to
the fcaffold, and a whole nation to mifery and
want.   Briffot was more frank than the Doctor,
and told us plainly, that the holy duty of infurrection, when ill applied, leads to anarchy and
mifery.

An Englifh nobleman can fcarcely think it an
honour to be fuppofed to patronife a work, the
author of which boafts that he is fo free from
prejudice, that his readers cannot find out, whether he approves moft of thofe who pillaged,
                                              plundered,

plundered; and maffacred the nobility of France,
or of thofe who were pillaged and plundered.
The Doctor, as a modern philofopher, may look
with indifference on the events of this world, and
fee the murderers and the murdered with the
fame eye, or the fpoilers and the fpoiled ; but in
his quality of an abftract philofopher, it is difficult to conceive why he preferred dedicating his
work to the Duke, when it might have been done
with juft as much propriety to the old woman
who fells ballads and oranges under his Grace's
wall; for as he balances between the nobleman
and the fans culotte, there can be no evident
moral reafon for preferring the nobleman. As
to the *material advantages, the advantages of
truckling commodity*, that's another affair, and is
beft known to the Doctor himfelf.

The French Jacobins have one good rule
amongft many bad ones, and Englifh noblemen
would not do amifs if they were to adopt the
fame rule---" We fear our open enemies lefs, and
we hate them lefs," fay the Jacobins, " than
thofe *gens gris* * who are of no decided opinion."
The doctor profeffes himfelf to be one of thofe
grey gentry who are ufelefs to all parties, dangerous to all parties, and fcouted by all parties.

But though the compliment paid to the Duke
in this Preface is equivocal, as applied to the perfon to whom it is addreffed, the intention of the
addreffer is abundantly evident, as it regards himfelf; for as it is not to be fuppofed that the Duke
accepted of the Dedication without knowing the

* Alluding to the colour grey, which is neither black nor
white.

b   nature

nature of the work, (though it is very probable
he did) it leads indirectly to the conclusion, that
one of the first noblemen of England for rank
and fortune, and for the reputation of an honest
man, is as undecided about the merits of the
French murderers as the man whom he appears
to protect.   Such a manœuvre is not unworthy
of a real Jacobin, and if the Doctor had not accused himself of belonging to the *grey squad*, I
should have done him the honour of putting him
in the class of frank Jacobins, whom, I own, I do
not dislike so much as that non-descript fuilant,
who conceals his want of feeling under the appearance of impartiality.

With regard to myself, I own that I should be
ashamed to have it doubted on which side of the
question I am, when speaking of limited monarchy compared with French republicanism, founded on their declaration of the rights of man.

I neither deprecate, nor despise criticism ; I expect it, and I know I am within its reach.   I
know that there is a periodical publication, *
which watches with *critical* care to attack whoever
presumes to meddle with Jacobinism.   An attack

---

* The publication here alluded to, is to be considered as
one of the periodical efforts, made by writers on the side of
French liberty.   It seems to have three objects in view, to
bring down its more candid rivals, to bespatter all who write
on the side of monarchical government, and to protect publications that come from a certain quarter.   England is the
only country in Europe where fame and falsehood are sold
out by the sheet at regular periods, and where the oracles, as
in times of old, conceal their persons, but proclaim aloud
their temples.

upon

upon me is, therefore, a matter of courfe : only
let thofe, who fet about it, recollect, that the
French nation itfelf has begun to turn againft Jacobins, and treats them worfe now than ever I
did, though I have excited their criticifm and fevere reproach for faying, that peace could not
be made with Jacobins. Well, the French nation fays the fame thing now, that I did then;
and will, before long, fay what I do now : *that the
abfurd and dangerous declaration of the rights of
man muft be exploded; and that, in order to avoid
the laft exceffes of Jacobins, it will be neceffary to
abandon and difclaim their firft principles.*

June 4th, 1795.

CONTENTS.

VOLUME I.

═══════════

CHAP. I.

CHAP. II.

CHAP. III.

CHAP. IV.

CHAP.

CHAP.

CONTENTS.

c

PREFACE.

AS I have frequently obtruded myfelf upon the notice of the public by writing againſt the Jacobins; as I have been held up by ſome of thoſe perſons, who, under the protection of an anonymous criticiſm, have attributed to me motives which probably might ſeem to them natural ones, judging of others by themſelves; I conſider it as a ſort of juſtice I owe to the public and to myſelf, to ſhew, that when I wrote about the Jacobins, I knew ſomething of my ſubject, that when I wrote againſt them, I had the reaſons which I alledged, and that I am a greater advocate for liberty than thoſe who call themſelves reformers and patriots. Though I have a ſovereign contempt for thoſe perſons who make ſo free with the truth as to ſay that I am paid by government; or, that becauſe I am of opinion that it is impoſſible to make a proper peace with the Jacobins, I am a promoter of eternal war.

I appeal, therefore, to the hiſtory of the ſect againſt which I have written, to ſhew that the moſt diſorderly and cruel deſpotiſm was exerciſed under

under the appearance of liberty and juſtice; that far from being an enemy to liberty, I am its friend, though I do not chuſe to join in the general deception that has been practiſed with regard to what has been called French liberty.

If thoſe ſupporters of the French ſyſtem were to be attacked with the ſame deciſive tone of voice that its enemies have been, they would certainly be called advocates of deſpotiſm; for though they might be impoſed upon during the firſt two years of the revolution, they ſcarcely can be ſuppoſed not to have opened their eyes ſince. The admirers of Bailly, of Rabaut, and Barnave, can they be admirers of their murderers? The Briſſotins, can they admire the party of Robeſpierre? and, finally, when one flood of murderers followed another flood in ſucceſſion, like the waves of the ſea; and when wearied out with their own exceſſes, the party of Robeſpierre, and the Jacobin club itſelf has been deſtroyed; when the whole of France is filled with aſtoniſhment and drenched in blood, by the abominable ſyſtem againſt which I write, can it yet have any advocates? No, it can have no ſincere ones, and I can venture to ſay, that there is not a man in Europe who knows any thing of the matter, who will not confeſs that it has been a ſyſtem of abominable cruelty and deſpotiſm, under the falſe appearance of liberty.

Thoſe perſons, then, who, in defiance of example, are ſtill the advocates of this plan of government, muſt excuſe me if I attribute to them other motives than a love of liberty; I ſhall change

change my opinion if any one of them will stand up, and either refute my arguments, or deny my facts; I challenge no man through bravado, nor an idea of possessing any superior abilities, but I defy the whole set of Jacobin amateurs in the present case; I trust only to truth and justice for victory.

Uniform in my attachment to the cause of order and of liberty, I have been, and I shall always remain, reserving to myself, however, the right of .... those who mistake the shadow for the re........ .... for the thing. I do n..... .... com....... the simple m..... .... phrases of a Brissot, and I have told him so to his face; nor do I conceive liberty to consist in a systematic disobedience of law, and invasion of property, which I always conceived the jacobin system to be, and so I always plainly expressed myself to jacobins themselves, till all law being overturned, there did not remain even the shadow of protection, and when open force put an end to argument.

I am an enemy to violent reforms, and of consequence a friend to those smaller reforms, which, without touching the main principles of the constitution, keep it pure; and I confess that it is not without considerable mortification, that I see a sort of indifference with respect to smaller abuses, which at last bring on a general change of things.

The following history is intended as much to shew, that abuse of power and disregard to public

lic opinion brings on revolutions, as to fhew the
danger that attends them when they are brought
on.   When abufes in the adminiftration of juftice
creep in, which it is the bufinefs of the legiflature to reform, but which it will not reform,
then men are naturally led to wifh for a reform
in the legiflature itfelf.   Had the court of Verfailles been willing to make the reforms wanted,
it would not have been itfelf reformed and deftroyed.   Had the nobility and the clergy been
willing to facrifice to the juft claims of their fellow citizens, thofe privileges which were ufelefs
and unjuft, we fhould not now have feen them
ftraying like vagabonds over the face of a ftrange
country feeking for bread.   It is impoffible for a
leffon to be written in more legible characters,
and it muft be confeffed, that till the Parliament
of England fhews a difpofition to crufh the abufes
which exift and augment in many departments
of the ftate, the mouths of thofe who cry out for
reform will never be effectually ftopt.   Such
would be the way effectually to crufh Jacobinifm,
as it would have been the way to prevent its
ever exifting; and until it is put in practice, Jacobinifm never will effectually be crufhed.   It affumes many forms, and is fo well adapted for
deceiving, that reafon will never completely get
the better; men will prefer a fyftem that offers
change to one, that preferves abufes, which,
though known, are not attempted to be reme-
died, for when men are difcontented, reafon has
not its full effect.

Men fhould learn to know, that if a difregard
to experience and to what has hitherto exifted is
a dan-

a dangerous thing, a too bigoted regard for precedent is dangerous alfo; although the fyftem of deftroying all the old laws to eftablifh an entirely new code is dangerous to the greateft degree, it is by no means well, to piece and patch eternally at old laws, and to render juftice fo expenfive, and the law fo unintelligible, that men can never expect to obtain their right, except in matters of great importance.

There are but two voices in the kingdom on this head, and the one is that of the whole nation, lawyers excepted; the other is the voice of the lawyers themfelves only. Let our judges vindicate themfelves, and root abufe up, fo that the peaceable citizen may enjoy tranquillity; it is not by fhewing a juft indignation at the practices of a vile attorney now and then, whofe imprudence, rather than his villainy, draws down punifhment, but it is by putting it out of their power to commit fuch abufes; it is the caufe that fhould be attended to rather than the effect. Our law lords will be liftened to when they apply to parliament, and furely the people will be relieved from a great burthen.

If there are abufes in the church, let the clergy themfelves fet the example of a reformation, and then they will avoid thofe terrible confequences which are but too certain to arrive when force is refulted to.

A revolution is fomething like a battle, when it begins, a general defire of conquering the enemy is the only feeling, but in the courfe of
the

the action, man comes to be oppofed to man,
and perfonal danger makes ferocity too often
take place of what at the beginning was only the
love of one's country.   Following the comparifon ftill farther, pillage and plunder fucceed to
victory, and individual motives overtop the feeling of general intereft.

Perhaps it may be confidered by fome, as making rather an apology for the infamies with
which the hiftory of the revolution is filled, to
fay that they are natural to revolutions; but it is
by no means meant as fuch, neither can it be fairly fo conftrued.   It is a melancholy fact, that in
every great and wealthy nation there are numbers of men capable of the worft of crimes; and
a revolution, by letting loofe the bonds which
held fociety together, gives the weight and importance to the criminal and bold, which
in other times are acquired by an attention
to the duties of the peaceable citizen.   To fay,
then, that horrors and villainies are natural to
revolutions, is no more an apology for the per-
petrations of the crimes, than to fay, that where
there is no law nor police in a country, there
will be robbery and murder, would be making
an apology for robbers and murderers.

That human nature furnifhes men who will
commit crimes during a revolution, is not fo extraordinary as that their exceffes fhould be defended by men in other countries, who are fo
feelingly alive to the fmalleft appearance of oppreffion that may take place in their own government.

                                           The

The cafe is not one that requires any nicety of reafoning. Suppofe that two or three perfons have been banifhed from this country for practices that were unfavourable to government, and let it even be granted, that their punifhment was too fevere, yet it is not the men who have feen with indifference above 900 perfons put to death in one month in Paris, where fifty at a time crowded in oné accufation, and who did not know each other; perfons under the age of fixteen and above that of eighty, mounted this fame fcaffold, enveloped promifcuoufly in the fame judgment.

A government that committed fuch crimes is the objeft of the admiration of certain men; the fame government which punifhed with an unjuft feverity, was guilty of permitting the horrible cruelties at Nantes, at Lyons, and over the whole country; cruelties for which there did not exift any name, in any language, until their perpetrators invented, by way of ironical pleafantry, names which will eternize their infamy,* and aftonifh pofterity.

I fay that it is more extraordinary, that there are men to vindicate the fyftem which has led to fuch crimes, than that men were found capable of committing them; but it is ftill more ftrange, that they fhould be the fame men who are fo tremblingly alive to whatever may appear to be rigour in the government of this country.

* Noyades, Baignades, Deportation, Vertical Deportation, Republican Marriage, &c.

Such

. Such men will fay, that the exceffes of Carrier, of the revolutionary tribunal, and the maffacres of the month of September, were not the acts of government. I firft begin with maintaining, and fhall prove it in the courfe of this work. that they were juft as much the acts of the government as any other acts fince the 10th of Auguft; but even if they were not, is it not the bufinefs of government to protect men from fuch things? or does it deferve the name of government, which does not afford protection againft fuch injuftice?

In following the manœuvres of the Jacobins, we find them changing fhape every time there is any occafion; when it is their view to be cruel and ferocious, they talk of juftice and the general good, of the fword of the law falling upon the heads of the guilty. When it is not their immediate aim to feek victims, they fpeak of patriotifm oppreffed, and *errors committed through an excefs of virtue and zeal,* and not from bad intention. Thus Hebert, and Danton, and Briffot, changed their language, when from oppreffors they thought they were oppreffed: and thus Tallien, that commanded maffacres at Bourdeaux, and of September at Paris; Collot d'Herbois, the moft cruel of all men, at Lyons; and Barrere, who had alternately been fubfervient to all the factions, fpoke of the tyranny of Robefpierre. They were right in that, but they were wrong when they pretended to exempt themfelves from having participated in thofe tyrannies; and if there is now a more moderate fyftem, it is only becaufe it is their intereft that it fhould be fo.

When

When men differ in opinion, facts muft be reforted to, and it is with this view that I appeal to facts, to prove that the firft principles of the revolution have led to a horrible fyftem of defpotifm under the appearance of liberty, and that thofe who are friends to the revolution, to whatever epoch of its exiflence they attach their admiration, are either ignorant of the fubject, or they are themfelves lovers of anarchy and defpotifm.

It is unfortunate for mankind, that the duration of the horrors of the revolution diminifhes the impreffion which they make on men's minds. The execution of the Marquis de Favras made more impreffion upon the people at the time, than when in later times feventy victims mounted the fcaffold in one fingle day; and when the ancient magiftrates known and revered for their exemplary lives, were executed by twenty-four at a time,

In other nations the impreffion is likewife diminifhed, for as horror is always accompanied with aftonifhment, and aftonifhment with novelty, it follows, that not only the horror is greatly diminifhed as novelty wears off, but the fyftem of France, fince the fall of Robefpierre, is called a mild and moderate one : three years ago it would have been accounted terrible. Such is the effect of habit on the minds and feelings of mankind !

In proportion as men feel lefs abhorrence for the crimes of the revolution, it becomes more and more neceffary to expofe them in their full
extent;

extent; and to fhew, that under the outward
appearances of patriotifm and virtue, men may
be led to participate in every fort of crime, and
lay a foundation for a feries of horrors, to which
they can fix no bounds nor termination.

Diforder muft naturally be prolonged greatly
by that corruption of manners which is the confequence of it, and no term can be looked for but
that which fatigue and depreffion of every kind
will at laft bring on, when fome tyrant or other
will feat himfelf in the throne, and the government of one will be preferred to that of many. It
is not when a country is fatigued out with every
fort of vexation and exertion, that men are capable of fettling a free government, for which
many things are abfolutely neceffary, that cannot be found in a nation at the end of a violent
ftate of agitation. The fullen repofe enjoyed under an arbitrary monarchy is the only thing that
is practicable after anarchy has worn out and degraded a people. The reign of Robefpierre
could not have taken place in the firft moments
of the revolution; but Robefpierre came too foon
to reign long as a fingle defpot, fome more fortunate tyrant will fill his place on a future day,
under whofe yoke all parties will indifcriminately
fall: it will then become the intereft and the
wifh of that defpot to enjoy fome tranquillity
himfelf, and let his people enjoy fome repofe.
By this means a new fyftem of order will in time
arife, and it will be well for the nation, if in feveral ages after they arrive at fomething like liberty
and happinefs.

In

In the following hiftory I have paffed over, in a very flight manner, fome of the moft ftriking moments of the French revolution, becaufe my only view has been to fhew the refults and confequences of the principles and practices of the revolutionifts. I have endeavoured to fhew, that the foundation of all the evils is to be found in the principle of perpetual infurrections, and the affiliations of clubs, which fupported each other; for without the clubs infurrections would not have been fo practicable, and without infurrection the clubs would have foon been deftroyed.

It is rather extraordinary, that of all the boafted rights of man, that of infurrection (which, allowing even that it were a right, is a very unpleafant and inconvenient one) is the only one which the revolution feems to have fully eftablifhed; for all the other rights have been moft fhamefully trampled upon and abufed.

The revolution is not now half fo interefting as in its firft moments, becaufe, though it is very curious and ufeful to know, how defigning and wicked men brought it on, there is nothing very curious nor ufeful in obferving thofe perpetual executions, plots, and confpiracies, which rife out of a ftate of depravity and confufion of interefts. At the beginning of the revolution, its fate depended upon the conduct of a few individuals, and an accident might have perhaps put an end to the reign of anarchy, becaufe diforder was not become the natural ftate of the majority of the inhabitants; but now the fall of a leader and of a whole party only makes room for more leaders and more parties,

There

There are in the interior of France at prefent above a million of its inhabitants who may be called brigands, or free-booters, and who cannot live but by diforder. Should peace be made, a million more will return from the armies, who will then be in the fame fituation. So that we may fafely fay, that one half the male inhabitants of France, who are of age, are and will be interefted in maintaining the reign of diforder; the probability of its continuance can, therefore, not be very doubtful.

I therefore, avowing my attachment to order and to liberty, fuch as we enjoy here in England, am an enemy to Jacobinifm, and the revolution *in all its ftages*, as being equally oppofite to juftice and real liberty; and it is to facts that I appeal to prove, that NO PORTION OF MANKIND HAS EVER BEEN LESS FREE NOR LESS UPON AN EQUALITY THAN UNDER THE MUCH-VAUNTED FORM OF A REPUBLIC.

HISTORY

OF

JACOBINISM.

CHAP. I.

*General circumstances that favoured the propaga-
tion of the Jacobin system.—Decline of the feudal system.—Changes in the state of society in
Europe.—Nobles hated in the towns.—Causes
why the clergy became obnoxious also.—Reasons
for discontents against the government itself.—
Novelty and innovation arise naturally from
discontent with the state of things.*

NO sect ever arose so suddenly, or carried its
principles into practice with so much violence,
rapidity, and success, as that of the Jacobins: in
less than four years from its first rearing its head,
this sect has overturned the first monarchy in
Europe for extent, population, and riches; has
made a complete revolution in property, both
moveable and immoveable; overturned the religion and laws, and effected a total change in the
manners of the people; so that the nation, which
for its politeness and urbanity used to serve as a
model for others to copy from, is become an ob-

A.   ject

ject of fear and horror, having turned favage and cruel, and trampled under foot whatever has been refpected in ancient and modern times.

That confufion and diforder are eafily brought about, is well known ; that it is much eafier to deftroy than to create, was never doubted ; but even deftruction and ruin could not have been fo completely accomplished in fo fhort a time, had not the ftate of fociety, and the nature of things, been favourable to that ruin and deftruction. When the hurricane comes, thofe trees which are moft expofed by their fituation, or rotten in themfelves, fall firft, and fall with violence ; and fo it was with France : for had not the nature of things in general, and many particular circum-ftances favoured the jacobinical efforts, violent as they were, their fuccefs could not have been fo rapid.

Every religious fect, and every political fyftem, had extended by degrees, and required ages and centuries to produce great effects, or extend widely, till in 1789 the Jacobins began their ef-forts ; their leaders did not exceed a dozen in number, and in lefs than four months the foun-dations of a powerful monarchy, eftablished during more than a thoufand years, were under-mined, and both the religious and political creed changed throughout the kingdom. The church of Rome, too, hitherto always encroach-ing on thofe who profeffed its faith, faw its autho-rity denied, and its profeffions invaded, whilft what remained of the feudal fyftem was nearly done away. Want of time, and not want of power, alone prevented this work of invafion
and

and deftruction from, even then, being complete; what has followed fince has not been lefs aftonifhing, and if the rage for deftruction feems abated, it is only for want of materials to deftroy.

To follow the rapid and wonderful courfe of thefe events, will be lefs our bufinefs, than to examine into, and fearch out, thofe extraordinary exertions, both open and concealed, which have been the caufes of a revolution fo unexampled in the hiftory of mankind.

They muft be ignorant indeed, of the proportion which exifts between human force and natural caufes, who imagine that either the genius or efforts of men could have produced fuch a change, had not the nature of things been favourable to it. To ufe a familiar, but an apt expreffion, thofe revolutionifts failed with the wind and tide in their favour. Before, therefore, we begin to follow the Jacobin fyftem, fince it became vifible and active, and began to predominate, we muft fearch for thofe general and particular circumftances which preceded it, and were fo much in its favour.

Our firft object fhall be to trace out the *general caufes*, fome of which we fhall find not to be of a very recent origin. The particular circumftances exifting in France at the time when this great revolution commenced, will come naturally next in order : we fhall then have the canvas upon which the Jacobins fet to work with fuch advantage.

When

When the incurfions of the favage nations from the north had deftroyed the Roman government in the weft, the invaders wanted both the means and the inclination to eftablifh another in its place. To be poffeffed of a richer foil, and enjoy a better climate than their own, was the firft aim of the barbarians; which, when by force of arms they had wrefted from the former mafters of the world, they endeavoured to preferve, by extinguifhing thofe arts and habits, which had, as they imagined, rendered the Romans effeminate and weak. It required but a fmall effort in favages to remain in a favage ftate; and thus the unpolifhed conquerors, mixed with the polifhed conquered, foon became a race of ignorant and unprincipled oppreffors and oppreffed.

The natural freedom of men who roamed about for exiftence, and who had by their bravery got poffeffion of thofe countries, which had formed but one ftate under the Roman government, did not admit of any regular or fixed obedience in times of peace to their chiefs, whom in war they had without murmuring followed and obeyed. Diforder and pillage amongft themfelves were the natural fruits of this ftate of things, and protection, not againft a diftant and powerful foe, but againft their neighbours, became abfolutely neceffary. Europe then became peopled with nations, perpetually employed in attacking the property of their neighbours, or defending their own; and from this ftate of things arofe, by a progreffion very eafily to be conceived, a fort of fyftem, by which the lower claffes were fubfervient to the lords or barons, in a manner very difgraceful to human nature, and which muft have been very terrible

terrible to thofe who were obliged to fubmit to it. This which has been called the feudal fyftem, extended all over Europe, and it is wonderful how nearly thefe fmall governments (for fuch they may not improperly be called) refembled each other, even in the moft diftant parts. In the fouth of France and the north of Scotland the rights of the proud baron were nearly the fame.

The feudal fyftem which was fo univerfally eftablifhed, and fo completely put in force, was well adapted to the ftate of mankind at the time. It was natural that lands taken from their ancient proprietors by the fword, fhould be preferved by it; as the fear of the old inhabitants reduced to flavery, but not exterminated, obliged the man who poffeffed the lands, and thofe who lived upon and cultivated them, to make one common caufe in their defence. Thus the original tye between the landlord and the vaffal was founded not only on mutual intereft and advantage, but on abfolute neceffity. It is not to be wondered at, if in times of grofs ignorance, and when there were neither arts nor commerce, the vaffals became totally fubmiffive to thofe mafters, to whofe protection they looked up for fafety, and upon whofe bounty they depended for bread. This double claim made it extremely eafy for the lords of lands to increafe what they termed their rights; fo that befides flaves, who were completely the property of their mafter, free-men, as they were called, became at laft little better than flaves. In another place, when it will become our tafk to relate the horror and aftonifhment which an enumeration of thofe rights occafioned, we fhall mention fome of them; at prefent, it is

fufficient.

fufficient to fay, that the power of life and death,
and of judging in all civil and criminal cafes, lay
in the ignorant barons, whofe knowledge was
confined to the art of war and plunder, and who
placed their honour upon objects very different
from that of adminiftering impartial juftice:
men who even defpifed the knowledge neceffary
to render them capable of judging between their
dependents, and who, though not ignorant of
their own privileges, paid very little attention to
the rights of others.

The feudal fyftem, like many others, as it approached towards perfection (not perfection in
goodnefs) in itfelf,* brought along with it the
caufe of its decline; for, being fully eftablifhed,
and having procured men fome degree of fecurity
and repofe, their condition ameliorated by degrees, they then became more wealthy, and the
chiefs found it their intereft to attach their followers to them by affection, rather than to truft
to force alone; fo that, towards the eleventh
century, when the crufades engaged almoft all
the barons in Chriftendom, in an enterprife which
coft them vaft fums of money, and did not very
immediately touch the intereft of their vaffals, as
the petty wars between neighbours always had
done, the lords became ftill more dependent upon
the vaffal both for money and perfonal affiftance.
Thus did the ftate of men become better by degrees; but from the feudal fyftem, when in its full
force, to any thing like liberty, the road is too long

* A fyftem may be very perfect in itfelf if all the parts
anfwer each other, although the whole may be founded in
grofs error and imperfection.

for that small progress to have been very perceptible.

During the same period, commerce and the population of towns had operated likewise in diminishing the rigour of feudal chiefs; but, in proportion as the proprietor felt his power disputed and curtailed, he employed himself in attaching his vassals or retainers to his person. The means of doing this, very fortunately for the chiefs, increased as it became more necessary; for, as riches and civilization advanced, the barons reaping the first fruits of both, had the means of increasing the attachments of their adherents both by gifts, and by exciting admiration and esteem. Men, as they become polished, attach themselves more easily from favours received; and it must not be forgotten that, during all this time, as the administration of justice remained in the hands of the barons, and as wars amongst neighbours, though diminished both in their violence and frequency, were not at an end, the protection of the chief was by no means become useless, although considerably diminished.

Thus, then, till towards the fifteenth century, the feudal system was supported by the mutual interest and the mutual inclination of the lord and the vassals; and, therefore, its evils and enormities, though felt, were submitted to without much murmering; and though by this time the different kings of Europe had established their power on a pretty solid basis, yet, as the prince depended upon his barons for support in war, he took care, while he endeavoured to weaken their priviliges with respect to himself, not to touch

too

too feverely upon their power with the vaffals, otherwife he might in the end have deftroyed himfelf.

Charles 8th. The first Standing Army.

It was not, then, till Charles the Eighth of France eftablifhed a ftanding army, the firft in modern Europe, that the barons felt their importance with their prince and with their vaffals equally diminifhed. Soldiers regularly difciplined, and conftantly paid, were far fuperior to labourers taken from their ufual occupations. This inferiority was foon felt, and foon followed by great effects; the fovereign foon fet in earneft about humbling the haughty lords, on whom he no longer totally depended, and whom individually he was now able to reduce to obedience. Occafions were found where the opprefled vaffal appealed to his fovereign, and many exertions of power were found to have originated in fuperior ftrength, and neither in natural right, in mutual agreement, nor in mutual intereft.

The manners of the times ftill, however, favoured feudal authority to a great degree. The proprietors of lands lived upon their eftates, and continued to have many dependents from affection or from fear. The money arifing from the rents of land was fpent amongft thofe who cultivated them, and even a confiderable portion in entertaining them; fo that there feemed to be a very intimate connection, both in intereft and good fervices, between the proprietor and thofe who lived on his eftate. This was, perhaps, in the progrefſion of things one of the moft happy periods; it was not, it is true, the golden age, nor was it a refined one, but it was an hofpitable one.

one. That ferocity of manners which makes hatred and fear predominate in the human breast, had difappeared ; men began to have many of the conveniences and fome of the luxuries of life, and that focial feeling of man to man, which is one of the moft agreeable of which our nature is capable, was felt without alloy ; a feeling which in our prefent ftate of falfe refinement, and luxurious mifery, we feldom have. Let us dwell a moment on that happy period in the hiftory of the human race, when half the people of a county affembled with their lord to enjoy the banquet, or fhare the fports of the field ; when mutual affection and mutual utility encouraged bounty, and fweetened obedience ; when neither a difference of manners, nor of interefts, feparated the landlord and the tenant fo widely, as to deftroy thofe enjoyments which both could partake of, and enjoy together.

This was a happy, but from its nature not a durable ftate of things. The landlord, as he loft his own importance, became himfelf the vaffal of his king, and followed the court, from which he, in his turn, fought favour, or implored protection ; fo that by degrees, neither his revenues, which were fpent in following the court, nor the perfonal accomplifhments, nor the protection of the lord, ferved to attach his tenants to his fortune or his perfon. The connection became then merely a mercenary one, and the proprietor of the grounds was little known but by the harfh and hard exactions of his fteward,* or by his arbitrary

trary

* In France the bailli, who very abfurdly had the power of adminiftering juftice in inferior cafes, in his mafter's ab-

B   fence

trary and domineering conduct, and when as if
by accident the mafter paid a vifit to the feftive
hall of his anceftors, it was but a difgufting ex-
hibition of luxury, pride, and effeminacy, which
only ferved in general to augment the difcontent
and humiliate the feelings of his tenants. This
laft change may be dated from the time that
Louis XIV. came to the throne; and it is from
that time, that whatever was abfurd or unjuft in
the feudal laws was called to mind, and the rights
of the lord *(les droits du feigneur)* were held up
as an object of hatred and ridicule.

Louis 14.

Happily for England, this picture applies to it
but very imperfectly for many reafons, of which
the firft certainly is, that our conftitution having
reduced every fubject to the fame level as a man,
what was abfurd or unjuft in the feudal laws has
been done away; neither is Englifh hofpitality
in the country yet at an end. Our rich proprietors receive a better education than they did in
France, and comprehend much better the mutual
obligations of landlord and tenant. The fize of
England too, and the fuperior conveniency of
travelling, is in our favour; and a portion of the
year is always fpent in the country; whereas in
France, many nobles never vifited their diftant
eftates at all; and as from our court there is lefs
to hope and *much lefs to fear,* it is not neceffary
even for the courtiers to be always there. Let us
rejoice that this is fo, and join in wifhing that it
may continue; for, *the perfonal weight and influence*

fence; during the laft century they were in many cafes always abfent. The baillies were a great curfe.

of

of men of property on their estates is one of the closest, Important Observation.
and certainly one of the most pleasant bonds by which
order and subordination in society are upheld.

Although the feudal lords in France had thus
lost every kind of real importance with their
tenants; by a sort of folly which it is difficult
to account for, they had preserved the abfurd
power which they poffeffed in former times,
although the exercife of it was generally in a
great meafure laid afide: this ferved to humiliate and difpleafe one part of the human race,
while it was no fervice to the other, and only oc-
cafionally gave rife to individual acts of oppreffion
and infult.

During the former order of things, that is, till
the revolution, all murmurs or difcontents about
feudal rights were ftifled, but we fhall foon fee
with what dangerous confequences it was attended; for fome of the feudal laws and cuftoms
were as good and wife as others were bad; the
fame fate, however, as in moft cafes of innovation, awaited both: all were deftroyed, and
what is worfe, the legal invafion of property
began, and a door opened for moft of thofe in-
vafions which we are to fee the hiftory of in the
prefent work. The worft of feudal rights border
upon ravifhment, robbery, and murder; and
there are others as facred, as fair, and as much
founded in wifdom, as any other of the laws refpecting hereditary property: how dangerous
was it then to comprife under one name, rights
of fo different a nature, which endangered the
poffeffion of all property, and put in queftion
the

the equality of man ; a queſtion ſo dangerous, if improperly handled and if ill underſtood !

Let rich men and law-givers learn from this, that it is not enough to make good laws, that ufelefs or improper ones *ſhould be repealed ;* it is not enough that they condeſcend not to put what is ufelefs or unjuſt in force; they ought to renounce the power of doing it, and the good and wholeſome laws, · and a good conſtitution, will not have to fear reproach on account of bad laws, nor be endangered by, their application. In the moral, as well as the natural world, the rotten often carries the ſound along with it; and it is probable that if there is any efficacious receipt for preventing revolutions, it is an attention to this circumſtance.

Whilſt the proprietors of land had loſt their importance, and their old friends in the country, they had acquired no new ones in the towns. Their time was ſpent in following a court, where they acted only the part of dependents, and their money in paying ſervants who felt for them no perſonal attachment, or in other expences and pleaſures, which being generally carried beyond their power to pay, rendered them contemptible, and created them enemies.

It is to be added to this, that ever ſince the days of Louis XIV. the nobility and gentry *(les nobles et la petite nobleſſe)* had been in the habit of running into ſcandalous and enormous expenſes, which, inſtead of paying, they availed themſelves of their credit at court to be exempted from paying their creditors, whom they found various

means

means of harraffing, tormenting or evading.
But the noble did not, in leaving his inferiors in
the country, to follow and cringe before his fuperiors at court, leave his pride behind him; for
every petty privilege that gave a fort of fuperiority at public places, was kept up with an invidious induftry. All places of honour or profit in
church and ftate, were occupied, as were alfo
thofe in the navy and the army, by the nobility;
and the *roturicr*, as he was called, by way of   *roturier*
contempt, learned from his infancy to hate a race
of men who feemed born only to humiliate and
opprefs the fimple citizen.

It is a fortunate circumftance for fuch perfons
as poffefs honours and privileges which they do
not merit, when they have good fenfe or modefty fufficient to let them remain forgotten;
but the noble in France had not this advantage
under the moft affable and familiar outward
fhew, he reminded his inferiors of their relative
fituations, and of *his* nobility. If fuch was the cafe
in the common affairs of fociety, when any real affair was on the carpet, it was fifty times worfe;
then the *roturier* was fure to feel and pay dear for   *roturier*.
his inferiority, and in cafe of any injury received,
redrefs was generally out of his reach; if he appealed to the king in council, he had ten chances
to one againft him, and in parliament or court of
juftice, compofed of nobles who thought it not below their dignity to be folicited by thofe who had
caufes to determine (except in fuch flagrant cafes
as would have thrown open difcredit upon the
judges), the fupplicating noble had always the
better chance.

Could

Could the noble for one day have laid aſide the prejudices with which he had been brought up; and could he have calculated, like a wiſe and reaſonable man, how ill it became his dignity, how uſeleſs it was to his intereſt, and how hurtful to ſociety, that ſuch privileges ſhould exiſt, he certainly would have bluſhed for himſelf, and have abandoned them for ever; but this moment of reflection never came, or if it did, it was when it was too late.

Thoſe errors into which the nobles of France in general fell, more through want of thought than bad intentions, only ſerved at the end to heap coals of fire upon their heads; for every thing, either ridiculous or unjuſt, was enregiſtered in the minds of their enemies, and proclaimed at laſt with a loud voice; nobody could defend ſuch abuſes, and the order of the nobleſſe, inſtituted for good reaſons at firſt, and ſtill uſeful under proper regulations, became odious and deſpiſed.

what reaſons? for what uſe?

We ſhall frequently have occaſion to remark, how eſſential it is for the peace of ſociety, to prevent the advocates of anarchy from having the appearance of reaſon on their ſide, as by that they bring over to their party the innocent and the well-intentioned.

Clergy.

During the above period, the power of the clergy, formerly ſo great, had experienced a diminution, ſo far as it depended on opinion, not very unlike that which we have been deſcribing relative to the order of nobles; and this fall in their importance had ariſen from the conduct of its members being neither adapted to the original
ſpirit

ſpirit of the religion which they profeſſed, nor to the nature of the times in which they were living.

In the dark ages, when the precepts of our Lord and Saviour were firſt preached over the far greater portion of Europe, many abuſes crept in, which in thoſe dark, ignorant, and ſuperſtitious times, tended rather to aſtoniſh and create reſpect than otherwiſe. The apparent auſterity and manners of the clergy, their ſuperior knowledge and learning; but, above all, *l'eſprit du corps*, with which they were all filled, kept up the intereſts of the church with increaſing brilliancy and reputation for many centuries. The lower orders of the prieſts, crafty and intereſted, inſinuated themſelves into the good graces of individuals; and as independent of the advantages of ſuperior education and riches, they had their time at their command, they improved with great aſſiduity thoſe moments of weakneſs when men are ready to grant to their prieſts what they feel they owe to their God. Thus the church grew in riches, in power and pride. This unnatural order of things could not be permanent, the increaſe of knowledge, and the neglect which ultimately attends whatever is not intrinſically good, muſt have in time brought it to an end, but many circumſtances haſtened its fall.

Many of the ceremonies of the Church of Rome began to be conſidered as uſeleſs parade, and the wealth and luxury of the dignified clergy, who appeared in days of ceremony before the public in a blaze of gold, but ill imitating the poverty, and ſimplicity of life of their Divine Maſter:

Mafter : were now looked upon as a reproach to themfelves, and an infult to thofe who contributed to their fupport.

Proteftant

The progrefs which the Proteftant religion had made, the induftry and happinefs of thofe who profeffed it, as well as the good fenfe of men, which begins to exert itfelf as foon as the barriers of fuperftition are broken down, promoted an inquiry into the origin, as well as the application of fuch prodigious wealth, and it was foon difcovered that it had arifen from a fyftematical warfare, carried on at all times and on every occafion by the members of the Romifh Church, upon the minds and property of the weak and fuperftitious. Often had the widow and the orphan been reduced to beggary to fupport the licentious and finful indolence of a convent. The application of the immenfe revenues of the church, amounting to near twenty-five millions fterling, when examined into, was found to be not more pure than their origin; the far greater portion being employed to pay the high clergy, who were enormoufly rich, or to maintain indolent and luxurious monks; and a very fmall part applied to the payment of the poor and virtuous curates, who did all the hard duties of the church, though they received fo few of its good things.

25 millions

monks

curates.

high Clergy.

Many of the high clergy went into all the fafhionable vices of the age, one of which was to turn religion itfelf into ridicule, at the fame time that they neglected moft of thofe moral duties which are impofed on every member of fociety, but more particularly on men whofe bufinefs

nefs ought to be to inftruct and improve others by their precepts and by their example.

The felfifhnefs of the clergy, in matters of intereſt, was but ill calculated to conciliate the minds of their fellow citizens, who confidered, that if men in a ſtate of celibacy required ſo much money, and were ſo tenacious of its poſfeſſion, thoſe who had families to maintain, and were obliged to pay them, were but in a pitiable ſtate,

It may not here be amiſs to obſerve, that one thing which in former times was ſo well planned for the aggrandifement of the church of Rome, tended at laſt to accelerate its fall. The poverty of that portion of the clergy, confiſting of men who were continually going like poor dependents, or honourable beggars, into people's *mendicant* houſes, and who were to be found at every table, even ſharing his cruſt and fallad with the peafant, though formerly refpected as being of ſuperior knowledge and breeding to the maſter of the houſe, now excited a mixture of pity and contempt; they now appeared ignorant, vulgar, and cringing, and even amongſt the very inferior claſs of citizens, were become objects of ridicule; ſo that thoſe emiſſaries who formerly were very uſeful as the ſpies and runners of their ſuperiors, now drew down upon the whole body of the clergy a ſhare of that contempt which their own conduct and behaviour inſpired.

To ſuch as have never been in a Roman Catholic country, this picture may appear exaggerated, but it ſo happens, that (without pretending

to enter into the merits of the two branches of the
fame religion) there is not to be found in any
Proteftant country, men who refemble thofe of
whom we fpeak.* The pooreft curate in England, fpeaking in a general manner, is a character greatly fuperior, and in fpite of his cottage,
his ragged children, and his fcanty income, there
is no comparifon between them as to dignity of
character, and even in politenefs of behaviour. The feeling, too, which every man has
towards the Proteftant curate, on reflecting that
he has the fame intereft with himfelf, that he has
a family and a home, and is not continually
prowling for food, and meddling with the people's affairs, is greatly in his favour.

The policy of the Church of Rome has generally been very profound, and there is not a doubt
but that the ceremonies of its religion would have
experienced fome changes, according to the fpirit
of the times, had it not unfortunately been one of
its tenets that the fovereign pontiff was infallible;
any change or modification would therefore have
been inconfiftent with the articles of its faith, it
therefore was neceffary to leave things as they
were; and though the head of the church had
the prudence, in general, to fet afide, without
remorfe or ceremony, what did not fuit the times,
many of the clergy in their own parifhes had not

* So much were this fet of low abbés difliked, though
people tolerated them, that it was a vulgar and general belief that they brought ill luck to every houfe they frequented, and probably this belief had a more real foundation than
the prejudice that fome people have againft *black cats.*

that

that good fenfe,* and by this means drew down
ftill more difpleafure and contempt upon thofe
who were very relaxed in their obfervance of
their own duties, and very rigorous towards
others.

It was not unnatural that the French fhould
embrace the firft opportunity to copy their rivals,
the Englifh, and their neighbours, the inhabitants of Switzerland, in curtailing a little the
forms of their religion ; and we fhall accordingly
fee, that they did not let the firft occafion flip, but
in this, as in all other things, they did not know
where to ftop, and inftead of reforming, rooted
out all religion, and at once became as intolerant
to the clergy and their doctrines, as they had formerly been to thofe who prefumed to differ from
thofe doctrines. The French nation has difgraced
itfelf at all times by the extremes into which it has
run, and the maffacre of the Proteftants, in the
time of Charles the Ninth, is of the two lefs difgraceful than that of Sept. 1792, under the
aufpices of the Jacobin faction. The former was
lefs difgraceful, as being by the orders of a fingle
defpot, and executed upon men of a different perfuafion, than for the whole of France to fit down
peaceably and quietly with the imputation of
having in cool blood maffacred their own priefts,
without even a fhadow of complaint againft them.

Maffacre. 6.9th

Sept. 1792

---

* When the curate of St. Sulpice, in Paris, refufed
Chriftian burial to the body of Voltaire, the old Marechal
Duc de Richelieu obferved, " that curate is an old woman
" who does not underftand his trade *(c'eft un cagot)* : he
" fhould have pretended to have converted Voltaire, and re-
" ceived him into the church, all the parifh would then have
" taken it for a miracle, and believed more than ever."

In the former cafe, the orders of a cruel king were executed by his trembling flaves; in the latter, a portion of the people, as volunteers, converted themfelves into monfters, and executed, with a hardy and unrelenting cruelty, their abominable intentions, without the plea either of neceffity or of ignorance. The guilty hand which figned the order for the murder of the Proteftants, could fet a term to the maffacre, but a nation converted into murderers, knows not how nor where to ftop. This fhould be a leffon to thofe who ftir up the people, and may ferve as a fort of anfwer to thofe who are continually fpeaking of the vice and depravity of kings, and of the virtues of republicans.*

If the people at large were prepared for adopting, with pleafure, a change in the feudal and religious fyftems, to which may be attributed, in a great degree, the eafe and rapidity with which Jacobin principles fpread, we fhall find that they were not lefs indifpofed againft the forms of government itfelf, which gradually had become liable to many objections.

The French nation was originally one of the freeft in Europe; but not to go farther back than the time of Charlemagne, the right of the people to be reprefented by their deputies, at the affembly of the ftates general, was a fort of magna charta, as no taxes could lawfully be laid on without the confent of this affembly. Here was

Charlemagne

* Thefe were the common topics of the Democratic leaders for the fitft three years, till Robefpierre filenced all parties at once by his travelling guillotine.

a clear

a clear and folid foundation laid for the rights
and liberties of the fubject. It would be tedious
and foreign to our fubject, to fhew by what ftra-
tagems this privilege had been fet afide, and that
affemblies which fhould have been held twice a
year, were not held once in a century; and that
even when called, their purpofe was defeated by
the intrigues of the court, which fet the reprefentatives of the different orders at variance.

How bad kings abufed uncontroled power, is
not to be inquired into, becaufe it cannot be
doubted; but without feeking farther back than *Louis. 14.*
Louis XIV. we fhall fee how he involved his people in war, and loaded them with taxes, for his
whims, his pleafures, or his vengeance; how to *war*
the miferies of expenfive wars he added the injuftice and cruelty of profcribing fome hundred
thoufands of his moft induftrious fubjects, by revoking the edict of Nantz; how he eftablifhed *Revocation*
on a more firm bafis than ever the right of ban- *of E. of Nantz.*
ifhing or imprifoning his fubjects by letters de *Lettres de cachet.*
cachet, for which punifhments his fovereign will
and pleafure was the only reafon he had to give:
added to all this, the abufes already fpoken of *abufes of*
amongft the nobles and the clergy being protect- *Nobles and*
ed by the crown, the latter fhared in the odium *Clergy*
incurred by the other two.

The minds of men were thus prepared for a
new order of things by thofe general caufes,
which had been increafing in force for fo many
centuries; to thefe we have yet to add the more
recent and more particular caufes that operated at
the time when the revolution broke out, and
ce t inly

certainly our furprife at its violence and rapidity will be very confiderably diminifhed, when
we find fo many caufes operating, *in one direction*,
and that direction in favour of novelty, and under the idea of procuring happinefs and liberty.

C H A P.

CHAP. II.

*Ruinous confequences of the borrowing fyftem—Mr.
Necker comptroller-general—His pride and ambition—Madame Necker's hatred to the nobility—
Bad policy of the court with refpect to Mr. Necker's adminiftration—Monf. de Calonne fucceeds
him—Calonne's miftakes—The finances ruined—
Calonne's difgrace—The Notables—States General propofed as the only means of arranging the
finances—General difcontents increafe—American war, its confequences upon the public mind—
Archbifhop of Sens minifter—His blunders—Duke
of Orleans chief of a faction—Necker recalled.*

IN addition to thofe general caufes which had
more or lefs operated a change of opinion all over
Europe, with refpect to the laws and government,
we have to enumerate fuch others as were felt
only in France; or which at leaft had no immediate connection with the other nations of
Europe.

The mode adopted by France, as well as by
fome other nations, of borrowing money to defray the expences of war, it is obvious to every
reafoning and calculating man, if not ufed with
wifdom and moderation, is not only capable of
bringing about revolution, but muft inevitably
do fo. As the advantages refulting from war
(when any do refult, which is not always the
cafe)

cafe) are generally but temporary and small;* and as the burdens laid upon the people to pay the interest of loans are permanent and great, they naturally accumulate and increase. The power or capacity of bearing burdens is limited in every nation, but there is no limit to the embarrassments that may be brought on by borrowing; on the contrary, the more that a remedy for the evil becomes necessary, the more difficult does its application become, and that not in a simple but in a compound proportion. A multiplication of taxes not only draws the money from the industrious, but by augmenting the number of the agents of government, is vexatious, and diminishes the number of productive labourers.† It diminishes also the value of money, and thereby renders what may be called the *efficient portion* of the revenue insufficient, so that the wants and the embarrassments of the state are augmented with regard to the daily expenses.

The manner in which both France and England have seen their expenditures increase, is a proof of the justness of what we have been remarking; for since the beginning of the borrowing plan, their annual expenses have increased beyond any former example.

---

* The proper object of war is not to procure advantage, but to prevent loss. Robbers only make war to gain by it, therefore it is not fair, nor does the fact justify any calculation of gain resulting from war. The burdens are, therefore, in fact, only so much actual loss without any deduction.

† See the great Adam Smith's definition of productive labourers in his book on the Wealth of Nations.

The

The revenues of England, at our revolution in 1688, amounted to scarcely two millions a year; at that time our debts were too inconsiderable to be mentioned, so that the annual expenses were under two millions. Since we began borrowing money, not only have we contracted an annual expense of ten millions for interest, but our yearly expenses amount at present to more than five millions, for what we call a peace establishment,* that is to say, twice and a half its amount only one hundred years ago.

1688

In France, the progression would have been nearly the same as to expenditure as it has been in England, had not a bankruptcy during the minority of Louis XV. under the regency of the Duke of Orleans, reduced the debts contracted in the time of Louis XIV. so that, though their practice of borrowing began nearly thirty years before we adopted the same method in England, the beginning of the present debt of France may be dated rather from the year 1722, than from the arrival of Louis XIV. to the throne, at which time their revenues amounted to five millions sterling;† before the revolution they a-

Bankruptcy
Orleans Regent

1722

* It is in vain to lay this diminution of the value of money, as many people do, to the increase of the quantity of gold and silver in Europe alone; first of all, because in many countries, where gold and silver are not wanting, it has not taken place; and likewise, as at the time when South America was first discovered, and more gold came than at any other period of equal duration, the depreciation was not so rapid as it has been since loans and paper came in use.

† One hundred and twenty-five millions Tournois in the year 1665.

D   mounted

mounted to twenty millions fterling ; but as the expenditure exceeded the revenue about two millions and a half, we fhould fay twenty-two millions and a half.*

Befides the bankruptcy in the time of the regency, a great portion of the loans made in France confifted in life annuities *(rentes vigageres)*,† therefore the debts of France did not accumulate fo rapidly as our's, which accounts for their expenditures not increafing fo rapidly, and adds weight to what we have afferted with refpect to the evil tendency of perpetual loans for temporary purpofes.

The increafe of the expenfes of government, and confequently of the burdens upon the people, is in any ftate attended with great inconveniences and hardfhips ; not only does the mode of levying the taxes become vexatious, complicated, and oppreffive, but all tranfactions with other nations, in the way of commerce, become lefs advantageous and more difficult ; and as the price of every thing gradually increafes,‡ the time is

* Four hundred and eighty millions revenue, and five hundred and thirty-five millions Tournois of expenditure, in 1788.

† The ultimate advantage of borrowing on annuities is very great, but it cannot be done to great extent in England. A finking fund, equal to five per cent. on the capital borrowed, however, anfwers the fame purpofe. See a Comparifon between Annuities and Perpetual Loans, by Mr. Playfair, publifhed in 1786 by Debrett, Piccadilly.

‡ It is this that makes a bottle of good ale dearer now than a bottle of claret was in Scotland or Ireland thirty years ago.

brought

brought nearer when no farther fale of goods to other nations can be expected, on account of the highnefs of their price.

It would be tedious, and certainly here unneceffary, to dwell upon this fubject, as we ourfelves feel from experience, that every new loan of money is attended with many inconveniences; and as it is plain, that an accumulation of inconveniences muft finifh with deftroying the fyftem in which it arifes; juft as the man who has continually recourfe to mortgaging his property, or his time, muft in the end finifh by ruining himfelf, however great his refources may have originally been.

The taxes in France had increafed to a degree that, under a bad adminiftration and a defpotic government, made them extremely heavy and vexatious.* The mode of letting them out to *Farmers General.* farm was, in every refpect, diftreffing to the fubject, and oppreffive; for under an arbitrary government, what redrefs can an individual expect in cafe of injuftice, by going to law with a company compofed of fixty of the richeft men in the kingdom, who held the court itfelf in dependence, by the advances made, or rather which they pretended to make?—Such was the company of farmers general in France, who employed 22,000 clerks, fpies, and emiffaries, who paid *Twenty two thoufand Clerks Spies &c* monthly into the royal treafury half a million fterling on account, and at the end of the year the balance of what might be due to govern-

* A free people may bear equal burdens with much lefs inconvenience, becaufe they know the amount of the evil, and, in cafes of oppreffion, may expect juftice.

ment.

ment.   Oppreffion was not only to be dreaded, but expected from fuch a body;* and accordingly it exifted, and difcontents multiplied on all fides againft the court, to the extravagance of which every evil was imputed.

Sale of Nobility & Places

From the time that Louis XIV. had adopted the method of raifing money, by felling patents of nobility and places of every fort, men who were not born to honours or to riches, found themfelves cut off from every fair chance of acquiring them, at the fame time that they could not help obferving, that when there were burdens to bear, they were thrown by preference upon their backs.   The mortification arifing from this was great; but what is unjuft excites anger likewife; and unfortunately the former ftate of things in France afforded too many occafions for both.

Courtiers & Nobles Slaves to Ufurers.

As the court had become the flave of monied men, or what they termed financiers, but what we may venture to call by their proper name, money-lenders and ufurers, fo alfo had the nobles individually, with only a few exceptions.   Their eftates were generally mortgaged, or their revenues anticipated, by this ufurious tribe, whom they hated, defpifed, and envied, at the fame

---

* Without any imputation upon the judges, yet the forms of juftice, and its expenfe, prevented the individual from getting his right.   The farmers general had a clerk who defeaded all actions in their name, and without any trouble to themfelves, the expenfe being no object to the company, the individual was ruined by delays and appeals from one court to another.

time

time that they were obliged to cringe to them for
pecuniary aid.

Such had been the ftate of things in France
during the long reign of Louis XV. and continued *Louis 15.*
with only this difference, that it was gradually
getting worfe, till the American war began, and *American War*
haftened that revolution which without it would,
perhaps, have been twenty yea 's longer in coming to a head.

It would be neceffary to go on with this relation, in order to enter into fome details concerning M. Necker, who, while he was acquir- *Necker*
ing for himfelf popularity and reputation, as an
able financier, honeft man, and philofopher, was
ruining the French nation, deceiving the world,
and betraying his king.

Monf. Necker muft certainly be confidered as
being one of the principal caufes of the revolution
breaking out when it did, and in the manner that
it did. We fhall at prefent only confider him as a
finance minifter ; it will be our bufinefs on a future occafion to examine his conduct as a poli-
tician.

The management of the finances of France
were entrufted to a minifter who was called the
comptroller general, who might either have a
feat in the King's council, or not, as circumftances permitted and required. M. Necker, a
Proteftant and a ftranger, when called to that
important office, on account of his credit amongft
the monied men, and his fkill in operations in the
banking way as carried on in Paris, was not admitted

mitted to the honour of a feat in the King's council ; and it is no fmall proof of the degraded ftate
of the court, that it refufed fo neceffary an honour where merit was acknowledged and obligation received.* There was a fingular degree of
want of policy, and, we may even fay, of injuftice, in refufing M. Necker a feat in council,
where his prefence, as being at the head of the
finance, was fo neceffary ; but, as M. Necker's
ruling paffion wa. ambition (to which his love of
money was fubfervient), as this was well known,

Madame Necker and that Madame Necker, a woman of no inconfiderable merit, and of a very decided character,

vain & ambitious was ftill more vain and ambitious than her hufband, whom fhe governed, the imprudence of
trufting them and humiliating them at the fame
inftant, is beyond any common degree of folly.

*Enemy to the Ladies
at Court* Madame Necker was always an enemy to the
ladies of the court, into whofe circles fhe could
not be admitted. This hatred was no fecret in
Paris, any more than her influence with her hufband. From two ftrangers, rich, vain, and exaf-
perated, placed at the head of the deranged finances of the country, much good could not be ex-

---

* M. Necker's merit was acknowledged by the very act
of appointing him to the place, and, as he received no falary,
the obligation was not to be denied, *by thofe who had confidence in him,* though the fact was quite otherwife ; it was
the intrigues of the bankers in Paris that raifed M. Necker
to the comptrole generale, that he might favour their ftock-
jobbing manœuvres ; and, as for falary, his own vanity was
gratified by not receiving any, and the people were blinded
with refpect to his character ; though, being partner in the
banking houfe of Girardot and Haller, he could get more
money by ftock-jobbing in one day, than by his falary in ten
years, had he received one.

Girardot & Haller

pected ;

pected; and affuredly, if their wrath was great, their vengeance has been greater ftill; it has fucceeded beyond any other example.

M. Necker began his adminiftration by making his court to the people, and he at laft got public opinion entirely on his fide, by fetting the example of publifhing an account of the receipts and expenfes,* intituled An *Account Rendered.* Much indirect praife of his own talents, and a moft decided eulogium on his heart and intentions artfully interfperfed through the work, ferved to raife him highly in the opinion of the public.

Necker courts the People

Compte rendu. praises his Talent & heart.

This *Account Rendered,* calculated in every refpect to gain friends among the people at large, produced its effect; but how great was the admiration of all Europe, and the adoration of the

* M. Necker had already been known as a writer. His firft production, and, perhaps, his beft, was a pamphlet in anfwer to an attack made upon the India Company by the Abbé Morèlet, in which he difcovered precifion of reafoning, and confiderable talent for controverfy. His latter works have been fpoiled by his vanity and egotifm, his profeffions of virtue, &c. except that voluminous work on the *Legiflation of Grain,* as he called it, which is a compofition fcarcely to be paralleled for ignorance of facts, falfity of reafoning, and inconfiftency with itfelf. An Englifhman in Paris, hearing this character of the book, went and bought it. " A book that contradicts itfelf," faid he, " has a " chance to be right fomewhere at leaft." It is probable M. Necker wrote this book for popularity, and not becaufe he felt he underftood the fubject; for it does not bear that appearance of his knowledge of trade and commerce, that is to be feen in his other productions. M. Necker's books are generally interfperfed with good things, well expreffed, and conveying real information, the work in queftion is, however, an exception.

French

French to a minifter who boafted of giving liberty to America and of humbling Great Britain, without laying on a fingle tax? A minifter, who, though a ftranger, did this great fervice without receiving any pay from the ftate, and who for the firft time, and as an example for others, fhewed that his hands were clean, by rendering a voluntary account of his tranfactions. Words feemed unequal to his praife; and even in France the fuperlative degree was feldom ever more employed than on that occafion, unluckily, alfo, it has feldom ever been worfe employed, as all parties will now readily confefs.

M. Necker knew perfectly all the manœuvres of banking and ftock-jobbing, having paffed through every ftage of the bufinefs from the clerk at thirty pounds a year to the partner of the firft houfe in France; he knew extremely well how to make loans and raife money, and his fecret in not laying burthens upon the people confifted in nothing more than in paying the intereft of all former loans by that which he had made the lateft; thereby giving the people a momentary cafe, concealing the growing evil, acquiring a temporary fame and reputation for himfelf, but preparing a cruel reverfe for the nation, and a difficult tafk for whoever might be unfortunate enough to fucceed him in his office.*

Loans

* It is wonderful that M. de Calonne, who fucceeded Necker, and who had fo long a conteft with him about the finances, did not confider that, as the world could not follow out an intricate and long difcuffion, it would have been the wifeft way to give this fimple and true ftatement.

When

When the American war was finished, it was impossible to go on with the perpetual resource of borrowing, and the impropriety of laying on taxes in time of peace is evident to all, particularly so when it was believed that M. Necker had carried on so expensive a war without rendering any new burdens necessary. The odium of this measure fell upon M. de Calonne, who had succeeded Necker, though not immediately; and upon the court for its extravagances, which were such, indeed, as could not be expected greatly to conciliate the public opinion. M. Necker retired to his own country, to contemplate from a distance the ravages of the flames which he had kindled, and under the appearance of defending his own reputation, blowed the bellows with all the ardour possible, and with all the effect he could have desired.

Calonne

Court Extravagance

The monied people and bankers made a common cause with M. Necker; they had participated in his fortunes, and they shared in his disgrace; his humiliation seemed to be their own, and the consequence was a general wish to humble the court and the nobility.

Monied Men

M. de Calonne, attached to his king and country, and desirous of serving them, was imprudent and unskilful in the way of doing it. Precisely the reverse of M. Necker in his way of thinking and acting, and having been long covered with debts, he wanted that order, reputation, and external appearance, which are necessary both to conduct things, and to inspire confidence. Besides, he mistook the manner of serving his country, he wanted to imitate Colbert,

Calonne

E

bert, when he fhould have endeavoured to have imitated Sully.

Economy in the court, reforms of fome abufes in the laws, and order in the finances, were what fhould have gone firft. M. de Calonne, perhaps, defpairing of bringing about that economy, wifhed, by encouraging trade and manufactures, to enable his country to bear thofe burthens, which want of economy rendered neceffary. An attempt of this nature requires time to bring it to perfection, and tranquillity to allow its operations to fucceed; and the confufed and difcontented ftate of things afforded neither of the two; fo that, unfupported by public confidence, which he did not take the way to acquire, M. de Calonne was obliged to abandon his projects, with the mortification of having by the attempt rather inflamed the wound which he meant to heal.

The dilemma of a minifter who wifhed really to ferve his country, but who had not in himfelf the means of doing it, made him advife his Majefty to affemble the NOTABLES, which is an affembly, as its name plainly indicates, of notable or chofen perfons throughout the kingdom.

The affembly of notables, by its ancient rights, had only the privilege of advifing and inveftigating, but could do no act of a legiflative nature.

The nature of public affemblies, and the modes of managing them and leading them to an ufeful end, were totally unknown in a defpotic kingdom, where, for many ages, none had exifted.

ifted. Each individual brought his own opinion, and many fpoke it with vigor and boldnefs.
Although the advantages that might have been
expected from this affembly, were not derived,
yet, as it was the opinion of the majority of the
members that an affembly of the *States General*
could alone introduce order in the finances, and
heal the wounds of the ftate, their opinion was
generally adopted, and, from this general belief,
the remedy they propofed became more neceffary
than ever.

The almoft univerfal fpirit of innovation ; the
reforms which the Emperor Jofeph had attempted, and was then attempting, in the Auftrian
Low Countries, and in his hereditary dominions,
added to the other caufes we have already fpoken
of, and of which we have yet to fpeak, contributed greatly to make the members of this affembly
wifh to fee an amelioration effected in the order
of things in France. They have been accufed,
and perhaps with fome reafon, of wifhing individually to become members of the ftates general,
when they fhould meet *not to advife, but to act.*
This was natural enough ; and, if in other re-
fpects they had good intentions, it is difficult to
fee why they fhould be blamed for it. Let, however, the queftion of individual virtue, and wifdom, reft where it will, the refult of all was this,
that the difcontents of the nation were greatly
augmented by a remedy being pointed out for all
their ills, which the court feemed unwilling to
employ ; and the whole bulk of the people looked forward to this affembly of the ftates as the
term of their woes ; fo that every day that it was
retarded

retarded added to the difcontent and odium
thrown upon the court and courtiers.

In this ftate were the finances, and thus was
public opinion, when M. de Calonne quitted his
place, and foon after the kingdom. As it is
our bufinefs to trace the caufes of the difcontents,
which laid the foundation for the fudden and total change of opinions in France, we fhall not
follow the Archbifhop of Sens, who fucceeded
as prime minifter,* in his ridiculous attempts to
arrange matters of finance, becaufe that would
only be the hiftory of the blunders of a man totally ignorant of what he was about; we fhall
only fay, what thoufands of living witneffes can
atteft, that an oppreffed people found their miferies augmented in a two-fold manner, by the
profpect of a remedy, and by that remedy being
withheld by a court, of which the expences and
luxury were by no means concealed; a court,
where the prodigality of Louis XIV. was equalled, but not imitated. Louis XIV. was great
even in his follies; he was an encourager of merit and talents of every defcription, and by a
kind of theatrical manœuvre, rendered his court
the envy and admiration of all Europe. Louis
XIV. was expenfive and cruel upon the great
fcale where his ambition interfered; but if he
was the fcourge of the nation in which he was
born, and of the age in which he lived, he was
alfo their ornament, and his fubjects bore with

Sens

Lewis 14.

* In Calonne's time there was no prime minifter; he,
therefore, was at the head of the finances; in the Archbifhop's time the comptroller general was only to be confidered
as an under fecretary of ftate.

patience

patience burthens which were conducive to the gratification of their great national paſſion, vanity. The palace of Verſailles was the grandeſt in Europe, and its gardens the moſt magnificent; the flatterers whom his bounty or vanity fed, compared his days with thoſe of the Emperor Auguſtus, and in doing ſo, pleaſed the nation as much as they pleaſed the king.* But the court of Verſailles, in its latter days, had loſt regard for public opinion, and with that had vaniſhed thoſe uſeful or brilliant qualities by which it is obtained.

Whilſt thoſe who profited by the ancient order of things, ſeemed totally indifferent as to public opinion, and that to ſo great a degree, that one would have thought they were ignorant of its importance, thoſe men who wiſhed for a change, ſeemed inſtinctively to know which way to go to work, and not a ſtone was left unturned, and no method untried of converting all the errors of the court to advantage.

The ſupport given by the king of France to the *Americans* Americans, when they threw off the yoke of this country, had alſo operated in changing the opinions of the French with reſpect to their own government. The Americans were then ſtill known in France by the name of the INSURGENTS; the king of France had ſupported them in their inſurrection againſt their ſovereign, and had aided

* Thoſe who chuſe to trace national character through its windings, will ſee a great ſimilarity between the vanity of imitating Auguſtus, and many pieces of republican affectation, ſuch as new names borrowed from Rome and Greece, an imitation of Spartan ſimplicity, new calendars, &c. &c.

them

*Moderation
wife laws*

them in eftablifhing a republic. The moderation
of the Americans in their fuccefs, the wife laws
which they had made; but, above all, the example of men who had fully fucceeded, operated
ftrongly in favour of infurrection and republican
principles. The advocates of the late virtuous
and unfortunate monarch could not deny, that
he had himfelf fupported an infurrection, and
been the principle friend of the American republic; and although there was a difference between the two cafes, it admitted of a difcuffion
which could not but be unfavourable to the
king. Whilft fome faid that the Americans had
been ill treated by England, and merited fupport, others argued that there never were any
baftiles in America, nor any letters de cachet,
nor any gabelle; that though America had a
right to complain, France had a ftill greater
right, and that the king who had fupported the
caufe of liberty on the other fide of the Atlantic,
ought not to preferve the power of oppreffing his
own fubjects. Thefe arguments feemed pretty
convincing, for nobody could fay there ever had
been abufes in America that were in any fhape to
be compared to thofe in France. The advocates
of the French monarch were thus reduced to
filence, for either Louis XVI. acted wrong in
fupporting the caufe of freedom, or the caufe of
freedom ought to be fupported againft Louis
XVI. While this and other reafonings took place
amongft a certain fet of men, the great majority of the the people decided the matter by a very
fhort mode; " infurrection was in all cafes," faid
they, " infurrection, and liberty was liberty, and
" the king who kept from his own people what
" he had wafted their blood and treafure to
                                        " procure

" procure for ftrangers, was a tyrant, and fo it
" was lawful and right to force him to give them
" what they wanted."

rebel.

The queen, fo fair, fo amiable, and fince then *The Queen*
fo unfortunate, and who, had fhe fallen into
better hands,* was capable of fetting the example
of whatever was good or great, had efpoufed
along with the French monarch, many of the
follies and prejudices of that nation. Young,
beautiful, and generous, fhe was foon led into
all the expences that fplendour and donation are
capable of occafioning. The defire of humbling
England had always been a ruling paffion in
France, and this the queen fhared with thofe
around her. It was no lefs a perfonage than the
queen herfelf that firft brought the American revolt into fafhion at court, and of confequence
many young men of family and ambition fought
fame and diftinction by going as volunteers to
America ;† and when they returned, flufhed with
victory, and full of republicanifm, they affected
to give the ton to the age, fo that what the people
cultivated from intereft and inclination, thofe of
higher rank did from fafhion, and perhaps fome
few of them from principle.

The writings of Voltaire, Roufeau, and Raynal, *Voltaire*
had produced great effects upon the minds of that
clafs of men, who, by their own writings and

---

* It is not meant her hufband, who was perhaps one of
the moft virtuous men of the age, but the people around the
queen when fhe firft arrived, and who never left her.

† The Duc de Lauzun, fince Biron, La Fayette, the
two Lameths, General Rochambeau, Gouvion, &c. &c.

reafoning,

reasoning, when they are left at liberty, always
finish by swaying those above them, as well as
those below them; so that all ranks in society
were prepared for changes ;they formed hopes on
a new order of things, and were much displeased
with the present order, to which nothing attached
them whatever.

Thus, by a concurrence of circumstances,
which could scarcely have been more complete
than it was, a field was prepared upon which
Jacobin Principles Jacobin principles were to be sown ; not that we
mean to confound Republicanism and Jacobinism,
but that the French confounded them ; not that
liberty and anarchy can be mixt together, for
where the one is, the other certainly never will
be found, but that the French mistook anarchy
for liberty, and were thereby led into those violent extremes for which they have always been
so famous, and which are often so fatal and so
difficult to retract.

Thus have we seen, that, previous to the revolution, every thing favoured a change, which
therefore became unavoidable. We must next
examine into the immediate causes of the violence
of the change, that so soon after took place.

First of all it is to be observed, that though all
parties wished for liberty, they were unacquainted
with what true freedom is ; the first principles of
it were misunderstood, and therefore, while they
were seeking liberty with all the energy which so
good a cause inspires, it was not difficult for de-
signing and ill-intentioned men to lead them far
beyond the mark at which they wished to aim.

Of

Of those ambitious and defigning men who were inclined to miflead the people, and who had the means of doing it, the Duke of Orleans muft be confidered as the chief; poffeffed of revenues equal to royal, he was diftinguifhed for moft of thofe low vices (carried to a great excefs) which are in general only to be found in the lower clafs of vagabonds. Every rank in fociety has the vices natural to itfelf, but this Duke, as if to fhew mankind what an affemblage of vice might be produced in the fame perfon, had the vices of all different ranks of fociety. Firft prince of the blood, he was a faithlefs and cowardly chief of a wicked faction; a bad hufband to an excellent wife; a bad father; the murderer of a near relation, that he might inherit his fortune; given to every fort of knavery in regard to the tenants upon his eftate; a gambler, without honour or integrity, and full of all the tricks practifed by the loweft of the fort. He had but one crime to add, which he took care to do, that of murdering his fovereign, to complete the catalogue.*   An enemy to the king, whofe perfonal character he difliked, as it was a reproach to his own, and to the queen, from motives of pride, he longed for an occafion

righthand margin annotations: *Orleans described.* / *what a Portrait!*

---

* This portrait of the Duke is fo black, that it may feem exaggerated. As to his debaucheries, his gaming, and his tricks of the little villain, they are known in England as well as in France. The incurable difeafe communicated to one of the beft of wives; his cruelty and neglect of her; his having killed the Prince de Lambelle, his brother in law, by leading him on purpofe, where he was to contract a mortal diforder; his letting all the fhops and houfes in the Palais Royal, and exacting a fum for the leafe, and then felling them all (a fale in France breaks the leafe) immediately, are well known. His private tranfactions were fuch; of his public ones we fhall foon fee plenty.

to humble both. Far from being deſtitute of
talents, poſſeſſing energy and activity, which are
frequently allied to a bad diſpoſition, he ſeized
with alacrity and avidity the firſt moment of
trouble, to put himſelf at the head of a party.

M. de Calonne was no ſooner at a diſtance
than his ſucceſſor endeavoured to raiſe taxes, and
to bring the receipts to a level with the expenditures. It had been the cuſtom, ever ſince the
ſtates general had been laid aſide, to have the
new taxes enregiſtered by the parliament of Paris,
and the other parliaments of the kingdom ; not
that their enregiſtering was neceſſary to make it
legal, but it had ſome appearance of doing ſo ;
and had become a cuſtom ſo well eſtabliſhed, that
it would be dangerous to put a tax in force that
was not ſo enregiſtered. Beſides this, as the
parliaments were the judges in civil and criminal
caſes, refractory people would not have been
puniſhed by them for refuſing to pay a tax
which they themſelves had refuſed to enregiſter.

*Parliaments refuſe to
enregiſter.*

The parliaments refuſed to enregiſter the new
taxes ; the Duke of Orleans ſupported their oppoſition with all his influence, and that of his dependents, and by this he increaſed the embarraſſ-
ment of the court, and procured for himſelf conſiderable popularity.

The ſquabbles between the king and the parliaments do not merit any exact relation, becauſe
they have no other connection with our ſubject
than as they tended to inflame the minds of the
people againſt the king, and attach them to thoſe
who eſpouſed their intereſts.

It

It has never, perhaps, been the lot of any man to be *always* playing the part of a fcoundrel in the eyes of mankind, and accordingly M. d'Orleans, for a few months, was banifhed from Paris on account of his having oppofed the abitrary will of the court !!!

orleans banished

The minifter finding himfelf incapable of making things go on at all, and no money being to be had, the treafury was very unequal to the unavoidable expenfes of the ftate, although the payment of the annuities at the town-houfe were retarded ; fo that the court finding it impoffible to go on, it was refolved to recall M. Necker, in order to reconcile the people to the taxes, which it would be neceffary to lay on ; or by his credit with the monied men to procure, at leaft, what was abfolutely indifpenfable. It is from the moment of M. Necker's recall, that we ought properly to begin our hiftory ; for it was then that the public voice obtained the firft complete victory, and put the court entirely into the hands of its enemies ; for from that day forward, the fame faction that has fince overturned every thing, begun openly to cabal and to act ; and though the heroes that we are now going to fee ftrutting upon the ftage, have been fince then maffacred, guillotined, put to flight, or have perifhed by their own hands, that does not prove that they were not exactly of the fame band with thofe who have guillotined them or put them to flight ; and in following them through their different windings, we fhall fee that they were all *intrinfically the fame ;* that private intereft and particular circumftances only has made a difference ;

Necker's recall, the 1st victory of the public voice!

ence; that the fame man affumed the guife of a philofopher or an affaffin, according to occafion; and that the principles laid down by the firft innovators, in the firft moments of their power, led to the laft and greateft crimes, of which, any of what we call the fect of Jacobins have been guilty.

C H A P.

C H A P. III.

Necker's administration of finance—His politics—
His alliance with the Duke of Orleans—Popu-
larity of the Duke—He puts himself at the head of
the reformers and factious, and protects them—
Election to the states general—Intrigues of the
Duke—The Abbé Seyes elected—His pam-
phlet—Democratic principles circulated every
where—Indolence of the other party—Confe-
quences natural from this opposite conduct.

F R O M the time that Lewis the Sixteenth
found himself compelled by public opinion, and
his own necessities, to recall M. Necker, he was
no longer the ruler of France; and what was
still more, the whole tribe of courtiers lost their
influence also, not with the king, but upon pub-
lic affairs. M. Necker, too well acquainted with *Necker absolute*
the urgent reasons of his recall, to be ignorant
of his importance, or to fear his being dismissed,
acted entirely as a master ; not, indeed, in outward shew, for he affected a stiff and philosophi-
cal modesty and simplicity of manners, but in
reality. His opinion was law, and the king was
exactly reduced to the state of a bankrupt who
had surrendered his effects to his creditors.

M. Necker found in the royal treasury, on his
entering upon office as comptroller-general for the
second time, only about sixteen thousand pounds
sterling

sterling in cash, which was equal only to the current expenses of a few hours. As the most con-
summate ignorance of affairs was alone capable of
having reduced the treasury to so empty a state,
on his arrival it was soon replenished ; not that
M. Necker enjoyed the same confidence as when
formerly in the same place in more prosperous
times, but that he had sufficient credit and resource for any momentary supply. This was in
the month of August, in the year 1788 ; the recall of the banished members of parliament, and
an apparent peace amongst parties soon succeeded.
As the necessity of preserving M. Necker at the
head of affairs was generally known, and as it
was also well known that no danger was to be
apprehended of being punished by him for any
freedom of speech, or of the press, Paris became
a sort of debating club ; every opinion was discussed there, and every assertion hazarded with
boldness and rashness that plainly shewed that it
was a new privilege to those who made so ill an
use of it.

August 1788

Although M. Necker was, properly speaking,
minister of finance, he was, in fact, sole minister ;
or rather, if it had not been for the sake of form,
he was the whole council, and the king was only
there to lend his signature when it was wanted.
If M. Necker had formerly suffered in his importance from not occupying a seat in the council,
he now was amply compensated, for he, in fact,
occupied all the seats. The automata around
were all moved by the man, to whom both king
and people looked up for deliverance from a state
of very disagreeable embarrassment.

Necker Sole Minister

If

If there are perfons, who yet recollecting the enthufiafm which the name of Necker once infpired, feel hurt at what has fince happened to him, let them put their minds at eafe, for M. Necker, by entering into a cabal with the Duke of Orleans, whofe vices and villainies he well knew, has himfelf fet the feal upon his boafted morality and virtue. The agents of the faction that oppofed the court, promenaded the bufts of the philofopher and the debauché together; they were equally the idols of the people, and of the fame portion of the people ;* they both fpoke the fame fort of language to the people, and appeared like two meffengers of Heaven, fent down to cure the wounds of the ftate, and alleviate the miferies of individuals.

Necker cabals with orleans

Amongft the ftrange propenfities of the French, carried to excefs, is that of being led away by found and fhow. Thofe who knew the two chiefs in queftion, compared them to the quack doctor and the merry andrew of the fair; and the fimilitude was not a bad one, for they completely duped the lookers on, by appearing what they never were, nor ever wifhed to be, and by giving them remedies that were worfe than the difeafe.

* The other members of parliament who had been banifhed for oppofing the king, were more efteemed then the Duke, and for fome time more popular, but their popularity was of a different nature, it was with the public at large; with the fober citizen: that of Necker and d'Orleans was with that clafs of men fince then not improperly named *fans cullottes,* from their ragged and haggard appearance.

Necker & orleans popular with the Sans cullottes.

M. Necker,

M. Necker, it is certain, had enough of virtue and good intention to have preferred serving the people to doing them an injury, provided the one and the other had equally served his own ambition ; but where ever thefe two objects have come in competition, he has uniformly given the preference to what concerned moft his own perfon.* Though the two firft heroes of infurrection were capable of acting together at firft, yet it is not from that to be inferred, that their turpitude was equal, for between them there certainly was a wide difference ; their conduct was the fame while they thought their objects the fame, but they had different objects. M. Necker did not conceal his (though he concealed his meafures as much as he could) which was a new order of things, more favourable to general liberty, over which he thought to prefide. He had the vanity to °imagine that public opinion would be always at his command, that he was to be the regenerator of France, and that the affembly of the

Necker a ftockjobber
and
Gambler

* As it is of importance that fuch men fhould be viewed in their true light, let us confider that M. Necker, who came a ftranger into France, had amaffed a princely fortune in a few years. Thofe who know banking bufinefs, know, that though it is a good one, it is not poffible to rife fo quickly by the fair line of bufinefs. M. Necker acquired his fortune by ftock-jobbing, that is, gambling, and by the artificial rifes and falls, which he and the other Genevefe, his countrymen, underftood better than the French. This was much eafier in France than it is in England, there being upon Change, at Paris, twenty different forts of ftock, both of government, of the India company, and of private companies, the capitals of which not being confiderable, a few monied men, by buying and felling, could raife or lower them to a certainty, at pleafure ; it was no better than keeping a gaming table with falfe dice. Such was M. Necker's moral practice ; as to his moral profeffions, the world has been furfeited with them.

ftates

states-general would allow itself to be governed by him. Madame Necker, in the fulnefs of her *Madam Necker* glory, was heard to exprefs herfelf to this purpofe, adding, that fhe actually believed that if her hufband were to conceive the idea of fubftituting another religion in the place of the Chriftian faith, his genius, his combinations, and his influence over the minds of men were fuch, that fhe believed he could bring mankind to adopt it. M. Necker knew the art of ftock-jobbing well, and the intrigues of the court a little, but he knew nothing at all of his influence with the people when once they fhould have no more ufe for his finance manœuvres, when once the court fhould be humbled, and his affiftance fhould be no longer neceffary. No man in a time of political difficulty had lefs refource than Necker, he was clumfy, ufelefs, and inconvenient, and of confequence was the firft public man whom the revolutionifts difcarded from their fervice with difgrace.

The Duke of Orleans, on the other hand, had no idea of eftablifhing order, but diforder; " *Make the water muddy, faid Philip, and I will* " *fifh in it.*" D'Orleans trufted to his money, his intrigues, his agents, and his new-fangled popularity, for profiting of whatever chances a ftate of diforder might throw in his way. This was precifely the view of that immenfe number of innovators who fo foon after appeared; all of them calculated right as to the firft outfet of the affair, but every one of them was miftaken as to the ultimate confequences. It was a perfpective, in which the immenfe revenues and riches of France were reprefented as wrefted from the

G hands

hands of the king and his feeble court, by men of energy and enterprize. The accumulated riches and honours of a thousand years, lay all before them, and the means of poſſeſſing them ſeemed eaſy by the intervention of the good people of Paris, whoſe opinion was entirely in their favour. Saturated with the view of ſo rich a proſpect, and giddy with ſuch a variety of objects, the eye did not perceive the gallows and the guillotine, the poignard and the torch, that were in the back ground. The people, obedient to their leaders when they commanded plunder, ſeemed to them a certain means of acquiring wealth and power, but they did not ſee that this ſame people would in the end turn againſt themſelves, and tear from them the fruits of their firſt exceſſes. M. Necker, who thought he had influence enough to overturn the Chriſtian religion, and eſtabliſh another in its place, and d'Orleans, who calculated that he could always rule the mob, were equally miſtaken in the end ; but in the firſt part of their experiments their road was the ſame, deſtruction of the preſent order was the object ; and, in planning this, the latter months of 1788, and the beginning of 1789, were employed.

1788. 1789

Whilſt the two chiefs were occupied in this manner, a number of ſpeculators in anarchy, acting either as ſubalterns, or for their own proper account, were buſied in preparing to aſſiſt openly, ſo ſoon as things ſhould be a little farther advanced.

Speculators.

The aſſembly *des amis des noirs*, under the appearance of ameliorating the ſtate of their fellow-low

Amis des noirs.

low creatures in the West India islands, held meetings which had a very different object. This assembly, called Friends of the Blacks, might with more propriety have been termed the enemies of the whites; it was a school for equality *School of Equality* and abfurdity. There people of different sexes, and of all ranks, might be admitted; but it was exprefsly forbidden to take off the hat or salute the company; so that Briffot and conforts, spe- *Briftol* culating on the revolutions they could bring on, and the plunder they could gain, were jumbled into one affembly with the virtuous Madame de la Rochfaucauld, without more ceremony than *Rochefaucauld* porters in the tap room of an ale-houfe.

-The humanity of relieving our fellow creatures led the virtuous and good to fuch an affembly, and the juftnefs of the caufe gave its members a cloak for circulating writings, which tended to prepare the way for the new fyftems that were broaching. The circumftance alone of not being allowed to take off the hat, nor to return a falute, was a clear proof, that the affembly was for another purpofe than that which it profeffed; and if that can be doubted, we may eafily be convinced, when we find that Condorcet, Cla- *Condorcet, Claviere* viere, Briffot, and a number of thofe perfons, *Briftol* who fince have propagated with fuch effect the fyftem of riot, robbery, and murder, were its leading and active members.

The ftate of fenfelefs inactivity, and of ftupid torpidity, into which men of rank and fortune had fallen, who no longer now made any noife, or appeared to be of any importance, left the field open to adventurers, who had occafion to
fpeculate

ſpeculate upon the public mind; and as credulity, and the diſpoſition to adopt whatever is new, have always been known to predominate in Paris, it was therefore neceſſary to attract public atten- tion by what was extraordinary ; in the center from which moſt of the faſhions, the cuſtoms, and rules of behaviour in modern Europe have come, it would have been difficult to eſtabliſh any thing more new than a total diſregard to eve- ry cuſtom, and to every form, neceſſary not only for politeneſs but even for decency in ſociety. The cloak of humanity and philoſophy recon-, ciled people to it in ſome degree, and they began to reaſon on the natural equality and artificial in- equality of man ; ſo that to the diſcontents occa- ſioned by real evils, and the hopes of bettering their ſituation, people began to unite that ſort of modern philoſophy which has ſince led to ſuch fatal extremes.

The great art of beginning commotions conſiſts in ſeducing the minds of men by the appearance of what is good and virtuous, and of what will make them happy ; but above all, of what ſuits the intereſt, or flatters the paſſions of the greater number. It was in correſpondence with this plan, that the words of *liberty, equality, rights of man, humanity, virtue, friends and brothers, uni- verſal benevolence,* &c. were perpetually in the mouths of the firſt innovators. The people be- lieved they ſaw a number of beneficent deities deſcended from heaven to give them happineſs, and ſell them bread and wine at half price ;* and
of

* The French began to have caricature prints at this time, and a very famous one was that of a poor cobler, who was
ſaying

of confequence they were prepared, whenever the occafion fhould offer, to aid and affift with all their might in a *reform* (for the revolution was announced under that fpecious name) that promifed fo great an advantage, and which they confidered as being founded upon right and juftice.

The winter of 1778 and 1779 was one of the *Winter of 1789* moft fevere, both on account of its great length and the intenfity of the cold, that had been feen for many years ; fo that, in addition to the ftagnation which uncertainty always gives to trade, the feafon was fuch as to occafion a great deal of mifery. Wood for firing was no dearer than ufual, it is true, but it was more neceffary, and the price was at all times exorbitant. Bread, which is the great nourifhment of the people of France, was dear, and not fo good as ufual ; the loaf of bread that ufed to be at eight fols having rifen to eleven and twelve. Butcher's meat, too, was dearer than ufual, and the productions of the garden could not be had in fo rigorous a feafon. The miferies of the poor all through France were by this rendered extreme ; and here it is no more than juftice to fay, that the rich and opulent, and

faying to his wife, juft returned from market, where every thing was very dear, " Patience Margott, we fhall foon have " *three times eight ;*" which fignified bread at eight fols the loaf, beef at eight fols the pound, and wine at eight fols. Such were the views of the people ; they were good and laudable, but were foon perverted. This caricature was foon fucceeded by the *Calculating Patriot*, who reckoned up the number of heads already cut off, and the number wanted to infure the happinefs of the people. Hogarth's Harlot's Progrefs is not more curious, than the Progrefs of the Wants of the People, which began with bread and wine, and ended with blood and murder.

in

Clergy and Nobility.

in particular the clergy, performed wonders in relieving their fufferings. It would have feemed, that Providence gave to the rich one laſt opportunity of ſhewing what the Chriſtian charity of the church, and the generoſity of an ancient nobility, were capable of doing. The poor and needy, whom ſhame prevented from feeking aid, were themſelves ſought after, and relief was forced upon the poor ſtarving family in their cold and hungry retreat, by thoſe fame clergymen and nobility who foon after were driven from their own abodes. Surely theſe acts which did ſuch honour to thoſe who performed them, and are a full proof that their follies and luxury, and the oppreſſion they occaſioned to the people, were not from badneſs of heart and from want of feeling. Theſe acts of charity were not the acts of a few, they were general, and were done without oftentation or ſhew, as ſuch actions always ought to be.

Orleans

The Duke of Orleans did not let ſlip this occaſion to fignalize himſelf; his charities were numerous and ſplendid, and induſtriouſly held up to public view; while M. Necker, who wanted to reform every thing, fent to St. Germain for an ox, had it weighed, killed, and weighed again, ſkin, horns, hoofs, &c. being deducted. The butchers were convicted of felling at twelve fols what, by calculation, coft only eight. But though this experiment ſerved to ſhew that things were too dear, no ſerious attempt was made to reduce the price, and the only advantage refulted to the miniſter, who obtained credit for his good intentions.

Public

Public works of charity were inftituted, where people were employed to grind corn at the public expenfe; this afforded the lower orders means of caballing, by bringing great numbers together for the fame object, and having the fame interefts. M. Necker has been accufed of having done fo with defign; but there feems little reafon for the accufation, which appears rather to be a fabrication of his enemies than a fact. It was really neceffary to do fomething to employ the idle, who were ftarving. Hand-mills, though a dear way of grinding, were ftill a refource in fo long and fevere a froft. Befides, M. Necker was never ferioufly accufed of wanting humanity; and to all this muft be added, that though he wanted to have public opinion to fupport his meafures, there was no probability that mobs or cabals amongft the lower orders could ferve his purpofe; it is therefore but fair to acquit him of this charge.

With regard to M. Necker, as well as moft of thofe who worked in the revolution (to ufe their own expreffion, *travailler à là revolution*), people are apt to attribute to defign and to diftant project what only arofe from neceffity or particular circumftances; and the proof of this is, that every one of the leaders of the revolution has fallen a facrifice to the refults of his own principles, which refults were, therefore, not forefeen: another proof of the fame thing arifes from this, that the greater number feem to have had *no fixed plan, only to deftroy order, and employ occafion to advantage.* Thus the pick-pocket creates a confufion in a crowd, and trufts to his own dexterity for the profits which he may reap from it. M. Necker was

was interefted in humbling the court, and rifing
as a fort of dictator between the king and the
people; but he was interefted, and that deeply
too, in preferving the force of a government, the
reins of which were in his own hands.

It was during the rigour of the winter that
M. Necker arranged his plan for the mode of affembling the ftates-general; fearing, that if
they were called in the ancient form, the nobility
and clergy would prevent innovation; he gave it
as his opininion that the third ftate, as it was
called, or the commons, fhould have a double
reprefentation; that is, be reprefented by as many deputies as the other two.

Whilft mankind has been improving in arts,
fciences, and amongft others, the art of leading
each other into errors by falfe philofophy and
metaphyfical argument, we do not find that they
have improved much in common fenfe; there are
even fome reafons for thinking, that it is become
more rare than it was formerly. As common
fenfe arifes from the action of the mind upon
itfelf, and upon the objects which naturally come
before it, that methodical way in which people
are brought up to fpeak about every thing, and
to judge of every thing, hinders the mind from
keeping itfelf company, as it were, and, under
the influence only of factsand obfervations, forming a judgment. The old times, when the ftates
general were firft inftituted, are therefore not
by any means to be defpifed; and there feems to
have been very great reafon, fince the ftate was
compofed of three different orders, to give each
an equal fhare of power that it might preferve itfelf.
M. Necker

M. Necker was unwilling to take the refponfi-
bility and the confequence of this bufinefs upon
himfelf; he therefore advifed calling a new affembly of the notables, in order to regulate the   *2ᵈ. Notables*
method of calling the ftates general, hoping that
it would be eafy to make that affembly chufe the
mode which he himfelf approved. In this, however, he was difappointed, the notables did not
think proper to determine it in his favour; fo
that, after having called them together on purpofe to follow their advice, he difmiffed them on
purpofe to follow his own.

The double reprefentation of the third ftate   *double Reprefentation*
having been refolved upon, letters for their elec-
tion were expedited.   M. Necker had publifhed
his reafons for changing the form, a precaution
fufficiently ufelefs, as the far greater number
wifhed it; thofe who did not wifh it had no
means of oppofing him; and his reafons were too
flimfy to convince any one.   It was evident, that
by giving double the number of voices to one
party united in intereft, the other two, who were
not in one intereft, muft fink under the conteft.
That was precifely what every thinking man expected, and what M. Necker wifhed.   He was
the minifter of the people, and he thought to
govern their deputies as he had governed their
king; but he was not long before he difcovered
his miftake.

In the election of deputies every thing was
againft the court and the nobility.   M. Necker,
the minifter who acted for the court, favoured
the election of Proteftants, of poor clergymen,
and of lawyers; in order the better to have them

H   at

at his command, and in order to be the more certain of humbling the rich proprietor and dignified clergyman. In this last hope he was not deceived, but in the former he was, as we shall soon see.

Orleans

The Duke of Orleans, with his extensive lands, great revenues, and numerous dependents, made great efforts every where. Accustomed to intrigues, and surrounded with men who were so too, he succeeded wonderfully in a country where election manœuvres, so disgraceful to those that employ them, were little known. As the manœuvres at a horse-race and at an election are very much of one stamp, the duke, who was always surrounded by jockies, gamblers, and men of such description, succeeded pretty well. He was also

Grand Master

grand master of the order of masonry, and had, by that means, a good opportunity, at a very small expense, of giving a bias to the elections in different parts.

The lovers of change, having all the same cant phrases at command throughout the kingdom, easily knew each other, and, as if by a sort of sympathy, without any previous arrangement, they lent aid to each other; so that in the election matters, the great majority was on the side of reform and change.

Great, however, as all the efforts and exertions of M. Necker and the duke were, they never could have had any considerable degree of success, had the proprietors of lands and the dignified clergy set seriously about getting themselves chosen; but they neglected this opportunity of

serving

ferving their country entirely, whether through ignorance of the neceflity of exertion, through indolence, or trufting to fome other method of preferving their weight in the ftate, or to a combination of all the three, the fact was exactly as it is related; perfons were reprefented, but property was not; and as property cannot protect *Property not reprefented* itfelf, the ruin which it has experienced is not any great reafon for aftonifhment.

Amongft the deputies who were by the duke's *Portrait of Sieyes.* intereft elected to the ftates general, was a man who, to the caufe of anarchy, was worth an hoft; a man of a taciturn, cold difpofition, a clergyman with much erudition, but no religion; cruel and a metaphyfician, determined to ftick at nothing to advance his fortunes, and capable of laying deep plans and guiding their execution. Such a man was the Abbé Seyes, elected deputy for Paris, to fill up the laft place that was vacant.*

When deputies were chofen, it was the ancient cuftom, and was ftill adhered to, for the electors to draw up their intentions and their wifhes in the form of inftructions, which were called CAHIERS; *Cahiers*

* The election manœuvre in Paris was a very complete one. Paris alone fent forty members, and the duke propofed feveral, amongft others this abbé, who was totally unknown; he had never been heard of. The elections were protracted by different delays, till the members from every quarter of the kingdom were already arrived; till the electors were all tired out and fatigued; and, in fhort, till they had neither any time to lofe nor to fpare; fo that he might be actually faid to be forced upon them, as by delay and fatigue large affemblies are often led to do what the majority of members never intended.

thefe

thefe were intended as a rule for the conduct of the reprefentatives, and by a comparifon of the different cahiers, by extracting and comparing their contents, the real wifhes of the nation might have been known.

Orleans's cahier   The Duke of Orleans, by his fituation, had a right to give a cahier to fome of the deputies chofen on his eftates, and it was there that he made his great ftroke at popularity. The Abbé Seyes was faid to have compofed it, and it is more than probable that he did fo ; but whoever was its author, the duke gave the example of the firft prince of the blood ftanding up the advocate of the rights of the people againft his own intereft. Thofe who knew his real charac-ter vented exclamations of wonder at his villainous duplicity; and thofe who knew him not, were as much aftonifhed at his virtue and philanthropy. The lower clafs were in ecftacy, and he obtained by his popularity amongft the fifh-women and fellers of fruit, the title of King of *Roi des Halles*   the Markets *(Roi des Halles)* which, to thofe who know Paris, will appear equivalent to king of the rabble.

What is the 3ᵈ Eftate?   Previous to the opening of the ftates-general, when public expectation and anxiety were wound to their higheft pitch, a pamphlet made its appear-ance, written by the Abbé Seyes, compofed with much art, plaufibility, and falfe reafoning, and entitled, *What is the third ftate?* This title plainly implied the queftion of the importance of the people at large. " The third ftate," fays he, in this pamphlet, " is at prefent as nothing—it
" ought

" ought to be every thing, and it only wants to
" be fomething."

Such a pamphlet, printed and fpread abroad
with the money of the duke, at fo important a
period, and when men were yet unufed to in-
quiries of the fort, could not but excite great
notice; it was accordingly confidered as a mafter-
piece of argument and philofophy, and Monfieur
l'Abbé was confidered as the moft profound metaphyfician of the age, the ableft ftatefman, and
the moft liberal-minded writer who had ever
enlightened the human race.

In the pamphlet of the abbé may be found *Jacobin Creed.*
the foundation of the whole Jacobin creed, dif-
guifed, indeed, fo as not to offend by too abrupt
an introduction of principles which are of a nature to revolt any reafonable man; but leading
on imperceptibly to conclufions, of which the
reader was not at firft aware, and at which he is
the more certain to arrive, that he does not fufpect where he is going.

It is one of the evils attending metaphyfical
reafonings, that their refults are frequently not
difcovered till men are led into errors from
which it is difficult to draw back. The work in
queftion appeared to the bulk of its readers at *The Majority oppreffed*
firft only to prove, that the majority were op-
preffed, and that they ought not to be fo, but to
feek redrefs by affuming that importance to which
their fuperior number gave them a juft title. The
pamphlet appeared to contain little more at firft;
it feemed to be a fimple ftate of facts, told in a
ftyle that announced a calm, unprejudiced, and
inftructed

inſtructed mind, good intentions, and a found judgment. When, afterwards, the third ſtate had not only become ſomething, as he modeſtly had announced, but had in fact engroſſed every power, this ſame pamphlet hinted at the uſe they ſhould make of that power, in a way that was become intelligible, ſince the poſition of things had changed, though it was not ſo at its firſt appearance. To give an example of this :—Men had already learned, that the minority was to be governed by the majority in the deciſion of political queſtions; from this a deduction was artfully drawn, that the will of the majority was the law of the whole; and that the intereſt of the majority ought to be their guide. Thus though the firſt principle laid down is fair; the two others, that ſeem to the perſon who does not reflect to riſe out of it, are the moſt falſe and dangerous that can be imagined, and from which it would reſult, that the will of the majority becomes law and juſtice. But it goes ſtill farther; for the majority is to judge what is for its good, and therefore the life of the individual is at the diſpoſal of the great number. This doctrine was contained in the book, but couched in ſuch terms as only to become evident as the minds of men got ready for it, ſomething like a ſympathetic ink.

We muſt dwell the more upon this pamphlet, as it was a production that operated ſuch amazing effects, and becauſe it contained the baſis of all thoſe principles which have ſince been carried to ſuch pernicious exceſſes. Perhaps no production on either ſide of the queſtion has been written in ſo artful a manner. The ſteps by which people were

were led on to falfe conclufions, as matters ripened, was of more importance than may at firft fight be imagined; for had the SAME principles been contained in different productions of the SAME man, they would not ftill have produced the SAME effects; moderate and well meaning men became at firft converts to the principles of the Abbé Seyes, they had approved of his work openly, and both inclination and pride hindered them from retracting. It is true, they found the book contained more than they had at firft underftood to be meant; but it was not fo eafy for a new-fangled patriot to confefs that he had read and not underftood, and approved without comprehending; fo that many perfons who never thought of any fuch thing, but who did not know how to extricate themfelves from the metaphyfical labyrinth, became unreafonable and unjuft from having too haftily committed themfelves.

As all the writers, and moft part of the talkers, *Writers & Talkers* were on the fame fide of the queftion, the political opinions of the Abbé Seyes were almoft univerfally adopted and approved. There were, indeed, a certain fet of men who, from fuperior knowledge or from a natural foundnefs of judgment, faw through all thefe fort of reafonings, but they had no means of counteracting their evil effects. More than half a million of copies of *half a Million Copies.* the pamphlet had been circulated, and any anfwer that could have been given to it, would never have exceeded a circulation of one or two thoufand, perhaps not fo many hundreds, and thofe would have chiefly fallen into the hands of reafonable thinking men, who did not want them; the

the ignorant and acting many would never have heard of them.

It is certainly here a proper place, while we are recording the energy, activity, and art of the Jacobins, to record also the opposite and contrary qualities of their rivals. At the time when the Duke of Orleans first began to set with activity to work, though with an immense fortune, and M. Necker with the royal treasury in his hands, yet the money that was at the disposition of the proprietors and dignified clergy, was more than fifty times as much, and it was their property and consideration in the kingdom that was attacked; they might, therefore, have made a powerful stand. Their revenues amounted to at least fifty millions sterling, and any sum that their enemies could dispose of, certainly did not amount to half a million. Yet, in this state of things, did the proprietors pay a single man of merit to plead their cause? No. If by chance a man of merit refuted their enemies, did they make a small sacrifice to give publicity to his work? No. He who pleaded the cause of murder and plunder saw his work distributed by thousands and hundreds of thousands, and himself enriched; while he who endeavoured to support the cause of law, of order, and of the proprietor, had his bookseller to pay, and saw his labours converted into waste paper. It is true, he had the consolation of his own mind, and the esteem of the few to whom his good intentions were known; but, with regard to effect upon the public mind, he produced none; his main object was, therefore, unattained, and the revolutionary arguments remained triumphant.

With

This has been the case in America as well as in France, — Witness Paines Writings — and the Defence &c.

With energy, some money, and a disposition to make use of it, on one side; and on the other, indolence, pecuniary means in abundance, but not the will to employ one shilling of it; can we be surprised that things went in favour of those who had the energy and will? It would have been surprising if it had not: and, accordingly, we have since seen the shirtless, shoeless vagabond burning the castles and title deeds of the proprietor, and, with a high hand, put himself in his place.*

It would be useless and absurd at this moment to give the History of Jacobinism, with the avowed intention of stopping its progress, without adverting in a pointed manner to the blameable conduct of those who were both by interest and principle bound to make a stand.

It is in vain to imagine that, in the present state of society, any order of things will long exist, that is not supported by general opinion. Men

* In this country, we have had something like an example of this in Paine's Rights of Man. It has been supposed by those, who have good opportunities of knowing, that above two hundred thousand copies of his book have been dispersed. So much for that clumsy advocate of anarchy. An advocate of order, and defender of proprietors, would not have sold, perhaps, five hundred copies, and would have had money to pay his book-seller. While this remains so, can men of property wonder if the minds of the lower class are led astray? they cannot buy books, and bad ones are given to them; so they hear only the wrong side of the question. Nor is it sufficient to suppress a book by authority; on the contrary, it appears to many to be a proof, or, at least, a presumption, that what was thus forcibly suppressed, was unanswerable, although with respect to Paine that was far from being the case.

I have

have of late learned the art of revolting, while
that of governing is becoming daily more difficult; and this difcovery is too important, and
too fatal to the human race, not to merit oppofition.   Public opinion, and not force, is the only
firm, folid, and durable foundation for power;
even Robefpierre himfelf, with his armies compofed of millions of foldiers, and thoufands of
executioners; with all his poignards, his cannons,
and his guillotines, was obliged to devote moft
of his time and his efforts to preferve public opinion; and he funk like a wretch the moment
that he ceafed to govern that opinion.   The different fects of Jacobins, have they not all fallen,
as their turn came to lofe the fupport of the public voice?   But, if the example of the efficacy
of opinion amongft the Jacobins of France is not
thought applicable to a well regulated ftate,* let
us call to mind the revolutions from kingly power to republicanifm at Rome, and from a republic to an empire: let us remember our own revolutions, whether they were in fupport of men
or of meafures, opinion and the general will
were the forerunners of all thofe changes.   We
have juft finifhed taking a review of the change
of opinion that preceded the revolution in France;
and can we for one moment doubt of the neceffity of preferving argument on our fide, if we
will preferve peace and order?   Fortunately, the
arguments on the fide of law and order are much
ftronger than any that can be employed by its
enemies, if we chufe to employ them; but it is

* Opinion, in fact, is of lefs importance as governments
are more arbitrary; that of England not being arbitrary at
all, it is here abfolutely neceffary.

not individual effort that will avail the cause. Defence requires as much exertion as attack; and the Jacobins themselves have set us the example how it is to be done, and that we ought rather to have recourse to acting upon mind than upon matter.

The history of all nations has shewn that persecution and oppression have given vigour to the opinions of the oppressed. Did not the christian *Christianity* religion extend over a great portion of the world under oppression? Did not the Protestant church *Protestantism* flourish under a cruel persecution? And what is still more, did it not cease to extend the moment its enemies ceased to persecute? The Jewish reli- *Jews* gion, too, professed by erring vagabonds, whom mankind have joined in all countries to oppress, whose interest seems to be their ruling passion, and whose interest would have genera'ly been greatly advanced by changing their faith; has all this converted them? No. The poor despised Jew continues to keep his sabbath as he did three thousand years ago. Such is the effects of force and power upon the mind, and no great depth of thought is necessary to form a conclusion.

Such as we have described, then, were the first efforts of those men who, few in number, had conceived the plan of overturning every thing that they might get something, and of destroying a great deal that they might get a little; until the opening of the states-general gave them a wider *States General* field to act in, from which moment we shall find them assume a confidence that makes their actions and their maxims more easily followed, and their motives traced with a greater degree of precision and certainty.

CHAP.

C H A P. IV.

Affembly of the ftates-general—Conciliatory difpofi-
tion in the king—Oppofite difpofition of the depu-
ties of the third eftate—The grand queftion of the
manner of voting—Public opinion in favour of
one general affembly of the three orders—The
king's offer on the 23rd of June—Obftinacy of
the deputies of the third eftate—Divifions in the
affemblies of the other two orders—Members of
the clergy and nobles join the third eftate—The
court becomes ferious—Miniftry changed—Troops
march againft Paris—Energy and activity of the
people—The revolt begins openly on the 12th
of July.

THOUGH we have already feen fome of the
heroes who entered as reprefentatives of the people
into the ftates-general, yet the names of moft of
thofe who are juft about to become confpicuous,
had, according to the common expreffion, never
before been heard of; and the few who were already known, difplayed in general a fort of character, which they had never before been fufpected to poffefs, fo that we may confider it almoft as an affembly altogether of new men.

The number of deputies for the whole kingdom
amounted to twelve hundred, which, according
to the new method of election, giving the tiers
etat,

etat, or third eftate, a double reprefentation, allowed three hundred for the nobility, three hundred for the clergy, and fix hundred for the third eftate.

The place of affembly was fixed at Verfailles, in a hall called the Menus Plaifirs (where the dreffes belonging to the opera and the theatre of the palace ufed to be kept); in this hall the affembly was to be opened by the king and his minifters, which, when done, the deputies of the different orders were to feparate, and to difcufs their interefts; after which, in following the old form, they were to meet again to adjuft matters, and reconcile whatever might be different in their views and interefts.

When the affembly was opened, M. Necker *Necker* explained, in a long memorial, the ftate of the finances of the kingdom, and the embarraffments, giving at the fame time plainly to underftand, that the king himfelf *poffeffed the power*, and had the means of arranging every thing, but that the beneficence of his majefty had made him liften to *his* advice, and call together the reprefentatives of the people.

After this day of opening, which was rather a day of ceremony than of bufinefs, the deputies of the nobles, and of the clergy, retired to two adjoining halls, of a fmaller fize, which were appointed for them; the deputies of the third eftate, being the moft numerous, remaining in the hall of the general affembly. The different difpofitions of the king, of his minifter, and of the deputies of the three orders, were evident from

different

different circumſtances, otherwiſe in themſelves but of little importance.

When the king entered the aſſembly, the uſage was not to take off his hat ;* the nobles and the clergy were to follow his example, but the deputies of the third eſtate were to uncover themſelves. The king, though he entered at one end of the hall, having the clergy on the right hand, the nobles on the left, and the deputies of the third eſtate at the oppoſite end, perceived that though they uncovered themſelves, it was done with reluctance, and not with that alacrity which might be expected. His majeſty, on beginning to addreſs the aſſembly, took off his hat as if by a natural movement, and found means, without appearing to do it deſignedly, to remain uncovered during the whole time that he remained. The nobles and clergy were thus obliged to uncover themſelves too, and tranquillity was reſtored, by eſtabliſhing that dearly beloved equality, which was already uppermoſt in the minds of almoſt every one.

The conciliatory diſpoſition of his majeſty was very viſible, even by this trifling circumſtance. which was likewiſe a proof of his penetration, for though none of the ſpectators were ſo far off from the members of the third eſtate as he was, yet very few of them obſerved the difficulty, and perhaps not one of them would have thought of ſo quick and complete a remedy.

* The king and nobles wore Spaniſh hats, with white feathers, and the whole dreſs was nearly that of the nobles of Spain.

M. Necker

M. Necker's views of perſonally dictating, in matter of finance to the aſſembly, wer very evident, by the diſcourſe which he had read; and his declaration of the king's having it in his power to make the arrangements neceſſary, without the ſtates-general, was a proof that he was a favourer of abſolute monarchy, unleſs it was only meant as a hint to give them to underſtand that they were there only during pleaſure.

The nobility and clergy on that day exerciſed, as was uſual, their privileges, without any effort either to conciliate or irritate the third eſtate, which, by their murmurs on the firſt moment, ſhewed exactly the ſame diſpoſition that has ever ſince been manifeſted by all the innovators. An ancient cuſtom, which could not then have been changed, as they had not yet begun their reform, might have reconciled philoſophers, as they pretended to be, to an empty ceremony, of which it would be as ridiculous in us to defend the utility, as it was in them to find in it a cauſe of offence. The impatience of the third eſtate, their unanimity, and the diſpoſition of not paſſing over the leaſt circumſtance that tended to diſtinguiſh them in honour from the other two orders, are very evident. It was impoſſible to begin ſooner, or upon a more frivolous occaſion, nor, it may be added, more improperly; it was not to reform uſeleſs ceremonies, eſtabliſhed a thouſand years ago, that their conſtituents had ſent them there, but to aſk and obtain a redreſs of real grievances, to reconcile oppoſite and jarring intereſts, and not to

[handwritten margin note] An empty ceremony! very wise & philoſophical! yet the Mob will always know that by ſuch empty ceremonies, they themſelves and their Superiors too are governed, a tri coloured, or orange Cockade, a Tree of Liberty &c are empty ceremonies yet We have ſeen them full of meaning.

to throw obſtacles in the way of general arrangement, by exciting ſuch trifling diſſenſions.

Whether with deſign or not, it had been ſo
ordered by the miniſter, that the third eſtate,
conſiſting only of between five and ſix hundred
members, held their ſittings in a hall capable of
containing, with eaſe, two thouſand perſons, ſo
that there was room for the curious of all de-
ſcriptions to witneſs their debates. The hall of
the nobility was not capable of containing five
hundred perſons, ſo that as the deputies themſelves amounted to near three hundred, the number of ſpectators could be but few. The place
of aſſembly of the clergy was nearly about the
ſame ſize with that for the nobles.

From this circumſtance it naturally reſulted,
that the debates and reaſonings of the third eſtate,
ſo popular from the cauſe they tended to ſupport, were widely ſpread abroad, and repeated
with eagerneſs and enthuſiaſm by that crowd of
ſpectators of all ranks, who went every day from
Paris to be witneſſes of what paſſed.

The reaſonings of the nobility and clergy, leſs
popular from their nature, but not leſs eloquent,
were little known, and inſpired no intereſt; the
third eſtate ſeemed already to be the only aſſembly,
and their opinions became thoſe of the public,
almoſt in an inſtant.

The change already made in the numbers of
the repreſentatives, for the three orders, not only
opened a door for other changes, but rendered
ſome others abſolutely neceſſary.

The

The orders ufed formerly to difcufs the queftions feparately, and the fimple majority in the
affembly of each order determined the queftion.
The determinations of the orders being thus
fixed feparately, they had to meet and reconcile their interefts in a general affembly ; or
when they could not fettle a point amicably, the
opinion of two of the orders carried it againft
the third.   As his majefty, by the advice of his
minifter, had doubled the number of reprefentatives of the third eftate, it was naturally a queftion to be difcuffed, whether the manner of
taking the votes fhould not be changed.   This
was therefore the firft queftion that came before
the deputies.

where is this to be. found.? It was never very conftitutionally fettled I believe.

It was evident that to increafe the number of
voices and to continue the old manner of voting,
would have been perfectly ufelefs, for if the refult of the deliberations of 600 perfons was reduced to unity, and that three hundred in each
of the other affemblies conftituted one vote alfo,
there was no ufe for having named fix hundred
deputies for the third eftate.   The people were
witneffes to all this reafoning, and the queftion
whether they fhould vote by head or by order,
as it was called ; that is to fay, whether the total
majority of voices fhould determine a queftion,
or the majority of orders, was foon decided with
the public in favour of a majority of voices.

Voices not orders.

The nobles and the clergy, on the other fide,
infifted, that as they had feparate interefts, they
ought to vote feparately ; that two bodies of three
hundred each, with different views, could not
with any effect vote againft fix hundred, all

K   united

united in opinion and interest, and who discussed
their affairs in one assembly, whilst they were
separated from each other.   This reasoning was
perfectly good, but it was not of any weight with
the public, who scarcely knew what was passing
in these two assemblies. Suppofing, indeed, the reasonings on all sides had been known, it would
not have resolved the difficulty, because the new
change of a double representation had rendered
the whole an absurd combination.   The debates
on this subject were warm, and occupied all
France ; which ever way they turned, there seemed to be either difficulty or absurdity in the arrangement, except by joining all the members
together in one assembly, and debating their interests in common ; though even this did not ob-
viate the difficulties arising from the nobles and
clergy not possessing the same common interest,
while the other six hundred deputies did.   The
deputies of the third estate, so far from denying
this, allowed it to be true, and it was from this
very circumstance that they made themselves certain of victory ; but they argued that the nobles
and clergy were Frenchmen, that a noble was a
man like another, and that if he had any separate
interest, far from that being a reason for voting
separately, that difference of interest only arose
from abusive privileges, and was a reason for
their being all united in one assembly.

We have already seen, by tracing the fall of
the feudal system, and of the influence of the
Church of Rome, how much men were inclined
to listen to such an opinion ; there was accordingly a great majority of people, and of the deputies themselves, in favour of *one common assem-*
bly ;

bly; this was precisely what thofe who wifhed for a revolution wanted, and it is clear that the minifter who changed the original form of election, muft have had it in view, if he was not totally ignorant of what he was about, and only meant to gain popularity, by adding an ufelefs number to the depuţies of the third eftate.

All Authority in one Center and that Center the Nation from Franklin & Turgot had turn'd the heads of all France.

This was a moment when the court might have made one laft effort to regain popularity and power, it was a time when the necefïity of fuch an attempt was necelfary and very evident. The deputies of the third eftate had completely fhewn what were their intentions, but they had not yet abfolutely tried their force; fo that if the king had made the facrifices of power which were reafonable, and which the general fpirit of the cahiers dictated; if he had reiolved upon economy, and thereby fatisfied the reaionable portion of his fubjects, the revolutionary gentlemen would foon have been reduced to infignificance; but the court did nothing, and the laft moment of its power and influence faft approached; for when once a trial of ftrength was made, and victory followed to the third eftate, the foundation of the revolution was completely and folidly laid. No conceffions which the king could afterwards make, could be accepted, becaufe, arifing from necefïity, they were liable to be fufpected, and the ftronger party could not be fuppofed to accept conditions that neither gratified the ambition of individuals, nor fecured the general intereft.

The court ought to have known the number of members in each of the chambers on whom it might

might depend ; as for the intentions of its enemies, they were well known : it was, therefore,
the excefs either of careletinefs or folly to put itfelf in the power of a general affembly, decidedly
inimical to its interefts, without making any effort to avoid fo dangerous an extremity.

The fhort interval between the firft affembling
of the ftates-general and the meeting of all the
members in one hall, is one of the moft important in the revolution, becaufe it determined completely the conteft between the king and the people, as to power ; with regard to the manner of
ufing that power afterwards, that was not at all
the queftion ; and, certainly, if the greateft enemies of the people had fet to work to point out
the evils to be apprehended, they would not have
been able to do it, for the plain reafon, that no
ftrength of imagination would have been fufficient to have conceived then what has happened
fince.

To add, if poffible, to the impatience of the
public during this period, the only regular method of knowing what paffed in the three different chambers, was by the Journal of Paris, a
daily newfpaper, upon a fmall half fheet, that
had room only to enter into the heads of what
had occurred. This paper was under the direct
influence of the court, therefore was fufpicious
and fufpected ; befides, it never gave the debates
till four or five days after. It is not in England
that there will be any difficulty to conceive the
uneafinefs, anxiety, and difpleafure, occafioned
by fuch a method of reporting thofe important
debates ; this was foreleen by M. le Comte de
                                    Mirabeau,

Mirabeau, of whom we fhall prefently fpeak more, *Mirabeau.*
at large, who had announced a daily paper, containing always the debates of the day preceeding,
and the fubfcription for which had not been open
a week at his bookfeller's,* before the amount
fubfcribed for three months only was more than
thirty thoufand livres, or above twelve hundred
pounds. The court put a ftop to this immediately ; and, by this exertion of power, inflamed
the public mind ftill more, and did not do any
good ; for Mirabeau was one of thofe daring
men with a fertile brain, who foon found out a
means of publifhing a periodical work under fo
reafonable a form, that it would have been the
higheft oppreffion to have fuppreffed it, under
the name of *Letters to his Conftituents ;* thereby
appearing to render an account of the manner in
which he did his duty as a reprefentative, he not
only gave an account of what had paffed in the
affemblies, but he could with propriety add what
he thought proper of his own, which, in the fimple form of a journal, he could not have done fo
properly. Befides, he was not tied down to relate every thing as in a plain narration, and,
therefore, he paffed over in filence whatever did
not fuit his purpofe, and heightened the colours
of whatever did.

The Count de Mirabeau was one of thofe ex- *Mirabeau*
traordinary men, who never feel themfelves in
their element upon ordinary occafions, but who,
in attempts that are difficult and require genius,
carry all before them. Mirabeau, whofe whole
life had been a hiftory of crimes, of blunders,

---

* Monf. le Jay, bookfeller, rue de Léchelle.

and

*Portrait of
Mirabeau*

and of misfortunes, whofe name was confidered as a reproach, and whofe company was fhunned by every man who had money or reputation to preferve, made himfelf confpicuous the moment that the ufual order of fociety begun to be inverted.   Convinced that he could not obtain a feat in the ftates-general amongft the order of nobles, and which, if he could have procured, would not have fuited his defigns; he went to Marfeilles, where the people are of a lively and violent turn; there he became a retail grocer, with the affiftance of money lent him by his bookfeller; and, from behind the counter, dreffed with an apron, he diftributed his groceries, his bon mots, and his principles, amongft all the people of the town, the firft for money, the reft for nothing.   As there never fcarcely was a man who had a greater faculty of rendering himfelf agreeable, as it flattered the fimple citizens to fee a nobleman of an ancient family reduce himfelf to their level, Mirabeau had not found the fmalleft difficulty to procure a majority of votes in his favour.* Perhaps, the violence fince difplayed

by

---

* Concerning fo extraordinary a genius as Mirabeau, there have been a thoufand things afferted, as is ufually the cafe, and moft of them exaggerated, both as to his crimes and his abilities.   The fon of a man of fortune and a man of letters, he had a good education; but, very early in life, fhewed difpofitions which obliged his father to follicit as a favour a lettre de cachet to put him in prifon.   From one crime to another, and from debt to debt, he had paffed the greater part of his time in different prifons, where he had not, however, neglected to improve his mind.   In England, where he came for a little while, he got himfelf into a fcrape with juftice, by which he got into Newgate, and narrowly efcaped being fent to Botany Bay, or to the hulks at Woolwich.   A man, therefore, who had been continually at war with order

by the Marseillois, and, in general, by the inhabitants of the south of France, was as much owing to Mirabeau, as to their natural vivacity of disposition : but, be that as it may, it is certain that the Letters to his Constituents, which he published, produced a very inflammatory effect all through France, and prepared people more and more for those excesses and those persecutions of the nobles, which so soon after took place. By these letters the factious of all sorts were led to a point of re-union, and that point was their author. So that their violent spirits acting upon each other, and then upon the public, a sort of revolutionary volcano was created ; and, if we may be permitted to extend the comparison, it was from this volcano that the lava run, and the ashes flew, which have more or less incommoded every nation in Europe.*

der and the property of others, and who had suffered so much from it, could be no great friend to either : obliged, likewise, to obtain a precarious subsistence by his pen and his address, he wanted none of those talents which were necessary in a revolution. He is said to have been very deficient in personal courage ; but to this he replied, that, as he could not fight with one-tenth of his enemies, it was needless to begin ; when he received a challenge, he therefore cooly drew out a memorandum book, and put his antagonist on the list, to be fought when he should have time. This was attributed to cowardice, but certainly unfairly ; for, had he been willing to fight, and had twenty lives, they would soon have been all gone ; therefore, it was necessary at once either to renounce his revolutionary career, or do as he did.

* Mirabeau was assisted by three Genevese gentlemen ; one of them pensioned by the King of England ; another, who lives with a nobleman in England, and whose names it would be cruel to mention ; and Claviere, who jointly aided in writing his Letters to his constituents.

K

The

The bad moral character of Mirabeau was so much against him, that the first time he attempted to speak, the affembly would not liften to him; but he was not a man to be diverted from his purpofe by any fuch trifling circumftance; for, as he knew better than any one that was there the ftorm that was preparing, as his great penetration informed him of his being more capable of riding on that ftorm than any of thofe around him, he knew he would foon not only be heard, but liftened to; and he was not deceived.

Court affembles Military about Paris

The court, either difregarding or defpifing its enemies, but at the fame time wifhing to put itfelf out of their power, affembled great numbers of the military in and about Paris and Verfailles; but, by the fame fatality which feems to have been attached to all its meafures, no precautions were taken to put the minds of the people at eafe, nor to preferve the troops from fucking in the fame principles of rebellion and revolt, which were but too apparent in the citizens of almoft every defcription.

Parisian

The volatile difpofition of the Parifian is famous all over the world, but with this there is alfo an expedition, quicknefs, and enthufiafm, in what interefts him, that on occafion is capable of producing great effects. Uneafy, and apprehenfive on account of the affemblage of fuch a number of the military, and urged on by the real or pretended apprehenfions of the deputies, who reprefented themfelves as being in the moft imminent danger, the citizens fet to work to gain the confidence and friendfhip of the foldiers. They gave them money, invited them to eat and drink,

drink, and told them that " they also were citi- Seduction of Soldiers
" zens before they were foldiers, and men before
" they were citizens."* The foldier found that a
bottle of burgundy and fuch language were very
convincing; and thofe who could not be convinced
by this means, were attacked by a ftill more irrefiftible fort of arms. The regiment of French
gua ds, confifting of about 3,000 men, on which the Guards corrupted by Money, Women and Wine
court ufed greatly to depend, was feduced by the
three-fold attraction of money, women, and wine.

It was fince the fitting of the ftates-general begun, that a new vigour was given to thofe cabals which had long been carried on in Paris,
particularly in the Palais Royal which belonged Palais Royal
to the Duke of Orleans. This building, originally a royal palace, with a public garden attached to it, had been converted into one large
elegant hollow fquare. The duke's palace occupied only one end, the remainder being fi'led
with fhops, taverns, hotels for lodging ftranger,
gaming houfes, no lefs than three play-houfes;
the great bulk of what was let as lodgings, being
occupied by women of the town. The middle
ftill continued to be a garden in the form of an
oblong fquare, in which were feveral fmall book-
fellers' fhops and fome coffee-houfes under painted
pavilions. A piazza of very elegant architecture
went round the whole, fo that in rainy or in fair
weather it was equally convenient as a prome-
nade. The defcription of the Palais Royal,

---

* This fort of reafoning, fo abfurd in itfelf, feems pe-
culiarly adapted to a French brain; it leads to a quick conclufion: and to men who do not take the time nor trouble
to think, is plaufible enough: at any rate, it produced great
effects.

as it was called, is entered into, becaufe, during the whole of the revolution, it has been
a theatre of as great, and fometimes greater importance, than the affembly of the deputies.

Numbers of clubs, named fo after the Eng-
iifh manner, had been eftablifhed, under the
roof of this extenfive building, and the protection of its mafter, for being exempt from the vi-
fits of the ordinary officers of the police as a royal
garden, men there found fafety for cabal and
intrigue, when it was to be found no where elfe.
It was from this garden that meffengers were
fent every two or three hours on important occafions, to communicate between the factious
leaders in Paris and at Verfailles.   The garden
itfelf, which ufed to be the refort of wit and
beauty, became filled with groops of the angry
looking and wretched dregs of the people, mixed,
however, with the mechanics who had left their
fhops, and the loweft clafs of women, who had
left their children and families *to work at the revolution.*

The eyes of all the factious turned naturally
to Mirabeau, whofe former character put villainy quite at its eafe in making any fort of propofition, and whofe audacity and ability rendered him capable of being ufeful in whatever
he might undertake.

It was in the Palais Royal that every experiment upon the minds of the people was made ;
there treafon was fpoken and fedition circulated
with impunity ; and from thence were difpatched
                                            thofe

thefe meſſengers of confuſion who have ſince de- *Meſſengers of Confuſion*
ſolated that miſerable country.

At laſt, a ſort of revolt among the French *Revolt of Guards*
guards broke out, inſtigated and aſſiſted by the
people, and ſome of their number were ſecured
and lodged in the abbey priſon. The people *Abbey Priſon*
ſeemed to take an active intereſt in the fate of thoſe
mutinous ſoldiers, who, by every military law,
deſerved to be ſeverely puniſhed. Attempts were
made to break open their priſon, and meſſengers
diſpatched to aſk from the king their pardon, in a
tone that, addreſſed to a ſovereign, was rather that
of menace than of petition. The court had not
determined what party to take, when the priſon
was forced, and the mutineers in queſtion eſcaped *Rescue*
without difficulty to the common aſylum of inſurrection, the Palais Royal; and there, under
a pretence of hiding themſelves, they remained
in a room occupied by a woman of the town,
which they entered by a ſort of force; but ſo
little was their fear of being diſcovered, that a
ſmall baſket was hung over the windows, to col- *Basket*
lect money from the crowd that was perpetually
paſſing or aſſembled below; and in the courſe of a
few days, more than eight thouſand livres were *8000 Livres*
collected. Drunkenneſs, riot, and the pilfering of
thoſe who joined them in their retreat, prevented
an account from being kept of what was afterwards received. This, however, ſhewed the
general diſpoſition of people of a claſs who were
able to give money. The king had the weakneſs now to pardon a fault, which was become
ten times greater than at firſt; ſo that the whole
regiment, encouraged by the example of impunity
and reward, and led on by inclination, became
a band

a band of mutineers, and, in fact, were the first
to rebel when open force was resulted to.

States General

The states-general still went on ; the Parisians
attended it in crowds every day ; and on the Sunday, the deputies of the third estate and of the
low clergy went to pay visits in Paris ; so that the
Parisian with one hand gave to the soldier, and
with the other to the deputy.

*Minority of Nobles
and Clergy join
the 3d Estate*

The states had already been in this condition
for three weeks, when the assembly of the nobles
divided in itself, and the assembly of the clergy
did the same ; a minority, indeed, but not an
inconsiderable one of each, having declared they
would join the third estate in one common assembly.

Orleans follows

The Duke of Orleans, finding that it was now
time to shew himself, declared that he was ready
to pass over at the head of a considerable number of his order, and join in the common assembly ; so that the king and court, finding what
they had to fear, resolved to anticipate the storm.

23. June 1789

Accordingly, on the 23rd of June, the king came
to the assembly, and offered to abolish all the
grievances which it was known the majority of
the cahiers contained.[A] This declaration, which
a month sooner would have occasioned the greatest
pleasure, and would have, perhaps, defeated the
manœuvres of those who sought revolt and disorder, was received by the assembly with a cold
indifference. When his majesty withdrew, and

[A] There are at the end, notes, consisting of such letters and papers as it is essential to know, but which could not
be with propriety inserted in the body of the work.

the

the affembly, according to cuftom, fhould have adjourned till next day, the deputies of the third eftate remained, (in their own chamber where the affembly was) and began immediately to debate very warmly, and moft part of the fpeakers were for rejecting the offers of the king.

His majefty, finding that the affembly continued fitting, fent his mafter of the ceremonies with a herald, to fignify his will, that they *Herald* fhould not continue that day. The audacious Mirabeau anfwered, without rifing up from his *Mirabeau.* feat, with a loud voice and a menacing afpect, " Go," fays he, " and tell your mafter, that we " are here by the will of the people, and that " we fhall not depart but by the force of the " bayonet."

This was the firft open declaration of difobedience to his majefty, in which the whole affembly participated by their approbation, and by their continuing to fit.

It is well known, how reports are fpread with *Reports fpread and* rapidity and exaggerated with fuccefs, in a large *fwelled.* city, and on an important occafion. It was reported in lefs than two hours after in Paris, that the affembly was threatened with the bayonet, and imagination added, that they were actually become martyrs to their own firmnefs, and their duty to their conftituents.

This open act of firmnefs and audacity on the fide of the deputies not being refifted, either by force or any other mode, by the court, was confidered as a fair trial of ftrength and as a decided victory.

victory.   The deputies of the third eftate gained courage, and thofe of the two other orders, finding the difcuffions were not likely to terminate, begun individually to quit their refpective affemblies, and join the affembly of the third eftate. This method was certainly very irregular, but there was now no rule for any thing; and as the fyftem is in all matters of revolution, that a point gained is a victory obtained, no matter how, this defertion of their order, and the intereft of their conftituents,* was greatly applauded, and the deferters honourably received.   The hopes of being well treated, in cafe of an infurrection of the people, acted forcibly on individuals, and anonymous letters were fent to many of them, which ftrengthened both the hopes and fears which they might have concerning the conduct to be adopted.

a Point gained is a victory.

Mirabeau a Leader. Mirabeau, who had gained as much credit by his fpeech on the 23rd of June with the affembly, as the affembly itfelf had gained with the people, now became a leading man, and conceived the project of writing an addrefs to the king, in the name of the affembly, requefting him to fend away the troops who were furrounding Verfailles and the capital, who, faid he, were only ufeful on the frontiers against enemies, but who could do no good in the interior of the country, their arms directed against the reprefentatives of the nation,

* As the affemblies of nobles chofe deputies quite diftinctly from the other affemblies, the point of their remaining feparate was, in fact, determined; for if they were to be confounded, it fhould have been by a new election, in which the electors fhould have been mingled in one body.

employed

employed in feeking what tended to make the people happy.

This addrefs, written with great elegance and *Addrefs* force of language, was read by Mirabeau to the affembly, which was unbounded in its applaufe: a fecond reading was demanded, and again applauded. The addrefs was then refolved upon, and prefented by a deputation of the members, who waited on the king.

The court began now ferioufly to think of one effort before all fhould be loft. There were great numbers of foldiers, as they imagined, at their command. There was a camp of twenty thoufand *20,000* men within a mile of Paris, and military quartered every where in and about both Paris and Verfailles. The ancient courtiers feemed awakened from their lethargy, and affembled round their king; but M. Necker was an infurmounta- *Necker* ble barrier in the way; it was impoffible to take any fteps without his knowledge, and they could never expect to gain his confent to what they propofed to do.

The plan that was laid, had it been well put in execution, might perhaps have re-eftablifhed the ancient fyftem completely, but the fame want of *Irrefolution* energy on the part of thofe employed to put it in execution, that had all along been evident, and which has been evident in all the operations of that party ever fince, by mifgiving, overturned the monarchy completely in the fpace of a few days.

The

Necker to be dismissed The plan was simply this, M. Necker, and those who acted with him, were to be displaced, and sent to a distance. Ministers attached to the court, and whose fidelity was known, were to be put in their place, and a loan of one hundred and twenty-five millions Tournois was secured amongst the monied people, with which sum the court could go on, at least for some time; the states-general was to be dissolved by the king's simple authority, if it would not accept his offers, and it is never to be doubted *Force to be employed* that force was to have been employed in case of resistance.

This plan was arranged with a secrecy that did credit to those who conducted it, and accordingly on Saturday, at a late hour, when the assembly was dispersed till Monday; each of the ministers got his dismission in the usual form, and not being ignorant of what was meant, each departed that same night with all the secrecy possible. Such was the secrecy with which this was performed, that though M. Necker quitted his house at Versailles at eleven o'clock on the Saturday evening, it was not known amongst the servants of the house before ten o'clock on the Sunday morning: it began to be known in Versailles at eleven, and was spread abroad in Paris about one. The consternation was prodigious and general, but perhaps would not have been attended with any violent movement, had not the court by its imprudence and weakness rendered resistance necessary.

The deputies who remained at Versailles, dispatched messengers to Paris; they expected to be be all maffacred or imprifoned, at leaft. The people of Paris expected little better; their credulity was great, and their fear greater; fo that under fuch apprehenfions it only wanted a fignal given to make an infurrection break forth, and this fignal was not long wanting. Mirabeau, and all thofe who had openly acted againft the court, faw their laft hour, they imagined, approach; thofe who had planned and acted more fecretly, apprehended their actions were known, and would be punifhed; there was not any room for hefitation or delay; the combat was begun, and it.was become abfolutely neceffary to act immediately, or fink for ever. It was not now to the leaders, a fpeculation of intereft and intrigue, it was an affair of life and death, from the Duke of Orleans to the loweft emiffary. Every means that they could command of money, or other, was employed to overcome this difficulty, the greateft and the graveft poffible, but which, whatever was the event, muft be the laft, as it muft end in death or victory.

On the Sunday, in the evening, the approach of the military, with cannon, to a public walk, where the Parifians amufed themfelves with their families, brought things to a crifis. Some perfons thinking themfelve protected from the cannon, by the prefence of the great numbers of women and children who were there, threw a few ftones at the foldiers; a fort of battle enfued, and feveral were killed, and others wounded on both fides.

As it is not to write the hiftory of the revolution that we are employed, thofe circumftances,

M   the

the moft ftriking in themfelves are what fhould be dwelt upon the leaft, becaufe they are already better known than any others, and have not an immediate connection with our plan, which is to trace opinions, their refults, and the modes of fpreading them. It becomes therefore a matter of importance to know how the foldiery were gained; the faults of the court in lofing their affections; the caufes of the battle of the Thuilleries (as it was called), are alfo important to be known; but a relation of how it was conducted, is not effential to our purpofe; the plan of the work is not fufficiently extenfive to admit of fuch details, however interefting they may be. No blame can be laid upon the people in this conjuncture; felf-prefervation was their object; force was become neceffary, and it was equally juft and natural to employ it.

Battle of the Thuilleries

The Prince de Lambefk, who commanded this fatal expedition, began it imprudently, and finifhed it the fame; for except giving the people to know what they had to expect, it had no other immediate confequence. The military were withdrawn from the fpot, having irritated, but not intimidated; and the frightened inhabitants of a city, where there were at leaft feven hundred thoufand fouls, were left time to rally, and to take meafures for infuring themfelves victory.

Lambefk

The night was paft by the leaders of the people in combining their plans, and by themfelves in feizing upon all the arms that could be procured. Previous to the election of the deputies, Paris had been divided into fixty different portions, called fections; one church in each fection

Sections

tion was employed for the primary affemblies, who chofe among themfelves electors, who all affembled at the archbifhop's palace, there to *Archbifhops Palace* chufe the deputies. Thefe fections ferved as points of re-union to the citizens, who now affembled there, all ranks promifcuoufly; for the danger was general. Though there were undoubtedly many perfons who had nothing to fear from the court, they had a great deal to fear from their fellow citizens, if they did not join them, which they all did; and thus the court united the whole of that great city in one mind and intereft by its imprudence. Had the refactory deputies been feized, that fame night, the plan might have yet fucceeded, but this was left undone, and thereby the affair entirely failed.

From this time the revolt obtained a phyfical exiftence; and the greater force was on the fide of the revolted, fo that the undecided individual knew, by embracing their caufe, he had leaft to fear. This is the rubicon of revolutions; it is *Rubicon of Revolutions.* the belief that force is on the fide of government that conftitutes its force; the contrary idea produces its immediate fall, and whether the opinion is at firft founded in fact or not, it becomes realized in an inftant; for force lies where it is *Force is where it is* thought to lie, as the greater number are de- *thought to be.* termined only by the fimple feelings of fear and of hope.

It is not in what has hitherto happened that the *Democratic Party* democratic party is to be blamed. A few individuals were certainly guilty of wrong intentions from the beginning, but by no means were the people, who wifhed for liberty and happinefs; when

when that becomes a crime, life will become a
burthen, and the only fit retreat for a man who
has any spirit or mind, will be the silent grave.
It was more than probable that the court would
not have been faithful to the offers made on the
3rd of June, had they been accepted; the people wanted a bill of rights, and it was a bill of rights
alone that ought to have satisfied them; and those
who refused it; certainly may reproach themselves
with being, in part, the occasion of what has since
happened; they did not participate either in the cruelties or injustices of which they have been the
victims, but they were neverthelefs in a great
meafure the caufe. It is too late to be reafonable and juft when we are forced into it. Such
conduct excites fufpicion, blame, and contempt,
while a contrary behaviour abtains confidence,
efteem, and gratitude.

A greater leffon can never be given to thofe
who govern than this, and if the people and their
leaders, who turned to advantage with fuch addrefs the faults of the court, had been inftructed
by them, and learned juftice and moderation
when it came to their turn to reign, they might
long ago have enjoyed that happinefs which a contrary behaviour has fo completely banifhed from
their miferable country. It is with reluctance
that we can vindicate the conduct of men for a
moment, who have fince been guilty of fuch
crimes as make nature fhudder, and will not only
remain a ftain upon their nation, but will reflect
difhonour on the whole human race.

C H A P. V.

First motives of the insurrection good, but soon be-
came bad—Multitude armed—Bastile, &c.
taken—Beginning of cruelties—Adroit manœuvre
by which all France was armed—King visits
Paris—Triumph of the people is complete—JA-
COBIN CLUB begins its affiliation—destruc-
tion of liberty occasioned by them—Mistakes in
England on this head.

IF the beginning of this history has been employed in relating the misconduct and follies of a
state of society, where prejudice in favour of what
was ancient was carried too far ; what remains,
is destined to paint the miseries and crimes into
which men fall, when they, under the idea of
their being philosophers, lose all respect for expe- *Experience not always*
rience, thinking that they are getting rid only of *Prejudice*
prejudice.

The motive of the multitude being liberty and
happiness, was only what they have in common
with all mankind, but the unexampled vanity
with which their first successes were followed,
their ignorance of what liberty consisted in, and
the cruelty and want of any attention to principle, with which their possession of power was
accompanied, are proofs that violent revolutions *Revolutions destroy*
destroy the moral principle in man, by setting *moral Principle*
ambition and interest in too powerful a manner to *not always.*
work ; at the same time that by setting a great
object

object continually before the eyes of the individual, he paffes over without reluctance what would in other times have made him fhudder only to have thought of.

The enthufiafm infpired by continually fpeaking and acting in a common caufe, and fharing a common danger, gives a fort of electric fhock that is communicated from one eye to another, that raifes the man above himfelf in courage, and finks him below the brute in favagenefs. The happinefs of men, and extremes of all forts, are at variance; they are by no means, therefore, the friends of the people, who open a door to exceffes; and thofe who may in future attempt fuch a thing, will be doubly to blame; for the revolutionifts of whom we have been fpeaking, were, perhaps, ignorant of the evils they were bringing on; thofe who follow their example, will not have the fame excufe, for the experiment has been very clearly made, and its refult is recorded in the blood of moft of thofe who were guilty of fuch temerity.

Happinefs not in extreams.

The Monday which fucceeded the battle of the Thuilleries, found all the inhabitants of Paris either armed or affembled. Their fections affumed the appearance of fo many federal ftates, having the town-houfe for its center, to which deputies from the different fections were fent. Paris became thereby an organifed military government, capable of acting with fome degree of unity. The prifons were opened; and the fufpected perfons difarmed; a green cockade was ordered to be worn by all thofe who were *for the people*, as they termed it, but having reflected, that the livery

Green Cockade

livery of the Count d'Artois was green, it was changed for the party-coloured cockade, which *3 coloured Cockade* has been called the national cockade ever since, and which was the livery of the chief of the factious, Philip Duke of Orleans.

The whole of the Monday was thus spent in securing Paris against the attack supposed to be meditated by the troops; the court affrighted, or at least aftonished at the tumult it had occafioned, remained inactive. Not one effort was made either to feize the ringleaders of the people, *No Ringleaders seiz'd* or to diffolve the affembly at Verfailles, nor to difpatch meffengers to explain the affair to the diftant provinces. This inexcufable pufillanimity and neglect was improved to advantage by its enemies. The barriers or gates, where duty was collected on merchandizes on entering into Paris, were kept fhut, and furrounded by an immenfe crowd of people, fo that neither the peaceable who wanted to retire from danger, nor thofe who wifhed to depart with defign, were allowed to go. This fingle circumftance occafioned an alarm in the whole kingdom, as the poft and other daily communications failed, in the middle of fummer, and in fine weather, the minds of the people, already extremely uneafy every where, were prepared for fome great event, and being reduced to the laft pitch of conftern- *Consternation.* ation, were ready to receive with alacrity whatever impulfe might be given to them by the party that fhould remain victorious.

At the fame time that this was paffing in Paris, the affembly, afraid to feparate, continued to fit, thereby appearing to do from firmnefs, what
was.

was really done from fear; for it was much lefs dangerous for each member to continue in the common hall, than to venture to go home to his lodgings. The fame feeling acting upon all, produced the fame effect on all, and the affembly was *Affembly perma*permanent. It probably was this that difcon-*nent*certed the court, for it is impoffib.e that the firft fteps of Saturday and Sunday could have been taken without an intention to follow them up with vigour and efficacy; but as they were followed by no meafures of any fort, fomething muft have difconcerted their plan, and it was moft probably the permanence of the affembly.

The court fhould have been prepared for vigorous meafures, as it could not be fuppofed that its enemies, having all at ftake, would want energy, until all hope was gone of faving themfelves by energy. The affembly endeavoured to difplay that ferenity and firmnefs which were fo *Impofing Sereni*neceffary to impofe both upon its enemies and its *ty.*friends. News from the deputies to Paris, and from Paris to the deputies, could not go freely, but it went fo as to affure the leaders of mutual fupport, and to inform them, in general terms, of the manner in which things went on. During this time, all minds being fet to work in Paris, and fafety rather than revolt being the common object, the morning of the memorable Tuefday, *14. July.*the 14th of July, began by a more regular plan of operations.

All the arms in the workfhops of the armourers having been feized on Sunday evening, thofe belonging to individuals had been produced on the Monday, but ftill that was far from fufficient to

arm

arm one hundred and fifty thousand persons. As there were arms supposed to be in the Bastile, the *Bastile* arsenal, and the hospital of invalids, different detachments of a mob collected early in the morning before the town-house, went from thence to each of these places, but so little was an attack of the fort expected, that at the arsenal and *Arsenal* the hospital, not the least resistance was made. *Hospital* The French guards being debauched from their duty, as we have already said, mixing with the mob, gave a sort of conduct, regularity, and appearance of force to these detachments, which intimidated those who might otherwise, perhaps, have attempted to resist. The numerous detachment which went against the hospital having procured a considerable quantity of arms, marched immediately against the camp that was pitched *Camp* in the neighbourhood; the soldiers, partly debauched like the French guards, and the officers without superior orders, astonished at this audacity, and totally ignorant of the number and force of those who had come against them, and imagining that the people were every where victorious, abandoned their tents, and marched off without resisting.

The party that went against the Bastile, alone *Bastile* met with some difficulty from the nature of the building; it was impossible to walk straight into it, as it was built with all the precautions of an ancient fortress, though quite incapable of any regular resistance: without any advanced works, and the embrasures of the cannons (of a small calibre) seventy feet from the ground, those who might attack the drawbridge and the gate, run but little risk. The strength of the gate was the real
N   measure

meafure of the force of the Baftile; had it been occupied by a garrifon, and fupplied with what is neceffary for a fiege; but the garrifon confift-ed of a few invalids, without provifions for one day, and commanded by a man who had been very capable of acting as a keeper of a pri-fon, but was very incapable of defending a for-trefs as a governor. [*Note* B,]

The ftate of the Baftile only permitting a ne-gative defence, the proper way would have been to have kept the gate fhut, and to have waited, without any offenfive act: but de Lawnay, the governor, loft whatever prefence of mind he had; a few random fhot, which went to a diftance, were fired from the cannon on the top, and fome mufketry difcharged from the narrow windows that are to be feen in moft old fortifications, for the purpofe of ufing fmall arms. This only ex-afperated the mob, which from its numbers, and the fituation of the ftreets, could not retreat, as the crowds which were out of all danger would not make way for thofe who were foremoft, and who run fome little rifk. This tumultuous at-tack was continued from eleven o'clock in the morning till about four in the afternoon, at which time the gates were opened, upon a promife from thofe who directed the people at the town-houfe, of mercy to the governor and garrifon. All the accounts of bravery on one fide, and refiftance on the other, which were fpread abroad with in-duftry, were not merely exaggerated, they were abfolutely without foundation, though they were far from being without utility to the popular fide. On a pretence of treafon, the governor and the fub-governor were carried to the Place de Greve, before

before the town-houfe (with all manner of blows and ill-ufage on the road) where their brains were blown out, and, fhortly after, their heads cut off. Two private invalids were hanged to the lamp iron, oppofite the town-houfe, and were the firft facrificed by that mode, which was for fome time fo popular and fo highly in vogue amongft the mob in all the towns in France. The Prevot des Marchands, who had prefided at the Hotel de Ville, was treated in the fame manner as the governor, becaufe he was fuppofed to have betrayed the people, when, in fact, he had only betrayed his king. Thus the man who had prefided over the revolt during about thirty-fix hours, and who had figned the order for wearing the party-coloured cockade, fell a facrifice to thofe paffions which he had affifted to roufe, and endeavoured, without either fortitude or abilities, to direct. He was thus the firft inftance in the prefent revolution of the danger there is in conducting the people, as de Lawnay was of the folly of believing them ; for, when under the influence of fear, the people ftop at nothing that is thought conducive to fafety, and, when mafters of the field, their victims are pointed out by their caprice.

The taking of the Baftile furnifhed the people of Paris with an ample fubject for boafting and admiration, as well as with materials for inflaming the minds of the people, as they got poffeffion of a large collection of printed books and manufcripts that had been fuppreffed by government, and, befides thefe, of the regifters of that famous prifon.

The

[marginal annotations:] Lamp Iron — Prevot des Marchands — Taking the Bastile.

The fuccefs of this day which had put the ar-
fenal, the Baftile, and a great quantity of arms
in poffeffion of the people of Paris, was a death
ftroke to thofe who fupported the court. They
now confidered themfelves as undone, and fuch
of them as yet remained in Paris endeavoured to
efcape by every means in their power. There
was now a complete change on the countenances
and in the minds of the inhabitants; the confternation of the two preceding days gave place to

Triumph.

a joyful triumph. Their own bravery was celebrated by themfelves, and magnified without
difficulty on account of the confufion and general enthufiafm. They thought they had taken
the Baftile by ftorm and irrefiftible effort. The
French guards were at the fervice of the citizens,
who, by a fudden but not an unnatural tranfiti-
on, difplayed a confidence and fecurity equal to
their former fear; the only anxiety that now remained, was concerning the affembly at Verfailles.

Events not only had fucceeded with fuch rapidity, but had been fo multiplied, that it was impoffible to fend to Verfailles any diftinct or true
account of what had happened; accordingly the
news that arrived in the evening and night between the Tuefday and Wednefday, were all of
a very confufed nature. It was, however, generally underftood and believed, as in Paris, that
the victory had been obtained by unexampled
prodigies of valour. The heads of the men who

Heads on Pikes.

had been murdered, having been carried upon
pikes all through Paris as a fpectacle to the people, had afforded not only a certain proof of the
reality of the victory, but of the ferocious difpofition

tion of the conquerors. The whole being then seen under the complication of circumstances the most capable of astonishing, did not fail to produce upon the deputies and the court a complete change.

The assembly, which had considered its existence as menaced every hour, took now the tone of conquerors. and the deputies of the two orders who had hitherto seemed to join the third estate with reluctance, now assisted with cordiality; for though they knew that the victories of Paris might be false or exaggerated, they were sensible that the court was incapable of making any effort in their favour.

Conquerors.

The form of the states-general, deranged in the beginning by the new manner of election, had since been totally changed, by an early exercise of power, in altering the name from that of States-General to *National Assembly.* Secured by their own perseverance, by the energy of the people of Paris, and by the pusillanimity of the court, from any personal danger, the deputies assumed another tone; it was resolved, that they should dispatch messengers through the whole kingdom to inform their constituents of what had happened; to rejoice with them at the fall of a faction, which meant, as they pretended, to have burnt Paris, dissolved, and perhaps massacred the assembly, and established despotism on a more firm basis than ever. This was a natural enough measure, and something of the sort was even absolutely unavoidable. Here begun to be seen the immense advantage which a numerous assembly enjoys in swaying a whole people, when actuated

National Assembly

immense advantage of a numerous Assembly in Swaying a whole People.

actuated by one general intereſt.   Without loſs
of time, each deputy wrote to his own province,
and the aſſembly compoſed a general relation of
the affair, in which, if the bravery of the Pariſians was augmented, their own firmneſs was not
diminiſhed.   In the ſtate of France, all intelligence having been ſuſpended for three days, this
produced completely the effect intended.   The
whole of France turned to the ſide of the Pariſians, and approved their meaſures : but a ſim-
ple approbation was not what the leaders of the
revolt wanted ; they wanted ſupport and participation, that they might run no riſque from a
change.   The adminiſtration of the public affairs
in every town and in every province belonged to
people placed by the king, who could not expect
to be truſted, or remain in office, if the revolution continued.   From the governors of provinces, and magiſtrates of towns, who had the adminiſtration of all public affairs in their hands,
oppoſition was therefore to be dreaded, and was
not to be riſqued.   We are now going to ſee the
moſt curious and moſt ſucceſsful manœuvre that
has ever been practiſed in any revolution, and it
was Mirabeau by whom it was planned and conducted.

Before there was any time to recover from the
fear, aſtoniſhment, or enthuſiaſm, which the
firſt news had ſpread, men were ſeen going
through the whole of France, men who were
ſtrangers in the places through which they went,
announcing the arrival of ten thouſand brigands,
or plunderers.   The brigands exiſted no where,
and were dreaded every where.   Every town in
France, in proportion as the rumour arrived,
felt

felt itfelf in danger, nearly as Paris had done on the Sunday and Monday; fo that they armed, and in a few days after came a decree of the affembly regulating the national guards of Paris, and directing every town in the kingdom to follow the fame plan. The authority of the affembly might probably not have been fufficient to put arms in the hands of the people, contrary to the will of the magiftrates, and for the avowed purpofe of revolt; but the fear of the brigands, whom nobody ever faw, and every body heard of, had already done that, fo that it was now too late for the magiftrates to attempt to refift, and the example of the Prevot des Marchands, at Paris, was a fort of hint what the confequences of fuch an attempt might naturally be, and therefore ferved to co-operate with the other equal and active meafures which had been taken.

Thus was an armed militia, amounting already to above two millions and a half of people, *2,500,000 Militia.* inftituted in lefs than fifteen days over the whole extent of France, and not only were they inftituted, but in activity, and in a condition to operate whatever the affembly might order, or their own views of things might point out. It was a general force, capable of receiving an impulfe from one common center, but poffeffed of an enthufiaftic energy, that, had it always been directed to one good end, would have conftituted a power fuch as no nation ever poffeffed in the world.

While the leaders of the people created, as if by a fupernatural effort, a new military, as well

as

as civil power, all through the kingdom, the
court relinquished the small degree of authority
which it had till then possessed. Amongst the
cries of victory, imprecations and threats of vengeance against the enemies of the people had
been heard in Paris, and it was reported at Verfailles in the fame breath, that the Bastile was
taken, the governor murdered, together with all
thofe who remained faithful to the court; that
their heads were carried in triumph by the people, who had threatened to march to Verſailles
to be revenged in the fame manner on its opprel-
fors.   The Count d'Artois, famous for his pleafures, his expences, and what was termed his
ariſtocracy, together with all the new miniſters,
were menaced.   Between the moment of receiving this intelligence and their flight, the interval
was but ſhort.   The Count d'Artois, with all
his family, left Verſailles that fame night; the
new miniſters, who had not yet begun to act,
followed his example; the Prince of Condé from
other motives carried off his family likewife;
and, in lefs than twenty-four hours, the court
of Verſailles was almoſt deferted, and thofe who
remained ſhared in the inquietude and aſtoniſhment of the royal family.

D'Artois

Condé

It was of too great importance for the affembly
to be able to guide the movements of Paris, for
the attempt not to be made; accordingly, on
Wednefday evening a numerous deputation of the
three orders arrived to fraternife with the leaders
of the infurrection.   The different dreffes of the
orders at firſt excited amongſt the people a fenfation of approbation and pleafure.   The nobles
diſplayed for the laſt time their elegant Spaniſh
                                                habiliments,

habiliments, and the people faw with pleafure, which foon changed to a different fenfation, thofe defcendants of the feudal lords reduced to the clafs of fimple citizens. The fimple and inelegant, or rather boyifh, drefs of their own deputies afforded at firft view a contraft that by no means was agreeable, even when they reflected on what was, in times paft; but, when they turned their eyes to the prefent moment, and found the deputies were all of equal importance, with this difference, that the deputy of the third eftate was playing a willing part, while the other acted a forced one, vexation and anger foon fucceeded.

The people of Paris, equally occupied to give orders, and to execute them, had determined in their fections on the deftruction of the Baftile, *Fall of the Bastile.* and it was actually begun. An immenfe crowd had mounted upon its parapet, and by mere human force had begun to throw down the large ftones of which it was built. The deputies arrived from Verfailles confirmed the decree of is deftruction, and mounted upon its battlements to encourage the people who were at work. The Baftile had been employed only for prifoners fent by letters de cachet without any trial; it was, therefore, confidered, from its peculiar appearance and public fituation, as a fort of defpotifm perfonified, and there were few who did not feel a pleafure in feeing it fall; the enthufiafm of liberty was not a little increafed when the people faw the nodding plumes of the feudal lords commanding the deftruction of this remain of feudal power. It had a theatrical fort of effect, and infpired people more and more with the love of liberty, and a hatred for defpotifm.

O Two

Bailly

Orleans & Mirabeau

Two men had rendered themselves conspicuous in the assembly, Monf. Bailly, an academician and astronomer of a good private character, and who had already been president, who had distinguished himself for his presence of mind and firmness, and who was strongly imbibed with the ambition and philosophy of the revolution. The Duke of Orleans and Mirabeau saw in him a man fit for their purpose; and by raising a man of reputed integrity, and a man of learning, to such a situation, the confidence of the people would be obtained, and men of letters in general be attached to the revolution. This last was not, perhaps, immediately any great object, but promised ultimately to be so; for, as the new principles spread amongst the people were all of them supported by false reasonings, it was of a double importance to secure the support of those men, who, as friends, could support the new principles, or who, as enemies, might destroy them. M. Bailly

Mayor of Paris

F. lefselles.

Fayette

was proposed as mayor of Paris, the name of Prevot des Marchands being declared infamous, with the memory of the unfortunate de Flesselles, who had last borne it.

M. de la Fayette, already publicly known, not for any distinguished conduct in American, but for his having been there, his having the honour to call himself the friend of Gen. Washington, his having distinguished himself as a friend of liberty, such as they understood it in France, was proclaimed by popular assemblies, commander of the armed multitude.

M. de la Fayette was one of those men who, with a great concealed ambition, had patience enough

Portrait

enough to wait for opportunity to gratify it ; and who, being allied by marriage to the family of Noailles, one of the richeft, moft numerous, and moft intriguing at court, was powerfully ftimulated and fupported. La Fayette's other paffions being entirely fubfervient to his vanity and ambition, he had few of thofe vices that hurt a public man with the public. Although not agreeable to the Duke of Orleans, who would have preferred a man that loved money to an ambitious man, he was not at that time very difagreeable ; and there was not any method of bettering the matter ; he, therefore, met with his fupport alfo, and as both he and M. Bailly were of the firft deputation, they were propofed and proclaimed by the people. Infurrection was then, to ufe their own expreffion organifed, and two ambitious men placed at its head ; the firft of whom laboured under great perfonal obligations to the king,* and the fecond was going quite contrary to his inftructions as a reprefentative of the order of the nobles.

A fyftem, however plaufible it may otherwife be, that is founded upon a falfe bafis, muft in the end lead its followers to ruin and error. Bailly and La Fayette vindicated their conduct under the plea of the general intereft, the good of the people, and the caufe of liberty. Vain illufions and defpicable fubterfuge! as if the interefts of mankind and their happinefs could ever permanently be advanced by what was itfelf cri-

* M. Bailly had a penfion from his majefty, and apartments in the palace of the Louvre. His other faults might have been forgiven him, had he not added fuch black ingratitude, which ought not and never can be forgiven.

minal ;

minal; as if *their* ſtanding forward to head the
revolt were neceſſary, which confummate vanity
alone could make them think. Mirabeau had
never received the favours of a court, and he had
fometimes felt its oppreſſion; he did not, therefore, add ingratitude to his crimes; his conduct
was not unnatural, and his faults, great as they
were, might be forgotten; but the mayor and
the commander had not the pecuniary neceſſities
of Mirabeau to plead as an excufe, and Mirabeau had no ingratitude with which he could accufe himfelf.

We ſhall fee in what follows, that though thefe
men were unfit for a revolution, yet they were not
unfit for the beginning of one; on the contrary,
perhaps men of ſteady principle and firm conduct
would not have ferved the caufe in queſtion fo
well. Anarchy was the bufinefs, and the beſt
men to bring it about were fuch, as, having
double views and little means, make their court
to every party, and are ufeful to none in particular. It is true, that fuch men can never expect
to ride out the ſtorm, but that is their own affair;
and we never fee, that there is any difficulty in
finding thofe who are willing to try, when they
have it in their power.

It will be an important leſſon for all future
nations, as well as for individuals, to obferve how
their firſt errors ended, in bringing deſtruction upon all thofe who affifted in this revolution. The
only moment that the revolutioniſts had of real
glory, and where they are not to be blamed, was
in the interval of the few days between the dif-
miſſal of M. Necker and their being maſters of
the

the public force: that fhort interval had been employed in exertions, which were aftonifhing for their activity and energy, and which, being in felf-defence, can never be queftioned as to their motives; and if, afterwards, it turned to a difgraceful revolution, it muft be imputed to the ignorance and bad intention of the members of the affembly, who, not contented with turning to advantage an infurrection, muft endeavour to perpetuate it, by adopting it as a principle, that to revolt was a facred duty. They pretended to copy and to quote Roufleau, but in what man- *Roufleau* ner did they do it? The author of the Social Compact could never have conceived an order of things, where perpetual change being adopted as a firft principle, there could exift no compact.

If the court abufed power when it was in pof- *Ct abufed Power.* feffion of it, and if it let flip opportunity, the *loft opportunity.* revolutionary leaders did the fame. As to abufing power, they have done nothing but that from the time we fpeak of to the prefent hour; and as to letting flip opportunity, they now let flip one which will never return.

The firft infurrection being in a manner ended by the complete victory obtained, there was an opportunity of obtaining a *bill of rights*, and efta-blifhing law and order, before the people, who had only been the inftruments, fhould become accuftomed to exceffes, which would render the eftablifhment of law and order very difficult, if not impracticable. It is well known, that peace *Peace & order* and order can never be maintained amongft a *maintain'd by* turbulent people but by force and defpotifm; *Force.* thofe who love liberty fhould, therefore, take great

great care not to deftroy the love of order and
obedience to law in the general mafs of the people, as a ftrong building can never be conftructed
of rotten materials ; if, at that time, the leaders
of the popular party could have eftablifhed the
new order of things, as we had done in England,
before riot, pillage, and maffacre, had become
habitual to the people, it might have been a fhort
and a happy revolution ; but they let flip the occafion, perhaps, from ignorance of the confequences, but, probably, becaufe it did not fuit
their particular views.

Had the leaders of the affembly been men of
property and of plain good fenfe, as were our
Englifh barons at Runnymede, they would have
been contented with laying a folid foundation for
liberty ; but they were moftly men of no property,
fmatterers in metaphyfics and philofophy, who,
thinking themfelves equal to any tafk, would not
be content with laying the foundations of a better
order of things ; they muft deftroy the old order
to eftablifh a new one in its place, and rifk the
fafety and welfare of their country for the fake
of wild theories which they had invented, and
which were totally impracticable.

In the deferted ftate of the court, his majefty
had been at the affembly, to teftify his conftant
defire of making his people happy, and his will
and intention to co operate in every meafure that
might be thought conducive to fuch an end ; but
it was now too late ; he was willing to make a
facrifice of power which he no longer poffeffed,
and offered to his enemies what they had already obtained ; fo that he only increafed their
                                                  pride

Runny mede

This writer is not
Senfible of the
Influence of Clarke
Foucault & Con-
dorcet at this time
and their neat
opinions & writings

pride and audacity by this humiliating ftep; humiliating, becaufe it was forced, and doubly fo,
becaufe it was rejected; though the fame offer
made at an earlier period, in a willing manner,
would have been equally honourable and ufeful.

The Duke de Liancourt, the friend of his king, *Liancourt,*
and of the people, though a courtier, and rather too much of a reformer, was the only perfon who would venture, or, at leaft, who thought
proper to fpeak ferioufly to his majefty about
fome mode of reconciliation with the people; he
advifed him to go to Paris to fhew himfelf, and
to convince the people that he was their friend.
Louis XVI. who never refufed any perfonal facrifice, and who, as he has fince fhewn, was not
deftitute of refolution and courage, immediately
undertook the dangerous and painful journey.

It was announced in Paris early on Friday
morning, that his majefty would be at the town
houfe at two o'clock in the day. On his road he
was met by the armed guard of Paris, who lined
the way for eight miles with a double row of
the new-made foldiers, forming a motley, but
to him a horrible fpectacle. The greateft part
were armed with pikes, fticks, and fwords, and
a few with mufkets, for there were near 200,000 *200,000 Men*
men, and they had neither uniforms nor leaders.
Some of the revolted foldiers were interfperfed
in the ranks.

It was circulated in Paris that the Duke of
Orleans had gone to Verfailles, and on his knees
requefted the king to pay this vifit to his people,
though nothing was more falfe; and it is fair,
from

from every circumstance, to conclude, that he would rather have prevented it, had it been in his power.

Jacobin Tactics

The tactics of the Jacobins began already to be put openly in practice. Men, whom nobody knew, and who were not in any oftenfible fituation, ran along the armed ranks, and threatened thofe who fhould fhew any marks of favour or approbation to his majefty. The factious were afraid that a reconciliation might take place, and their hopes and importance be blafted for ever. The monarch, therefore, arrived in the midft of an awful filence, mounted the Hotel de Ville,

Bailly.

where he was received by M. Bailly, who infulted him with an equivocal and ill-turned compliment on prefenting him the keys of the city. As no plan was laid by either party to make any folid arrangement, this journey could be of little advantage to his majefty, but was conftrued by his enemies as a fanction to every thing that had been done and certainly it had that appearance, and afforded an excellent reafon for all the provinces to follow the example of Paris. Whether it happened by accident or defign, this ill-fated monarch was always led into meafures that were fatal to himfelf; he had now put on the cockade

K. put on the Cockade

of revolt, the livery of the houfe of Orleans, and thofe who yet were attached to the monarchy, and who might have been prepared to make a ftand, could not any longer find a pretence for doing fo; and, at the fame time, the king derived not one fingle advantage. A promife to recall the minifters that had been difmiffed was made, and the applaufe of the people, which were now permitted by the fame unknown emiffaries

faries who had commanded filence, might rather
be confidered as cries of victory than of approbation. The king returned to Verfailles after
a fhort ftay at Paris, affured of the reality of the
revolt, but at the fame time convinced, that the
people intended him no perfonal injury, and that
he and his family might fleep in fafety.

Frefh couriers were difpatched into the provinces, to announce that the king had approved
of all that had been done, that the true friends
of his majefty fhould follow his example, and
acknowledge the power and juftice of the nation.
As the king was an infulated man in his own dominions, without minifters and friends, it was impoffible for him to moderate, in any degree, the
full effect of thefe meafures, which, otherwife,
might have been done, and which, if done in time,
might have hindered thofe exceffes which men
naturally run into, when they find their career
uninterrupted by oppofition.

A fort of tranquillity fucceeded for fome days
in Paris, and the well-intentioned citizens thought
the revolution was finifhed. Surely, faid they, if
it was to diminifh the power of the crown that
we revolted, that is done; if it was to deftroy
the Baftile, that is done ; was it to have back
the old minifters, in whom they had confidence,
they found likewife, that it was accomplifhed.
They conceived, likewife, as they could act as
they pleafed, and overturn every thing with impunity, they were free ; they thought, they enjoyed liberty already, and that of confequence
their evils were all at an end. They did not know,
that it was to give their reprefentatives the plea-

P   fure

fure of framing an abfurd conftitution, and of overturning the religion, the laws, and the property of the country, of corrupting the manners of all, and of ruining their fortunes, that all this had been begun, and that, of confequence, it would not be fo fpeedily finifhed : all this they knew but too late, and then, in revenge, they taught their reprefentatives their error. The reprefentatives, on their part, were foolifh enough to think, that they would always be able to command murder and pillage, and to reap the fruits of it ; and they did not know, that the day would come when the knife that they had fharpened would be turned upon themfelves; they never calculated, that in a ftate of revolution men muft be changed as well as meafures, and that it muft infallibly arrive fooner or later, that their principles and themfelves would become equally difgufting, and that he who imagines to make perpetually a tool of others finds himfelf deceived.

Jacobin Sect

The Jacobin fect, which now were the mafters, being all-powerful, holding the reins of government in its hands, fet ferioufly to work in fecuring the continuance of that power which had been obtained over the people.

As it was impoffible for any fet of men to make themfelves certain of always regulating elections, where the general mafs of the people was to affift in chufing the magiftrates and other authorities in the ftate, it became neceffary to evade the confequences of this principle without deftroying the principle itfelf.

We

We are now going to fee another of thofe curious and adroit manœuvres, by which the people were completely juggled out of their freedom
by the fame perfons, who pretended to make
fuch efforts and facrifices, to fecure it to them
upon a foundation fo folid as not to be overturned.

People juggled out of their freedom of elections

Let a fet of men in this nation commemorate
the glorious revolution that gave liberty to France
if they will, we may difpute about their intentions, which may be pure, perhaps; but there
can in that cafe be no difpute about their judgment and knowledge of the revolution, they may
be pardoned on account of their ignorance, for
they know not what they do. The revolution
changed but did not abolifh defpotifm in France,
and the change was from a mild and regular government, to a ferocious and diforderly one.

The Revolution only changed the Defpotifm.

The profperity of Charles IX. and of Catherine
of Medicis were no doubt prayed for by the col-
lege of cardinals, becaufe they had murdered
80,000 innocent men for the fake of religion; juft
as the 14th of July was celebrated by certain
amateurs of liberty in England; but the cardinals
and the amateurs of liberty, whether were they
ignorant or guilty? Did the former think the
Creator or the Saviour of mankind delighted in
blood and murder? or did the latter think that a
revolt which overturned a mild defpotifm, to
eftablifh a ferocious one, was favourable to liberty? Their own hearts only could anfwer this
queftion; but we muft allow that they were
equally ignorant of what conftitutes true religion
or true liberty, who were capable of approving
of fuch tranfactions.

Ignorance of Religion and Liberty.

The

The leaders having already felt that it was impoffible to obtain their ends by eftablifhing liberty, and equally fenfible that the appearance of it was neceffary, as that alone could obtain for them the fupport of the people, fet to work with their ufual energy, intelligence, and fuccefs, and the JACOBIN SOCIETY WAS INSTITUTED.

Jacobin Society inftituted.

Whilft, on one hand, they worked in making every place be filled by perfons chofen by the people, which feems to be the road to liberty and to the reform of abufes; the Jacobin club eftablifhed in Paris, and compofed of the ringleaders of the revolution, both in and out of the affembly, began by exciting the inhabitants of all the other towns in France to imitate them. The club in Paris correfponded directly with eleven hundred, and upwards, of thefe focieties, which eleven hundred focieties had each their circles of clubs in inferior towns and villages, with which they correfponded; fo that the total number of clubs amounted to about fifteen thoufand.

15,000 Clubs.

As thefe clubs were therefore fo numerous, and carried on a very active and vigorous correfpondence; and as they confifted of members actuated with one fpirit, there was no difficulty of regulating almoft all public affairs; and when they could not regulate, they could counteract any meafure, as whom they could not counteract they could denounce. That they did fo, we fhall fee inftances perpetually, for the hiftory of the revolution furnifhes them in abundance; but as thefe clubs were felf-created, as they were compofed of fuch men as chofe to affemble together, the government

of Clubbs

Self created.

government could not be called one founded upon the general opinion, nor upon the general
will, as it was a felf-created power that ruled.

The affiliation of the clubs, as it was termed,
was an invention the moft inimical to liberty that
hiftory has upon record, and the more fo, that it
deludes the people, by making the miferable voter
think that he is free, that it is his own reprefentative that governs, while it is only the Jacobin
club. That the conclufion which we have drawn
is juft, probably no perfon will venture to deny,
for it would be going beyond what the Jacobins
themfelves have ever ventured, for any one to
meet the queftion fairly ; we may therefore be allowed to call a government defpotic which is the
oppofite of liberty, and to fay that it is a very dangerous fort of defpotifm, which affumes the form
of liberty. The friends of that fyftem can have
only one allegation to make in its favour, that as
the clubs were numerous and felf-created, they
probably confifted of the majority of the citizens.
To this, facts are the beft anfwer.

Firft of all, in Paris, the Jacobin club did never
amount to eighteen hundred. The majority of
this club, which might be only about one thoufand perfons, could not be faid to be an affembly
of the people of Paris, where the total number of
inhabitants was above feven hundred thoufand.
At Rouen, where the number of inhabitants was
above feventy thoufand, the Jacobin club confifted of about fix hundred, and in the other
towns of the kingdom, nearly in the fame proportion. Allowing then the utmoft latitude in favour of the calculation, the affociated Jacobins

not one in 20 of the Males.

never amounted to more than one in twenty of the male inhabitants ; they therefore were wrong in calling themfelves the nation.

It may ftill be faid, that the nineteen out of twenty who were not reprefented by not being in the clubs, were free to be members if they chofe. The anfwer to this is, that befides the abfurdity, not to fay the impoffibility of the majority of the inhabitants of a country being members of a club, and affifting at fittings held two or three times a week, what right had any portion of the nation to infift upon fuch a condition, which was not confiftent with freedom? What right had the Jacobins to fay, we will rule over you, unlefs you join in our clubs, unlefs you leave your bufinefs, and vote with us, unlefs you affift at our debates, and aid in our correfpondence with the other clubs? What impofed fuch a condition upon a people who had thrown off the yoke of defpotifm in order to be free? But there were, befides this, means employed by the leaders, to prevent the clubs from becoming too numerous, men who were moderate in their principles, who did not applaud with enthufiafm the projects of the popular leaders, or who attended feldom, were denounced, threatened, and expelled. In times of crifis, there was ftill another expedient worthy of the French revolution, which was declaring themfelves permanent ; fo that at any time of the day or night, the prefident, or vice-prefident, affifted with the fecretaries, and a few members, could carry on the correfpondence and pafs refolutions ; in fhort, the whole was an infringement on the rights of the people, of the moft complete in its nature, that ever was known.

In

In Turkey, and in Morocco, the people know *Turkey, Morocco.* under what defpotifm they groan; they know who their rulers are, and they know that whatever injuftice they may be guilty of towards individuals, they muft have fome regard to the general intereft, to the prefervation of the whole. They have the fatisfaction too of complaining to a friend in fecret of their misfortunes; but the miferable French flave, who thinks himfelf a free citizen, does not know who his mafters are. He dares not complain, becaufe every one around him confiders that his miferies are the effects of freedom and philofophy, and like the philofopher Panglofs, though ruined and miferable, he has been taught to fay, that all is as well as poffible.

In the firft moments of the revolution, when the affembly was only occupied in pulling down the ancient fyftem, the emiffaries of the clubs *Clubs more popular than Magiftrates.* were every where much more popular than the magiftrates, who were fufpected of attachment to the ancient government; and as the affembly proceeded in organizing the new government, care was taken to preferve the power of the clubs, by putting fo many forms and delays in the way of the executive government, that it was impoffible for it to put in force any meafures that were not agreeable to the clubs. The king, according to the conftitution which was afterwards made, could not fend any orders directly to thofe who were to execute them; the minifter for the home department muft correfpond with the directors of the department, into eighty-three of which France was divided; thofe directors, when affembled, muft apply to directors of diftricts, which were
fubdivifions

fubdivifions of the departments ; and, laftly,
thefe were to give their order to the municipalities. The time for putting in execution fuch orders was more or lefs, according to circumftances,
but was in all cafes confiderable ; whereas the
Jacobin club of Paris could write directly to the
club in the municipality, and either be prepared
to fupport or oppofe the meafure in queftion.
Thus it was that the failing of troops from Breft
to protect the proprietors of St. Domingo was
prevented, by an order of the Abbé Gregoire
and M. Briffot, who excited the municipality to
difobedience before the orders of the minifter
could arrive. Thus M. Necker was ftopped by
the Jacobin club at d'Arcy fur Aube, when he
left France in 1790 ; and in the like manner,
every day, there were acts of oppofition to the
eftablifhed government in different parts of the
kingdom.

It would be very difficult to conceive any method of more effectually governing defpotically a
people under the appearance of liberty, than
this ; it is true, that there is no great depth of
judgment neceffary to fee through it, and nothing
is more certain, than that vaft numbers of people
did fee through it ; that even the lower clafs was
not entirely deceived, but then it was too late ;
what remedy could be applied ? The many-headed
monfter had fwallowed up the monarchy, and
covered the whole of France ; and what could
the opinion even of a majority of individuals do
againft it, when unconnected, and without any
poffibility of uniting ? Before any party could
obtain a fufficient degree of ftrength to make
head againft the Jacobins, they could eafily be
crufhed,

crushed, as, indeed, the moderates and the con- *Moderates. Constitu-*
stitutionalists always were, for the Jacobins kept *tionalists*
the correspondence and the place of meeting to
themselves, and were by that infinitely removed
from any danger from other clubs.

The government of the Jacobins was certainly
strongest, when it acted in concert with the
assembly, which it had, in general, the method of
governing also, as we shall presently see; but in
such cases as the assembly did not agree with the
club, the latter had a great advantage, because *Club. the advantage of*
the power of the assembly, till after the king was *the Assembly.*
entirely dethroned in 1792, was obliged to have
recourse to the circuitous mode already described
of the minister, the departments, districts, and
municipalities.

As long as there remained any regular form of
government in France, under the king, the club
was all powerful, and was out of the reach of
any danger, except that of a revolt in Paris, to
which fort of events, all governments, whether
despotic or not, must be liable in a greater or less
degree. The Jacobin club, it is true, lost a
great part of its importance and power, when
the king being dethroned, the assembly became *Assembly a Club.*
a fort of club itself, and expedited its orders in
the same prompt manner; it was then, indeed,
a different cafe, and had not the principles of the
assembly and of the Jacobins been the fame, the
club must have fallen sooner than it did. It
ought here to be observed, that till the club had
fairly brought the revolution to that pitch, that
the assembly became a club, it did not lose either
its power or importance; and when it did, it

Q   was

was rather a change of name than of nature that took place, for at prefent, the neceffity of going on as they have begun, and of fupporting meafures fo long adopted and applied, has rendered it unneceffary to continue, with all that energy and force that was indifpenfable in the firft moments of the revolution.

Such then was the organization of the Jacobin club, which took its origin from Mirabeau, and its name from the convent of Jacobin monks, where the affemblies were held; and certainly whoever are its advocates in other nations, muft either be the friends of defpotifm and anarchy joined together, or they muft be totally ignorant of the real Jacobin government.

Mirabeau the Founder of the Jacobin Convent the Place of Meeting

If there are any men who have been betrayed into an approbation of the revolution by the appearance of liberty and philanthropy, which an affectation of philofophy and virtue gave to the decrees of the firft affembly; and who are unwilling to believe that France groaned under fuch a great degree of defpotifm as that which we have been defcribing, let them fay whether they have found any of the decrees adhered to, except when it fuited the general fyftem of deftruction and plunder. Individual liberty, and the protection of property, decreed by the affembly, and included in their famous rights of man, were they ever attended to? and yet they are effential to liberty and order in fociety.

Will the greateft friend of the revolution fay, that it was entirely through ignorance that the conftitution was fo conftructed, as neither to be
capable

capable of being executed, nor of affording force
to protect itself? No, that would not pass; men
who succeeded so well in most of their endeavours
could not be so weak. They calculated that it
was impossible to be always representatives of the
people, but they might always be members of
the club; it was therefore their interest to have a
feeble government, that they might have a powerful club, and the calculation had but one fault,
which was, that in a state of confusion, such as
they were creating, nothing could be permanent,
every thing must be progressive, and that though
the club was the chef d'œuvre of the revolution, *Chef d'œuvre of the Revolution*
both for permanence and for power, still it must
partake of the nature of the foundation on which
it was built.

The success with which the leaders of the
French revolution found the work of anarchy go
on, and the ease with which they governed all
France, tyrannically, by means of the affiliaton
of their clubs, enabled them to make every apparent sacrifice of power to the good of the people. Supreme masters of France, the assembly
seemed superior to every consideration that its
own power and interest might inspire, and to attend
to nothing but the will of the nation. To those who
were at a distance, and did not know the double *Double Mechanism*
mechanism of the machine, justice, and a strict regard to the general good, might appear to be
the only guides for their conduct. But the ap-
pearance of the thing is completely changed, *The Assembly, only to deceive*
when it is discovered that the assembly, and the
laws which it made, were only the means employed to please, to delude, and to deceive. The
most humane and just laws seemed to spring from
the

the reprefentatives of a great nation, and infpired confidence, and afforded a profpect of being free and happy. The difficulties left in the way of the execution of thefe laws, feemed an imperfection, but an imperfection that it was thought had arifen from being too jealous of liberty and the rights of the people. The executive power which was the medium through which the people were to fee thofe good and humane laws put in force, was enfeebled; and it was thought, that through an excefs of delicacy and philanthropy, the affembly had enervated even the power of doing good, left it might be applied to do evil. So uncommon an appearance of moderation was very capable of leading thofe who obferved it into an error, and from this the Jacobins afpired at the hope of eftablifhing their government over the whole of Europe; in every country of which they found they had converts and admirers.

The Executive enfeebled.

It is certainly changing the appearance of things much, to draw the curtain afide, and fhew their real motives; that their executive power was only, as one of them faid *un hochet d'enfant* (a child's rattle), as were alfo their philofophical principles; they were made to pleafe and to amufe, while the true executive power lay in the Jacobin club, and its will conftituted the law of the land.

a Rattle.

It is no difgrace to ftrangers to have been miftaken as to the real ftate of things, becaufe they only faw them from a diftance; but certainly it may be expected, that men who were led into an error by the falfe appearance of things, through a love of liberty, will change their opinion when
they

they know the real state of the matter. Every
argument that can be used, and every fact that
can be produced in the history of the government
of France, will prove that the Jacobin government was such as we here represent it; and we
may challenge the world to produce an instance
wherein the laws and principles of the assembly
triumphed, when put in opposition to the will of
the club, during the first four years of the revolution.

first 4. years.

That the club met with occasional contradiction
from its own members, is true; a schism had
arisen, but the club itself always obtained the victory, and drew down signal vengeance upon those
who had dared so to oppose its will. When M.
Bailly had withdrawn from the club, and as may-
or of Paris wished to oppose the force of the
law to its arbitrary will: he proclaimed martial
law, and applied it to a disorderly mob. M.
Bailly was not after that re-elected mayor of Paris; he soon lost his place, and, finally, was ig-
nominiously put to death on the very spot where
the law had been executed. The momentary
triumph of M. Bailly far, then, from being any
proof of the submission of the Jacobins to the
law, is, on the contrary, a complete proof of
their being superior to the law.

Bailly

Jacobins Superiour to the law.

When any schism or division arose in the club,
the members who retired immediately invoked the
constitution, for they knew how much that and
Jacobinism were at variance; this occasioned numerous inferior squabbles, and finally terminated
in the revolution of the tenth of August, 1792,
when

10. Aug. 1792

when the club triumphed over every thing that had the appearance of law.

The assembly had no sooner made a sort of co-alition with the people who headed the Parisians, on the fourteenth of July, and the king returned to Versailles, than every possible measure was taken to destroy the ancient form of things ; even the names, in many instances, were changed, and there were people who already talked in public places of the agrarian law.

Agrarian

Voltaire &c

The writings of Voltaire, Montesquiou, Ray-nal, Rousseau, and Mably, were ransacked for whatever was favourable to republicanism, inimi-cal to injustice and to ill-founded prejudice ; but these passages were taken only as it suited those who took them ; they were changed, exaggerat-ed, and then from the mouths of the orators of the assembly passed into those of the lowest rabble. The social contract, and other ingenious reveries, were made use of to lead people astray ; for con-fusion and disorder could never be solidly found-ed, but upon wild notions instilled into the minds of those who were to be the instruments of the projected revolutions.

Mounier

Monf. Mounier, a deputy from the province of Dauphiné, was one of the most eloquent and reasonable men of those who were tinctured with the new philosophy and love of change ; of con-sequence, his projects for the rights of man [*Note* C.] was adopted, as being the best. It was to serve as a basis for the new constitution, and all laws made were to be framed so as to cor-respond with it.

Amongst

Amongst the articles of the rights of man, IN-
SURRECTION was not only one, but it was rank-
ed as a duty *(un devoir)*; and thereby the fatal
principle was adopted of the perpetual right of
the people to change their government at pleasure.
M. Mounier soon found out his error, but still he
found it out too late; and the very interesting
account which he rendered of his conduct six
months after, when he had been chased from the
assembly, is one of those that throws the most
light on the Jacobin transactions at the beginning
of the revolution.

[handwritten margin note: Insurrection a Right and Duty. a fatal Principle according to Mr Play fair.]

The principle of revolt is a very curious one, if
we consider it when weighed against *the will
of the majority being the law of the whole.* In a
small state like Athens, the majority might rise in
arms and change the government, because they
found themselves all in one place, and could see
which was the majority. A majority of the inhabitants of Paris might do the same; but then,
a majority of Paris was but a small number in
proportion to a majority of the kingdom, and in
the moment of rebellion it never could be possible
to know whether the revolt corresponded with
the general will.

[handwritten margin note: will of Majority the law of the whole.]

It has always been the practice of the Jacobins,
like other sects that want to lead people into
error, to make use of a sort of jargon that con-
founds the understanding, and, when new words
were not invented, to apply old ones in an un-
usual way. The very name of insurrection implies the effort of the weaker against the stronger,
or against the rulers placed over the insurgents
by the will of the majority; the insurrection then
must,

R.

must, from the nature of things, be totally incompatible with any fort of government whatever, as well as with the voice of the majority; for it is of no importance for nine-tenths of a nation to make laws, if the other tenth has a right to overturn them; which is not only the natural confequence of the principle, but has actually and literally taken place. Several infurrections in Paris have changed the whole fyftem of law and government, at different times, during the revolution, and not one of them confifted of fifty thoufand people. The infurrection of the tenth of Auguft, which deftroyed the conftitution and the monarchy, did not amount to half the number, fo that it was not at any rate one-hundredth part of the kingdom.

50,000 People 10 August.

Thofe who decreed the principle of infurrection, might, perhaps, be ignorant of its confequences at the time; but they did not remain fo long; they at firft found means of turning it to their advantage, but at laft, fell all of them facrifices to it.

Principle of Infurrection destroyed all its Inventors.

The moment that infurrection is to regulate a kingdom, the capital will become in the end the miftrefs of the whole; for, it is from the capital which the general movement alone can be given that fanctifies the infurrection. Thus we have feen every infurrection in Paris rendered facred by the fupport given to it by the whole kingdom; while the infurrections of Lyons, and other towns, have drawn down upon their inhabitants the heavieft and moft cruel vengeance.

Capital Miftrefs

Lyons &c.

By

By thus ftriking at the root of focial order, the leaders of the revolution, perhaps, only meant to fanction what they had done; but, if fo, they were doing what was unneceffary, for where ftrength and fuccefs are, no fanction is wanting, except what men receive from their own breafts; and that is not to be obtained by a creed of their own making.   But, whatever their intention might be, it ferved completely the purpofe of deluding the multitude, who did not ftand much in need of fuch a ftimulus, and who now no longer confidered obedience of any kind but as *Obedience, Slavery.* a meannefs and flavery.

It might naturally have been expected, that, *Deputies revolt* when the deputies found themfelves at leifure, *vs* they would confult their cahiers, that they might *their Constituents,* at leaft know the intentions of their conftituents; but this they never did, nor talked of doing; and it is not without truth and juftice that they have been accufed of having revolted againft their conftituents, as well as againft their king, and with ftill lefs reafon, for the king had given them fome caufe, and, perhaps, even the plea of neceffity might be urged; but they had no fuch plea with regard to their conftituents.

The manner of refolving this queftion was too fhallow to deceive any one; neverthelefs it ferved the purpofe amongft a people who talk a great deal, but feldom reflect ferioufly upon any thing. The reafon that they gave, was, that if they had *States General* continued under the name and form of ftates-ge- neral, they would have confulted their inftruc- *National Affembly.* tions, but, having become the National Affem- bly, that was not a neceffary form.   It was thus

R   that

Cromwell

that Cromwell, under the title of Protector, did what he could not have done under that of king.

If there can be any difference between two things where the effence remains the fame, and where the end to be anfwered is the fame, then this reafoning might have been good for fomething ; but, let the name be changed as it might, the deputies were chofen by the people, and were intended to procure happinefs for the people. Though the power which they had obtained by the victory over the court gave them the means of carrying their reforms fomething farther than their conftituents had dared to expect, ftill that was no reafon for not confulting their in- ftructions ; befides, as the change of name was their own act, and done without either the con- fent or knowledge of their conftituents, the re- lation between elector and reprefentative muft either have remained entire, or it muft have been deftroyed altogether, as no act of one fide only could change the original nature of the connec- tion between them.

*Change of Name
their own act.*

The intention, covered by the change of name, was feen through by moft people at the time ; it was confidered as a means of diminifhing their obedience to their king, and their duty to their conftituents, and fetting them above all thofe laws and formalities which exifted with refpect to the ftates-general. Befides this, they dazzled the eyes of the multitude, whom they flattered, by taking to themfelves the name of the nation ; a national affembly feemed to be a name above every name ; it feemed to comprehend powers of every fort by the appearance of national iden-. tity

tity which it affumed. Had the name been changed after the revolt of the 14th of July, it might have been confidered as a meer affair of neceffity; but it was done before, and therefore done by choice: or after it had been changed, if the deputies had confulted their inftructions, it would have been a proof, that they did not intend to fet them afide: but no fuch thing was ever mentioned by them, fo that the affembly might, in fact, be ftiled a felf-created one, as it preferved none of the marks of that body of reprefentatives of the people, which were effential to their exercifing legiflative power. It was the Abbé Seyes who propofed changing the name: as he has fince been the counfellor of Robefpierre, and ftill chamber-counfel to the ruling party, his ambition is as evident as his want of moderation.

The national Affem by Self created.

Sieyes changed the name,

That the affembly eftablifhed its right to legiflate by its having force at its command is true, and that it was, therefore, as legitimate a government as that of moft abfolute thrones muft be allowed; but when the members called themfelves the reprefentatives of a free people, were they faying true? No, certainly; to be fuch, another election and primary affemblies would have been neceffary; but it was very unneceffary for their ambition and private purpofes, and therefore neither a new election, nor the duties which the old one impofed upon them, were ever thought of.

As it is juft about this time, that the foundation of all the labyrinth of crimes and errors into which the people were led was firmly laid, it will be moſt conducive to order, to conſider the different principles that led to them under different heads.

Principles of Anarchy.

The foundations of the ſyſtem of anarchy, pillage, and murder, were laid on the following principles :

1. That inſurrection is one of the rights of man.

2. That the good of the public is the ſupreme law, before which all others are to give way.

3. That all men are born and remain equal in rights.

4. That men are never bound by what their anceſtors have done ; this laſt is only a kind of repetition of the perpetual right of inſurrection.

We have already ſeen how incompatible the principle of inſurrection is with the will of the majority, which never can be known at the time an inſurrection takes place ; and from this it ariſes, that as anarchy was what it was intended in the firſt inſtance to eſtabliſh, the jarring of the principles amongſt each other rendered them of a double utility. As every order of things eſtabliſhes an inequality immediately, the third principle was at all times ready to ſet the two others at work.

order eſtabliſhes Inequality.

Elements of Anarchy

The elements of diſcord and anarchy could not have been better choſen and perhaps, in future times, it will be conſidered as a diſcovery equal

equal to that of original colours; for let anarchy affume what fhape it may, its origin will be found in one or more of thefe principles.

The firft principle legitimates refiftance to the law, whenever thofe who refift fhall have the means of employing force, and obliging their fellow citizens to folow their example, where this is the general practice, a perpetual ftate of warfare and revolution muft be the inevitable confequence.

Perhaps, amongft a people like the inhabitants of North America, the fame principles might not *America* lead to fuch fatal confequences, becaufe there the people, both by their fituation as individuals, and their habits of life, would be led to make a different ufe of fuch rights. In a country where every man is either a proprietor, or has the profpect of becoming one by regular induftry, property muft naturally be refpected, and induftry confidered as the fureft road to obtain it, but in an old vitiated ftate of fociety, where fortunes were become very unequal, where nine-tenths were not proprietors, and had very little profpect of ever becoming fo, it was abfolutely neceffary to confider of fome manner of fecuring the peaceable inhabitant from the attack of that part of fociety, who having nothing to lofe, confider the *The world a fifh Pond,* whole world as a fifhing pond, in which they are to fifh as well as they can, and who compofe the majority at an infurrection, though common fenfe would revolt at their being admitted into a deliberating affembly, to become their majority.

The

unlimited Press.

The *unlimited* liberty of the prefs was alfo the confequence of thefe principles; fo that fedition, treafon, and every kind of calumny, became quite common, and rendered it equally impoffible to live peaceably in fociety, or to adminifter juftice and regulate public affairs.

Mistrust reigned.

Every man who chofe to do fo, fet to work with denunciations and fcandal, and did fociety thereby a great deal of mifchief; miftruft and fufpicion reigned, peaceable men, tired of a conteft where the anonymous villain had the advantage, or afraid to fhew himfelf as a mark for their arrows, withdrew from public affairs, which were by degrees left to the care of the abandoned and the defperate.

In fpeaking of the evils which might naturally be expected to arife from thefe principles, when applied to the government of fuch a large and corrupted nation, we do not by any means go beyond, nor even approach the miferable ftate to which they have fince reduced that country; it is even aftonifhing, that they have been carried to fuch length as we have fince feen, becaufe the pooreft individual has loft by the bargain. The maximum of perfonal enjoyment is now reduced below what formerly might be called the minimum; that is to fay, the general run of people are worfe in their fituation, than the pooreft clafs of working labourers was before the revolution.

The members of the firft affembly have faid in their own vindication, that though they at firft laid down, unlimitedly, the principles of things,
they

they afterwards fixed rules and bounds for their
application; as if a decree regulating the form of
an infurrection was not an infult upon common
fenfe. Why did not the philofophers of 1789
decree laws for the form of the waves of the
ocean, or affign bounds for the flames of the fire,
for they are all equally capable of being directed.
When the ftorm does not agitate, the wave ceafes
to rage, and the flame are regulated by the elements which furround them, and the food which
they feed upon: a mob in infurrection has likewife
its regulator, which is compofed of its will and its
power; where they correfpond, the infurrection
muft go on, where they do not, it muft ftop;
and thus we have feen the apoftles of the fyftem
of which we fpeak fall alternately facrifices to the
principle of infurrection; we have feen them torn
in pieces by thofe very men whofe paffions they
had ftirred up, and thereby taught, from fad experience, to know, that their tardy laws to regulate calumny and infurrection, and to explain
away their original definition of equality, was of
little ufe. They adminiftered the poifon, and let
it operate long before they applied a feeble anti-
dote, which could not have prevented the effect
of its operation, even if it had been fooner reforted to, but which, when thought of too late,
betrayed either a want of judgment or a bad
intention.

We might attribute naturally, and it would
be moft agreeable to us to do fo, to an ignorance of the confequences that would arife, the
throwing out a general principle in an unlimited
fenfe, and leaving a long interval before any attempt was made to fet bounds to its application;
but

but there are feveral reafons which fhew that it was done with defign and not through ignorance. Firft of all, it has been the conftant practice of the affembly ; fecondly, the ariftocratic party generally warned them of the danger of doing fo ; and, laftly, in fuch cafes as it fuited their own purpofes, we have always feen that they were not ignorant, but were acute in their examination of the probable confequences of things ; it would, therefore, be wrong to impute this to ignorance : however, if there can be any doubt on the fubject, that doubt is fully refolved by themfelves on different occafions fince. They

holy Infurrection
Condorcet, Briffot

have never dared to fpeak againft the holy infurrection ; but Condorcet, Briffot, and others, both in their fpeeches and writings, have fignified, that infurrection might laft too long, that it might at laft aliment itfelf with what was precious inftead of what required to be deftroyed ; and fuch jargon as this, from which nothing can be underftood, but that they difapproved of infurrection, in a general fenfe, as much as any of us do, but that they made ufe of it when it anfwered their own purpofe.

a general Principle
cannot endure too
long.

There is an abfurdity fo confpicuoufly great in confecrating, as a general principle, that which may endure too long, that it is aftonifhing there yet exift men who have any other fentiments than thofe either of horror or of pity, for thofe perfons who could lead a nation into fuch a labyrinth of error.

Sixty Sections

When the people of Paris had got the better of their fears, then the fixty fections, which were fo ufeful in the moment of danger, became the feats

feats of every fort of abufe that men could prac-
tife, under the appearance of juftice and the public good.

Each fection became a tumultuous affembly, *Each Sectiona a tumuly*
and had its orators, its prefident, and fecretaries,
exactly after the manner of the National Affembly. Decrees were made in the fame ftyle and
fpirit, and there was very little difference except
in the extent of dominion between the Sectional
Affembly and the National Affembly.

Although in any one fection there could not be *Sectional Affemblies*
any thing very important to do, yet the affem- *perpetual.*
blies were almoft perpetual ; under the cover of
giving advice or opinion, or of confulting with
each other, they examined every queftion ; and,
whenever it fuited their purpofe, thofe opinions
were printed and placarded : fo that with fixty
public affemblies debating, writing, publifhing,
and putting in force the new ideas of legiflation,
the minds of all the people were heated to a degree, almoft paft bearing. The confequence
was, that plots of every kind were imagined, and
oppreffion of every kind was put in practice ;
there was no reft by night nor by day, and the
moft cruel tyranny that is exercifed in any civi-
lifed nation would have been a ftate of happinefs,
in comparifon to what the Parifian began already
to feel.

Novelty, which has great influence in Paris, *Novelty*
and hope, which luckily comes to alleviate the *Hope*
pains of men on moft occafions, rendered the

S   citizen

Amour propre citizen content ; but, above all, his *amour propre*, was gratified by thinking himfelf free, and wearing an uniform.   Thus it is, that what is difficult and dangerous becomes often more fufferable than it would otherwife be, and at laft the neceffity *Neceffity of con-* of continuing added to the habit of bearing, *tinuing. Habit of bearing.* fupports us for a long feries of years under circumftances which would, without thefe alleviations, have become intolerable.

C H A P.

CHAP. VI.

The national affembly leads the people aftray—
Berthier and Foulon maffacred inhumanly by the
mob—the cool ferocity of the affembly, of La
Fayette, and of Bailly the mayor of Paris—Wo-
men are pufhed foremoft in all cafes of infur-
rection—Caftles of the nobles burned, and the
country people ftirred up—Many newfpapers
eftablifhed to preach rebellion—M. Necker's
return ; he lofes fome of his popularity—Que-
ftion of two chambers debated—The 4th of Au-
guft, and the feudal fyftem pulled down—Immedi-
ate evil confequences—General anarchy, difcon-
tent, and mifery—The affembly contradicts M.
Necker—A loan made—Mirabeau declaims
againft paper money—Neceffity of a change both
for the court and the affembly—A revolt and
maffacre on the 4th and 5th October—The king
brought prifoner to Paris—The affembly follows.

WHILE the members of the national affembly were neglecting to confult the inftructions
given by their conftituents, they were every day *Harangues*
employed in making harangues, which, by conveying an unlimited principle of liberty to the
people, was, in fact, ftirring up nothing but
anarchy and licentioufnefs.

                                    The

The end of the prefent century, fo much boafted of for its fuperior knowledge, has not, however, the merit of the difcovery, that it is only the vice of mankind that renders laws neceffary, or that renders a compact between men neceffary; if all were perfectly virtuous, it would follow, that all would be perfectly juft and happy, and that the fyftem of liberty and equality, as the French call it, might be put in practice. When we have quarries of diamonds we may build oriental palaces, but while we have but brick and mortar, we muft content ourfelves with European architecture.

Vice renders Laws neceffary.

Diamonds

National Vengeance

National vengeance and national juftice were words that the people ufed upon all occafions, with juft the fame attention to their application as the parrot from his cage. The mob had fcarcely got time to reft from the exertion of walking into the Baftile, when the door was opened, and maffacreing a few old men, before a new occafion offered itfelf for exerting a patriotic vengeance.

Foulon

Berthier

eat grafs.

Among thofe perfons who had accepted of a place in the new minifterial arrangements, when M. Necker was difmiffed, was M. Foulon, a man very rich, but by no means popular, and who, befides, was father-in-law to the intendant of Paris, M. Berthier. This M. Foulon, inftead of quitting France, retired only to a little diftance from Paris, and concealed himfelf on his own eftate, where he was difcovered, and brought from thence to Paris. The good people had heard fay, that this man had expreffed a wifh to make them eat grafs; it was confidered as a piece of of pleafantry and cruelty, that united to fatisfy the juftice of the people, to fill his mouth with grafs, and putting a bundle of hay on his back, to make him walk about twenty miles in the heat of the day in the month of July. No particular crime was laid to his charge, though he was not by any means a man without faults ; on the contrary, rich, vain, and felfifh, he could have few friends ; but he had never faid what was imputed to him, nor was he accufed of any act of oppreffion. He was firft carried to the Hotel de Ville, and from thence fent by M. de la Fayette, who commanded the national troops, under a feeble efcort to prifon. But there were men amongft the crowd, whofe purpofe was to prevent his arriving there ; Foulon was taken by force from the foldier citizens, hanged, and his head cut off. This was all but the affair of a few minutes, his head (the mouth ftuffed with hay) was carried in triumph on a pike, and the naked body drawn in a mutilated ftate, with all the indecency that it was poffible, through the ftreets. A number of furies, in the form of women, dancing round as it went along, and with words and geftures, which do not admit of a repetition, endeavouring to degrade a lifelefs corpfe.

Berthier, the intendant of Paris, was coming to town prifoner the fame day, under an efcort of an immenfe number of troops, and it was confidered by the mob as a pleafant piece of fport to carry the head of the father-in-law and throw it at the fon.

Berthier

Berthier arrived about ten in the evening, the same mob ftill attending to put him to death. It had even been advifed by numbers amongft them to put him to death before he fhould enter the town-houfe; this, however, was difficult to do, for there were more than twenty thoufand of the national guards there and in the adjoining avenues, fo that the mob had, in fact, been obliged to give up part of the ground to the guard. The General la Fayette, with all the cool deliberation of a philofophical and republican hero, fettled all thefe difficulties; about five hours before, he had feen the miferable end of Foulon, whom he had fent to prifon in broad day, yet he fent Berthier in the night to prifon, with a fmall guard only, and with orders to that guard *to do no violence to the people.* The confequence was, that the miferable victim had fcarcely defcended the ftairs, when he was feized and hung up at the fame lamp-iron, but the rope breaking, it was thought the quickeft method to cut open his body with a fabre, and in lefs than eight minutes from his leaving the council chamber, one of the mob appeared before Bailly and la Fayette, and all the deputies of the fections, with the victim's heart reeking in his hand.

Such was the commencement of the reign of liberty and juftice, fuch was the beginning of the adminiftration of M. Bailly as mayor, and M. de la Fayette as commander; with fuch a people, fuch a mayor, and fuch a commander, it was not to be wondered if the human character grew worfe, and if peaceable men began to wifh to be out of the kingdom.

An

An affembly that had feen fuch tranfactions, ought to have been quick to punifh.   They fhould have fearched out with feverity the authors and perpetrators of thofe horrid and difgraceful actions.   But what did they do? They permitted Barnave to pre- *Barnave.* ferve his place and confideration amongft them, though he anfwered to a member who lamented fuch atrocities; " What, then, and was the blood that was fpilt fo pure!" This Barnave fhould have been chafed as a monfter, from an affembly that pretended to be the fathers of the people; on the contrary, his reputation and importance in the affembly increafed, [*Note* F.] and the people finding advocates amongft the rulers, and no where any one to punifh, were prepared whenever there was occafion to repeat the fame.   There was no excufe to this affair, as on the firft day of the revolution, when they thought they had run great rifks, when they were heated with exertion, and not quite relieved from fear [*Note* G.]: it was a cool, deliberate act, and moft affuredly a very barbarous one.

It was upon this occafion the mob difcovered, that as the national guards were, in cafe of infurrection, to be their antagonifts, the beft way would be to make the women go foremoft. This *Women* they long practifed, and generally with perfect fuccefs; for befides that, the market and fifhwomen of Paris are generally full as ftout as the men, they were bolder, more daring, and more cruel; to this they added the advantage of the guards not caring to ufe violence with them; *Fayette.* fo that if M. de la Fayette fanctified infurrection, the people did it every juftice in the execution.

To

To prevent the nobles from exerting their in‑ tereſt in the countries which were not acceſſible to affiliated clubs and writings, in the ſame manner as towns, it was rumoured that the nobility were plotting a *contre revolution*. This word was invent‑ ed for the purpoſe, and *the people* were invited to burn their caſtles, and maltreat their perſons, by letters ſent to different quarters of the kingdom, ſignifying that the caſtles were the repairs and ſtrong-holds of ariſtocrats, from which they would ſome day or other iſſue out and maſſacre the defenceleſs inhabitants of all the villages.*

The

* Amongſt many tragical ſcenes which the burning of caſtles occaſioned, one pleaſant enough occurred in the pro‑ vince of Dauphiny ; the maſter of a caſtle being informed that the inhabitants of a neighbouring village were coming to burn his houſe, aſſembled all his friends and dependents as quickly as poſſible, and informed them of the buſineſs ; but, ſays he, defence will be uſeleſs, for other villages will join themſelves to that, and they will finiſh with murdering us all ; let us ſet off to burn their village. Off they ſet, and the two parties met on the road, when the following converſati‑ on took place.

People of the village. Well, Sir, you're ſetting off, we ſee ; do you know that we are going to burn your caſtle ?

Maſter of the caſtle. So, ſo, that's very well, for we are juſt on the road to burn your village. But whoſe orders have you to burn my caſtle ; are you properly authoriſed ?

Village. We act by the orders of the king and the nati‑ onal aſſembly for the public good.

Caſtle. That's perfectly right, nothing is more juſt, I do the ſame, don't let us loſe time, let each obey.

The chief of the village (after a little pauſe, in a low voice.) But what do you think of this affair, would it not be better' for

The people never could be led to these excesses but by inspiring into them fear, which has been the principal agent of the Jacobins. They knew well that under the influence of fear, men act more than they reflect or calculate, and that fear, with few exceptions, operates on all; whereas hope reflects and calculates, and does not operate so universally. Besides this, fear is the passion which inspires cruelty more than any other; the Jacobins therefore invoked fear, and employed it, from the beginning till the present day; it has continually augmented till the reign of Robespierre, when it arrived at its greatest possible pitch, it was then called the system of terror. The revolution, however, has only varied in the quantities it employed of the same thing, for it has been from the beginning spurred on by fear, conducted by fear, and continued by fear.

Fear the Agent of the Jacobins

Fear inspires Cruelty

Robespierre

System of Terror

The old government was no sooner deprived of all power, than a number of small daily newspapers appeared, some few of them only giving the debates of the assembly, and a little news; others giving news, reasonings of their own, and embracing whatever a newspaper may be supposed to contain. Three of those papers only deserve at present to be mentioned, that of the famous Brissot, called the French Patriot; another by Camille des Moulins, every week, entitled the Revolutions of France and Brabant; and the last the journal of Marat, called the Friend of the

French Patriot

Revolutions of France

Friend of the People.

for us both not to obey? we shall not burn your castle, and you will not burn our village?

Castle. Well, If you think so, I agree, let us each return home. Thus ended the expedition.

T   People.

Briffot

People. Of thefe the journal of Briffot was the moſt moderate; it contained fometimes good remarks, and though it laid down in their fulleſt latitude the principles of infurrection, of equality, and the faſhionable phrafes of the people's good, and the people's will, he never di-

Camille des Moulins

rectly adviſed murder nor robbery. Camille des Moulins, on the contrary, began by pointing out its victims to the people, and obtained from Mirabeau, who did not bluſh to treat him as his friend, the title of purveyor-general for the lan-

Marat

tern. Marat, fuperlative in wickednefs at the beginning, as he was at the end, preached nothing but maffacre and deſtruction. Thofe three publications, at a cheap price, were circulated through the kingdom, and having different degrees of atrocity, fuited different characters. The fate of their authors is a true picture of the progrefs and manner in which their principles gained ground. Briffot's principles at the end of two years were in the mode, and continued fo a long time; at laſt he fell, and then Marat and Camille des Moulins got more into vogue than ever Briffot had been, though at firſt they were objects of hatred and of horror.

Necker

The return of M. Necker on the 29th of July, was a fignal for general rejoicing, and Necker, who went to the town-houfe in triumph, thought to have completed his glory by propoſing a general amneſty for all that was paſt. He haranġued the common council, and brought them to confent to his propoſition; but he was fcarcely departed, when the fixty governments of Paris affembled, declared the common council had exceeded its powers, and revoked all. Thus was the

laſt

laft day of M. Necker's glory come; he was the firft who felt the effects of the infurrection upon himfelf, of all thofe who had worked it up.

The fame man to whofe will the nation had hitherto given a blind obedience, was now contradicted in the moft open and leaft ceremonious manner; and his fortune, like that of the great Pompey, took a decided turn. Till that day, *Pompey,* every thing had profpered with him, and from that moment he never had any thing but difappointment and defeat in all his projects.

The national affembly was employing itfelf in debates concerning the new conftitution that was to be made. It took an odd enough turn, and we muft naturally fuppofe with an intention to fpread general principles, by treating general queftions, and to complete the triumph of the people by oppofing their will and intereft to that of the king and the nobles. The queftion of whether the affembly fhould, as in England, be compofed of two chambers, or only of one, was de- *Two Chambers* bated, but probably never ferioufly, by the greater number of members who were decidedly in favour of one general affembly. The veto of the king, or his power of fanctioning, or refufing his fanction to any law, was alfo already mentioned; and all thefe difcuffions gave occafion to principles which led people to think that king, nobles, and commons were abfolutely oppofite to each other in their interefts; fo that no method of rendering the two former obnoxious to the general bulk of the nation could be better calculated, or for fpreading difcontents and jealoufies.

It

It was during thefe debates that whatever was wrong or ridiculous in the ancient feudal fyftem was held up to the public in the moft exaggerated language. Some privileges which infpire horror, but which were never ufed, and only exifted in fome particular places,* were confidered, or rather affected to be confidered, as dangerous to liberty; and ferved, however, to turn the general tide ftill more ftrongly againft the whole of the feudal fyftem than it already was.

One of the evils of having but one chamber is evidently the facility with which a decree may be paffed before it has been maturely weighed. This evil is particularly great in France, amongft fo impatient and lively a people, and where they are fo fufceptible of that enthufiafm which pervades men in popular affemblies upon the difcuffion of important fubjects. The National Affembly was regulated by no ancient form, nor by any new law, refpecting the manner of paffing a decree; fo that the feeling of the moment operated without reftraint; and as their fittings were almoft

It Seems Scarcely credible that Such Laws or Ufages Should ever exist.

* One of thefe was, that the Seigneur returning from hunting, had a right to kill one of his vaffals, by cutting him open, that he might foak his feet in his bowels, to refresh himfelf. The relation is fhocking, and the fact is true, but the general feudal fyftem had no connection with it. Another was, that when a Seigneur found himfelf ferioufly offended by a vaffal, he had a right to ufe the privilege of a hufband with the vaffal's wife, while the hufband was fhut into a ftrong wooden cheft, upon the top of which his wife fuffered violence. Another was the more generally known privilege of the Seigneur, called le droit de Seigneur, to confummate in perfon the marriage of his vaffals. All of thefe are fo repugnant to juftice and common fenfe, that they could not occafion the leaft uneafinefs to any perfon in the prefent enlightened times.

inceffant,

inceffant, being held from nine or ten in the
morning till three in the afternoon, and from
about half-paft four in the afternoon till ten or
eleven at night, the members got into a heated
ftate both of mind and body, that was extremely unfriendly to calm deliberation.

It was propofed to begin the work of forming
a conftitution; but M. de Noailles, a noble- *Noailles*
man in the party of la Fayette, propofed be- *'in*
ginning by facrificing the feudal rights of the
nobles to the general interefts. This was pro-
pofed in one of the evening fittings, and is a bet- *Sacrifice of*
ter example of the danger of one chamber with- *Feudal Claims*
out any counterpoife, than any thing that can
poffibly be faid upon the fubject. The rights of
hunting, fifhing, of having deer parks, rabbit
warrens, and pigeon-houfes, were done away
along with the other more unatural and more
unjuft of the feudal privileges. The nobles ftrove
which fhould be foremoft in abandoning their *and clerical Pri-*
rights, and the enthufiafm became general; the *vileges.*
parifh priefts, imitating their example, offered to
throw up their perquifites, and thofe of the clergy
who had a plurality of livings, offered in a voluntary manner to confine themfelves to one only.
Many particular privileges, which were enjoyed
only in certain places and towns, and, in particular in what was called the Pays d'Etat, were
given up by the reprefentatives from thofe places.
This enriched vaftly the fcene, and rendered it
extremely interefting.

The mixture of good and evil in this night's *4. Aug.*
labours was aftonifhingly great. No one who
contemplates it with the feelings of a man, can
refufe

Feeling.

Sentiment of Justice

refufe his approbation in a general view of the matter. It was the refult of feeling and of a fentiment of juftice which got the better of prejudice and perfonal interelt, though as to the manner in which it was done, prudence was left totally behind. Whenever the open and generous feelings obtain a victory over the calculating felfifh ones, it is a victory that exalts human nature, and fets criticifm at a diftance: and, certainly, though the confequences refulting from this night of the memorable fourth of Auguft have been terrible to the human race; though the manner in which thefe generous facrifices operated upon thofe on whom the favours were conferred is difgraceful to mankind, it is impoffible entirely to withhold approbation and applaufe from fuch a conteft of generofity and difinterestednefs as that fcene exhibited.

Invasion of Property.

In one night the ancient and Gothic fabric of feudal rights was deftroyed throughout the largeft kingdom in Europe; and that fyftem of deftruction and invafion of property was begun, which has known no other bounds, than that which nature has affigned to the moft terrible of its fcourges. Peftilence itfelf ceafes when there is nothing more to deftroy, and the invafion of property only ceafed in France, when there was no more property to invade.

The enthufiafm with which the feudal rights were deftroyed on that memorable night, only ferved as a fignal for deftroying the fmall remains of order and fubordination which remained in the kingdom. The people had already begun in fome parts to burn the caftles of the Seigneurs, they

now

now began every where to deftroy and rebel. If men through philanthropy have ever wifhed to annihilate the rights of hunting and fifhing; this decree, and its immediate confequences, may, perhaps, change their opinion. The whole pea-fantry of France turned itfelf loofe upon the birds and beafts—partridges and pheafants were for fome time cheaper than fowls from the barn yard, and other game was in as great plenty as butcher's meat. The people had rifen in a mafs for the firft time upon the timid race of ani-mals, which were exterminated in a few months. The pleafure of the chafe, hitherto confined to a few, were now entirely put an end to. The in-habitants of the rivers efcaped this general de-ftruction, becaufe it requires patience, induftry or art, to deftroy them, and the deftroyers pof-feffed neither of the three. Let us hope that the efforts of the fame armed banditti, as long as the deftruction of order is their aim, will at leaft be baffled by that fame element, and that the fea will at laft fet bounds to the vic-tories of thofe immenfe armies, which, like the locufts in Egypt, conquer and deftroy merely by their numbers: or let us hope, that in the end they will turn againft themfelves, for nature has fixed a bound to the deftroying principle by making it attack itfelf.

Birds & Beasts deftroyed.

A modification of the hafty decrees of the fourth of Auguft, regulating the manner of re-deeming the tythes of the clergy, and the feudal rights that were of a valuable nature, only ferved to augment the mifchief. Emiffaries were heard in all places harrangueing againft that many-headed monfter which they called the Ariftocracy,

Aristocracy.

and

and which they faid was going to revive. The
generous manner in which the firft facrifices were
made now loft all its value with the receivers of
the benefit, as imprudent generofity always does.
The nobles and the people became open enemies ; the burning of caftles and title deeds became an amufement, which the leaders of the
clubs and the orators of the affembly encouraged
by their words and actions.

In France, where they had been always accuftomed to the terms of Good God and the
Holy Church, and where, in general, every thing
is good or bad in the extreme degree, the name
of the people was feldom pronounced without
being preceded by the adjective Good, as that of
the king, priefts, and nobles, was ,by fome titles
either of reproach or contempt.

Thofe practices were begun in Paris, but imitated all over the extent of the kingdom with a
rapidity and exactnefs that nothing lefs than the
affiliation of the clubs could have given rife to ;
thofe who are any way acquainted with the manner in which uninftructed, as well as young
minds, are acted upon, know that epithets of
approbation or reproach, artfully and conftantly
applied, are the moft capable of deftroying old
prejudices or creating new.

It will be difficult for pofterity to believe to
what a ridiculous length the enthufiafm was carried, for it will never be credited, that the obedience of the child to the father was affected to
be traced to the feudal fyftem ; and thus one of
the moft facred bonds of the human race was
loofened,

loofened, and that for the firft time; hitherto,
by polifhed and by favage nations, by the Chriftian and the infidel, the facred rights of a father
had never been difputed. The philofophy and
knowledge of the eighteenth century had made
a new difcovery, and unluckily the ftate of fociety was fufficiently depraved to reduce it to practice.*

* In the Lyceum, an inftitution of a very refpectable nature in Paris, to which people were admitted for an annual
fubfcription of four louis d'ors, the democratic fpirit broke
out in all its extravagance. We are not, faid they, to read
fuch books and periodical works, and hear fuch lectures as
the proprietors of the eftablifhment think proper. We muft
no longer fubmit to fuch a ridiculous defpotifm: let every
thing be put to the vote amongft us, the fubfcribers, and
then it will be well. An Englifhman who was a member,
obferved in vain to them, that the proprietors had the undoubted and exclufive right of preferving the inftitution as
they pleafed, provided they did not make it worfe during the
courfe of the year; that this was not forcing them to read nor
hear fuch and fuch productions, fuch were offered to them
before they fubfcribed, and they could not complain. Debates and cabals went fo far, that the philofophical proprietors of the eftablifhment finifhed by giving it all up at
an inconfiderable price to the fubfcribers, who literally, by
noife and democratic buftle, became mafters of the field.
On many of the public roads the paffengers ftopped the diligence in order to fleep all night, when they pleafed; and
what was more, proved to the magiftrates of the towns
where they ftopped, that, as they paid, there was no reafon
why they fhould fubmit to the arbitrary orders of a conductor.
who was, in fact, their fervant. It was the people, a part
of the nation, that was in the diligence, and the conftituted
authority was glad, as well as inclined, to decide in favour
of the nation againft the poor humiliated public functionary,
who conducted this unruly portion of the fovereign. This
fort of jargon is the only one applicable to the defcription of
the confufion of names and things that was going on.

U   The

Opposition increased the Mischief.

The oppofition which the execution of thefe decrees met with from fome of the nobles only increafed the mifchief; and, as the ordinary courfe of induftry was ftopped (for nobody thought of building, planting, or improving, in a country a prey to diforder), the licentious and idle formed themfelves into regular bands, for the purpofe of burning and plundering, without paying any attention to whom the property belonged.

The decrees of the affembly to prevent thefe exceffes only increafed them, for the affembly had no power to put any orders in force. The affembly had no executive power but through the medium of the king and his minifters, whom they had fet the example of difobeying and ill-treating; fo that to expect obedience to themfelves was not only ridiculous but unfair. Though we cannot fee without difpleafure, as well as cenfure, the unruly and unprincipled conduct of the people, yet we muft fee that of the inftigators with feelings of the fame fort ftill more ftrong. The people have been, and are, and always will be, fubfervient to the will and views of thofe who have the art to manage them, by gratifying their paffions : incapable of any regular combination or unanimity of themfelves, they muft be guided by fome general motives. The affembly had power enough with the people when they chofe to decree any thing that correfponded with their wifhes, but whatever did not, was, as at the time we are fpeaking of, always left without force.

With

With one hand the affembly fet the people
loofe effectually, and with the other they fhewed
their defire to regulate their courfe by what might
have the appearance of wifdom and moderation.
It was by fuch conduct that, while they ferved
the caufe of diforder at home, they perfuaded
people in other nations that they were regulated
by juftice and found principles of morality. This
judgment may to fome people feem harfh, and it
is proper to fupport it with fome reafons.

Firft of all, the conftituent affembly continually perfevered in the fame plan of deftroying old
laws before they made new ones, by that means
leaving a fort of interregnum in law, which
could not but breed diforder. Again, that confufion of thofe empty, unjuft, or ridiculous feudal rights which demanded a total abolition, with
thofe which, being matters of real property, required a compenfation, could not have arifen
from ignorance, it muft have been done with
intention. The conftituent affembly was by no
means compofed of ignorant men, and their readinefs and acutenefs at comprehending was remarkably great; it could not then be from ignorance, particularly as the oppreffive and ufeful
parts of the feudal fyftem was not a new fubject
of difcuffion, but had been difcuffed at different
times, and in different countries; befides, it only
required common fenfe and a feeling of common
juftice to fee that the whole was not capable of
being comprehended under one general principle;
it is, therefore, very certain that the National
Affembly did not do fo. As a ftill further argument,

ment, we may certainly be allowed to quote the future conduct of the fame men; did not they profcribe the order of the nobles in lefs than one twelvemonth after? Did not they, likewife, lay violent hands upon the whole of the revenues of the church? and has not the famous Abbé Seyes, who affifted on the fourth of Auguft—who affifted Briffot, Danton, and Robefpierre, and who is ftill a leading man—did not he calmly fay with all the cruel *fans froid* of an executioner, when they were fpeaking of deftroying nobility, "De-"ftroy nobility," fays he, "that's impoffible, "you muft exterminate the nobles." All thofe reafons give a great appearance of probability to the intention which we have alledged; and though they will weigh more or lefs with people, accor-ding to the eyes with which they view the con-fequences which have refulted, yet to fuch as have had an opportunity of examining minutely the character and conduct of the leading men in that affembly, no doubts will remain.

The king fanctioned this decree with readinefs, as was to be expected. Under the lafh of a de-mocratic affembly, in danger from a democratic mob, and aided by the councils of a democratic minifter, he could not do otherwife.

"France, at this time," fays Rabaut de St. Etienne, (who wrote the hiftory of the firft period of the revolution) "might have been likened to "an immenfe chaos; power was fufpended, au-"thority difowned, and the wrecks of the feudal "fyftem were added to the vaft ruins. And "every thing tended to excite an apprehenfion, "that

" that the kingdom would become a prey to
" anarchy." So much for the admiffion of the
diforders introduced by one of the members of
the convention, who was long one of the leading
men. " But," continues he, " a people which
" hath grown old in the habitude of order feels
" the want of it, and cannot long difpenfe with
" it. The proprietors were all in arms, and this
" proved the falvation of France ; for that clafs
" of men who have nothing to lofe, and every
" thing to gain in a revolution, was reftrained
" from affembling any where through the fear of
" a repulfe."*

* See page 130 of Rabaut's Hiftory of the Revolution
of France, tranflated by James Whyte, Efq. publifhed for
Debrett, Piccadilly. Rabaut was the fon of a well-known
and much refpected Proteftant clergyman at Nyfmes, in the
fouth of France, of the name of Paul Rabaut. The fon
was by no means without merit and abilities, and as he had
been often obliged to preach, like John the Baptift, in the
defart, to an oppreffed body of induftrious, honeft, and loyal
fubjects, he naturally muft have felt ftrongly for the oppreff-
ions exercifed in former times ; he was, therefore, more to be
excufed than any other of thofe who went headlong into the
revolution. Monfieur Rabaut, in aiding to humiliate the
Church of Rome, could not be accufed of apoftacy, however he might be fufpected of being actuated by vengeance.
He abandoned the Jacobins during the fecond affembly, and
made, for a time, one of what was called the moderate party ;
but in the triumph of the Jacobins on the 10th of Auguft,
he joined them again, which is a fevere reproach, as it fhewed
the ftrength of a party weighed more with him than their
principles. When Briffot fell, Rabaut was condemned as a
fugitive ; he was taken and executed, and his wife, who had
contributed not a little, it is faid, to the violent conduct of her
hufband, put an end to her own exiftence. Such are the effects of revolutions upon thofe who otherwife would have
been happy and virtuous !

M. Ra-

M. Rabaut avows the exiftence of anarchy, but denies its confequences; and he fhews us alfo, that even democratic leaders expect the prefervation of order only from the exertion of proprietors who are interefted in it, and who dread diforder from thofe, who having nothing to lofe expect to profit by confufion. Truth, extorted from one of their leaders, this confeffion of faith, which but ill fuited a man who conftantly acted with the Jacobin fociety, whofe principles were fo different ; but Rabaut was ambitious and vindictive ; he had purpofes to ferve and paffions to gratify, and therefore did not act as he thought. With refpect to his opinion, that France was faved, and order reftored, his own miferable end, and that both of his firft and his laft affociates in the revolution, are proofs to the contrary.*

As

* As M. Rabaut's Hiftory contains fome good things, and the reputation of the writer, as well as the circumftance of his being an actor himfelf, will naturally give it confiderable weight with people, it is but well to obferve, that of every political event, fuch as the taking the Baftile, the 5th of October, &c. he gives what may be ftiled the moft vulgar verfion. He gives it juft as it was publicly fpread abroad at the time. Now the truth never was known at the moment. It is inconceivable how a man of talents, and of induftry, could be at fuch little pains ; and it is more than probable, that he wrote with fome particular defign. As an example, he fays, after the 5th of October the Duke of Orleans, with M. de la Fayette, prevailed upon the king to grant him a commiffion to the court of London. Now, in the firft place, M. d'Orleans had no commiffion to the court of London, and returned without leave to France nine months after. Secondly, La Fayette was become his mortal enemy. And, laftly, the trial inftituted at the court of the Chatelet proved to every unprejudiced man, that the duke was a principal leader in the affair of the 5th of October. Rabaut might entertain what opinion he pleafed, but why does he pafs over thofe facts? An

artful

As the affembly had not yet got full poffeffion of the executive power, for M. Necker was not prepared to follow them in all their mad projects, it was very defirable to reduce him by neceffity to yield at difcretion. No money had been obtained by any thing that the ftates-general had done, and therefore money was as much wanting as ever. M. Necker propofed making a fmall loan of thirty millions at five per cent. The affembly, though the loan was to be without fecurity, though credit, both public and private, was at an end, and money could not be obtained at eight or even ten per cent, thought proper to reduce the intereft offered to four and a half per cent. Six per cent, was the common rate of intereft in France; this reduction muft either be looked upon as a whim, as an infult to M. Necker, or as a means of depriving the court of the money, or, perhaps, a combination of all thefe reafons together: it is moft probable, that the real intention was to difguft M. Necker, and throw the court entirely into their hands; for the court enjoyed fome degree of public confidence in matters of finance as long as M. Necker fhould continue to adminifter them. We fhall fee many things that will confirm us in the belief, that this plan did actually exift.

This loan had no fuccefs; M. Necker was not accuftomed to meet with fuch treatment, nor prepared tamely to bear it. He remonftrated, and

---

artful hiftorian may give a falfe colouring fometimes, but it is in vain to attempt concealing what is publicly known. Rabaut juft gives it as it was believed among the people at the time, for foon after even the loweft rabble thought the duke guilty in that affair.

and having truth and juſtice on his ſide, threw the blame unanſwerably on the aſſembly.

Another loan, of eighty millions, was pro-poſed, with the intention, however, of only realizing forty, as, according to a method often practiſed in France, but which gave riſe to much ſtock-jobbing, one-half was received from the ſubſcribers in government paper already iſſued, and funded at a lower intereſt. This ſecond loan had better but not entire ſucceſs; and it was ſoon perceived, that as M. Necker was no longer the conductor, as the king was no longer king, as the levying of taxes was become precarious, and the aſſembly neither ſeemed to underſtand finance, nor to be governed by any fixed principles, loans would not do any longer; and that ſome other mode muſt be adopted, was not ſo much the talk of the aſſembly as of the whole nation.

Necker

Paper money, as it was then called, ſeemed to be the only reſource; but Mirabeau in the aſ-ſembly, ſpeaking of that, expreſſed himſelf with his uſual energy, ſaying, that paper money was an impoſt levied by the point of the bayonet *(c' étoit un impôt fait le ſabre à la main)*, that it was contrary to the rights of men which they were eſtabliſhing, and that it was the greateſt act of deſpotiſm of which the rulers of a nation could be guilty.

Mirabeau's opinion of Paper Money.

If at that time the court could have been fully ſupplied with money, the aſſembly ran a very conſiderable riſk. M. Necker was no longer its friend, but was become that of his maſter. He had reſources for raiſing money while the aſſembly

bly had none; and as he still enjoyed a portion of his former popularity, he was to be considered as a dangerous man. There is not, indeed, a doubt, but that M. Necker, whose aim in all *Necker.* that he had done was to gratify his own ambition, and who thought to rule the assembly, finding himself reduced to a state of insignificance, would have been very ready to join in any safe plan to arrange matters upon the old footing.

Mirabeau, with ambition and hardiness for un- *Mirabeau* dertaking any thing, and capable of executing a great deal, was pushed on by his friend and coun- *Claviere* fellor Claviere, who had an unconquerable aversion to his countryman M. Necker; so that there was on all hands reason for the one party to hate and mistrust the other. To prevent the court from having any effectual supply of money was the only probable method of gaining the victory for the party of Mirabeau, and therefore to deny the only resource was the best means.

Nevertheless, the misery and discontent of the people was extreme; no money was issued from the royal treasury to pay the renters in Paris who lived on the interest of money lent to the state; in return, they could not pay any body, the distress became general, and was prodigiously *want of Grain* augmented by the want of grain, which had now increased to a greater pitch than ever. The dis- *Caisse d'Escompte* credit which the paper of the caisse d'escompte had fallen into, in consequence of the discovery, that that company had lent a greater sum than all its original capital to government, augmented the evil, by decreasing the quantity of the circulating medium.

X It

Pinet

It was during this, that the party of Orleans is fufpected, by the fudden death of a money-broker, whofe bankruptcy amounted to above fifty-five French millions, and who was found laying with his brains blown out in the middle of a wood, to have procured a large fupply of money, which enabled the intrigues to go on with confiderable fpirit,* and prepared the way for a complete triumph over the court.

From the neceffity on one hand of procuring money to go on with the expenfes of the ftate, which was felt by the affembly itfelf as well as the court; and, on the other hand, the danger of allowing M. Necker and the court to be in poffeffion of a full treafury, it was determined to give the kingly power a deadly blow in time, fo as to have nothing in future to fear. This, however, could only be done by getting poffeffion of the king's perfon, or by putting him to death, and placing another on the throne, who

---

* M. Pinet was found in the Bois de Boulogne, with his brains blown out with a piftol; it was reported every where immediately that he had fhot himfelf; but the ftory, never before publifhed, of which, however, the proofs are in the hands of fome of his creditors, is too curious in itfelf, and too interefting, as fhewing to what lengths the Duke carried his villainy, to be omitted. After the revolt in July, when the Baftile was taken, it was a general opinion in Paris that the mob would pillage the bankers and rich money-brokers. Pinet, who was known to have large tranfactions, was the agent de change of d'Orleans, and for fecurity delivered to him his ftrong box, containing in notes and other value, for about twenty-two millions. The Duke gave him a receipt for the ftrong box, and when the end of the month arrived, peace being a little reftored to the capital, and the monthly payments coming round, he demanded the ftrong box. The

Duke

who should be in the true spirit of the revolution. (*See Note* I.)

An insurrection was necessary for either of these purposes. Those who wish for complete information on that affair, should consult the letter published by M. Mounier, who was president of the *Mounier* assembly when the insurrection happened, from which, as well as the trial instituted against the Duke of Orleans, it appears beyond a doubt that the plan was laid and executed by his party; that it failed as to the taking away the life of the king and his family, but that the plan was artfully changed to that of getting possession of his person. It would require a large portion of a volume to enter completely upon this subject; which would be totally inconsistent with the plan of this work, at the same time that it is impossible to pass over slightly so material an event, as that of the getting possession of the king and his family, and thereby of the keys of the royal treasury; and, in

Duke told him he had sent the whole to a country house, which he had at Passy, on the side of the Bois de Boulogne, invited Pinet to come and dine with him, and bring the receipt which he had given him, and the strong box should be delivered. The poor unsuspecting banker came and dined with the Duke, who contrived to persuade him to be conducted by one of his servants in a cabriolet across the wood; this he consented to, having an intention of going to his father-in-law, who lived at St. Germain. He was found two days after in that wood, with a pistol shot that had entered his *head from behind*, and the contents of his strong box, as well as the box itself, were never heard of. That this should actually happen, and no body dare to complain, is not surprising; it would have cost very little trouble to the Duke, and not a single reflection, to have destroyed whoever had ventured to unveil the mystery. [*For the rest of this, see note* II *at the end*.]

fhort, holding the unfortunate royal pair under the poignards of the Jacobins, till the moment fhould arrive when their deftruction might be convenient.

Feaft of the Guards

In the prefent plot, the errors of the court affifted as much as ufual in the aiding its enemies. At a feaft given by the life guards of the king to another regiment, they committed the imprudence of getting drunk, and expreffing in very plain terms their attachment to their king, and their contempt for his enemies. The royal family had honoured their faithful fervants by appearing in the room where the banquet was given, and if any thing could add to the enthufiafm which wine and mufic infpired, it was the prefence of the Queen of France; the guards became frantic, and their geftures, their words, and their fongs, were all, as might indeed have been expected, repeated to their enemies. Though the king and queen had only appeared for a moment, and had witneffed nothing of the mad fcene, yet they had heard of it without difapproving; and how was it poffible for human nature to teftify difpleafure, fituated as they were? Abandoned by the greater number of their former friends, and by the army, and particularly by the regiment of French guards, it was impoffible to feel difpleafure at the affection of the few faithful fervants who remained; and the king of France did not know what it was to affume the appearance of anger that he could not feel. In his profperity he never had done fo, and to his lateft hour he was never known to do it, neither did he probably think it neceffary. Without either plans or plots, at that time, the court was totally un-
guarded,

guarded, and its enemies confidered this as the fignal for ftriking the blow.

Reports had been induftrioufly fpread that the king had a defign of efcaping, and throwing himfelf and his family into the frontier fortrefs of Metz, but no traces of fuch a plan were ever difco-, *Metz.* vered, although they have been much fearched for ; and though a plot deranged is generally unravelled, and in this cafe ought not to have been very difficult, as the victorious party were left mafters of Verfailles, and therefore had every means of acquiring information that could be wifhed for ; information fo eagerly fought after, but which never was obtained.

Although the whole nation might be faid to be converted into fpies over the actions of the court ; although accufation as well as infurrection was confidered as one of the virtuous actions and duties of free men, yet no perfon ever came forward to offer a fingle fact that could add to the probability of the exiftence of fuch a plot. The feaft of the king's guards, and the unfufpicious conduct of the court, did not look as if a plot of this fort was in train, for then all parties would have been more on their guard. Befides, the evident intention of the court was to acquire fufficiently the affections of the regiment of Flanders, which was newly arrived at Verfailles, in order to be out of the reach of any ill treatment from the rebel foldiers of the French guards, who being incorporated with the national guards, claimed the right of guarding the king in rotation with the others.

Nothing

Nothing could equal the fears which the court entertained of the revolted guards, (who at all times had been, as individuals, every thing that was bad), fince the great victory of the Baftile, fince they had chaced away their officers, and were daily feen committing every excefs of which foldiers intoxicated, and without fubordination, are capable. They had obliged the town of Paris to diftribute a large fum of money amongft them, under the falfe pretence of its being their due; and were now decorated with an order inftituted to commemorate the victory of the Baftile, they were held in deteftation by all fober citizens, as well as by the court, fo that it could be no matter of wonder if the inhabitants of the palace were afraid of their mounting guard there. Though the method of fecuring the affection of another regiment was both uielefs and imprudent, it was not unnatural,* and accounts very well for what happened.

The fcarcity of bread in Paris, which was alarmingly great, was attributed to the court, although the court, it was notorious, had no means either of doing good or harm. It is true, that there was reafon to think that the enemies of the

---

* There does not feem to be any poffibility of reftoring difcipline to foldiers *by good treatment*, after it is loft; and undifciplined men can never be counted upon for any thing but revolt; it is therefore very well for thofe who want plunder and diforder, to employ fuch means, but not for thofe who wifh the contrary. On the affair of the 4th of October, women, who were in the moft fhabby attire, were feen diftributing money amongft the foldiers of that fame regiment, who did as the French guards had done in the month of July, they revolted againft their officers, and became a mutinous, ufelefs regiment from that very hour.

new fyftem, who were always ready to fpeak, *Scarcity of Bread.*
but never to act, did expect that the people would
be foon difgufted with liberty and no bread ; that
they had circulated a fort of *bon-mot* on the fubject, to the purpofe, that when the people had
but one king, they had plenty of bread, but now
that they had twelve hundred kings, they had
none. Scarcity of bread is too ferious an evil for
thofe who feel it, to give any relifh to a joke,
and it is as impolitic as it is cruel, to think of
producing any good in any cafe, by occafioning a
fcarcity of the neceffaries of life amongft the poor.
It would be juft as wife to think of employing an
eruption of Mount Vefuvius, to prevent the invafion of Italy, as to think of turning to any good
purpofe a tumult occafioned by the want of fo
neceffary an article as bread.

The impatience of the people was fo much the
greater, that they expected the revolution would
have been terminated before this time. The general notion was, that happinefs, freedom and
plenty would be eftablifhed before the winter
came on ; and now that it was faft approaching
they faw their mifery as quickly augmenting ; all
this put the Parifians, who are naturally the moft *Parisians*
impatient people in the world, in a fermentation,
that needed but the fignal for breaking out in
acts of violence.

The court was the only mark at which the
people could direct their fury, unlefs upon the
fuppofition of the national affembly being become
unpopular, which could not be the cafe, as it
had only been employed in making harangues to
pleafe, and deftroy whatever might difpleafe the
                                        people ;

K.'s Refusal of the Bill of Rights

people; whereas the king, by having refufed to fanction the bill of rights, and fome other decrees of the affembly, feemed to be the caufe of that ruin of credit and confidence, and that flagnation of the circulation of money, and of the neceffaries of life, which tormented and frightened every one.

Money distributed by unknown Agents.

Workmen

Market Women

Still, perhaps, the tumult would not have broke out with great violence, had not money been diftributed amongft the dregs of the people by unknown agents. The workmen who were employed from charity to remove earth upon the hill of Montmartre, were feen playing at petit palet with double louis d'ors, in the midft of this general diftrefs for money; and the loweft and moft abandoned of the market women were feen with their pockets full of pieces of fix livres.

4. Oct.ʳ

Went to Versailles.

Cannon

Women in Front.

It was this fame defcription of people, that on the Monday morning, the 4th of October, went in a tumultuous manner to the town-houfe, overturned the defks broke open the drawers, and from thence went off to Verfailles, about ten o'clock, upon the pretence of feeking bread. Along with this rabble went a portion of the licentious regiment of French guards; they dragged with them fome pieces of cannon, and forced all the women they met to accompany them. The women, particularly thofe who were better dreffed than the others, and were thus compelled to march, were placed in front, with the avowed defign of preventing thofe perfons attached to his majefty, who might be inclined to refift, from firing upon women, who, for any thing they knew, might be their own relations.

A man

A man of the name of Maillard put himfelf at the head of this unruly army, and was in fome meafure obeyed, fo that until they arrived at Verfailles, lefs damage was done than from fuch a mob might have been expected.

Maillard

But the national guards of Paris, as well as the more decent clafs of citizens who remained, were extremely uneafy. Great numbers of people having been compelled to march, every one was anxious that they might not be butchered by the life guards and the regiment of Flanders. This natural anxiety, more than any other reafon, determined them to follow to Verfailles. M. de la Fayette hefitated to obey thofe whom he expected to command, but was forced to comply by the unanfwerable argument of the lantern, which was juft ready within a few yards of his horfe, and which it is not to be doubted would have been employed.

Fayette.

About five in the afternoon this fecond emigration from Paris took place, and la Fayette went literally guarded as a prifoner by his own troops, and apparently with the greateft reluctance.* It is of importance to obferve, that nobody in Paris had any idea that they were gone to fetch the king and royal family, although they did not fail on their return to give that as their object. M. Rabaut fays in his hiftory, " that no

Rabaut

* Two American gentlemen, friends of la Fayette, met this cavalcade near the gate of Chaillot, by the Champs Elifées ; he feemed to them to be in a ftate of great confternation, and having ftopped his horfe only an inftant as they paffed by, one of the national foldiers took him by his bridle inftantly, and with an oath forced him to advance.

Y   pencil

frantic joy

" pencil can paint the frantic joy of the Parifi-
" ans on feeing the guards march with an inten-
" tion of feeking and bringing away their king."
It is very ftrange that he alone fhould have heard
of the joy, for it is certain, that except on the
firft night of the revolution, and perhaps not
even then, were the people of Paris fo uneafy
from fear of the cataftrophe that next day was
probably to witnefs.

The citizens who remained, applauded, indeed,
thofe who went, wifhed they might fucceed, and
return fafe; but the uncertainty of the event was
fuch, as could not in the nature of things admit
of frantic joy; there was fcarcely a family in
Paris where the father, mother, or fome of the
fons or daughters were not gone upon that uncer-
tain and dangerous expedition. It was very natural to wifh to fee it terminated peaceably by the
national guards, whofe arrival during the night
would at leaft prevent bloodfhed from continuing
fhould it have been commenced; but farther
than this, it was impoffible they could, in fuch
circumftances, carry their hopes.

The diforder on the arrival of the firft troop at
Verfailles was immenfe. The hall of the affembly was near the road to the palace, fo that naturally they muft ftop there firft. Maillard, the
commander, fpoke for the troop at firft, and demanded bread and reparation for the affront offered to the nation by the life guards.

The affembly fent a deputation to the king to
acquaint him with the demands of the mob, and
to require his fanction of the bill of rights, together

ther with fome other articles of the conftitution. The anfwer of the king to the demand of the people was a promife on his part to do every thing in his power to aid them, and to the affembly an acceptation of the act, but with fome obfervations. The affembly would admit of no obfervations, which they faid were a fort of proteft againft the fanction; fo that the king was obliged to obey, and thus once more made a facrifice of power, without gaining any credit or good will by what he did.

King obeys.

As it is our bufinefs to trace out thofe events that evidently took place by defign, rather than to turn our attention to what were merely the effects of accident, it is not very much to our purpofe to inquire into the inevitable diforders of that afternoon and evening. How could fome quarrels be avoided, although the king had given orders not to fire, and his guards did not fire? The people who had come from Paris, whatever might be the intention of the greater number, formed too promifcuous an affemblage to be all guided by any one fentiment; plunder was the end of many amongft them, and plunder could only be obtained by exciting diforder; for fo long as the iron rails and the iron gates facing the palace were kept fhut, there was no more chance of plunder than if they had been upon a barren heath. Several attempts were made to force the gate, and in the dark the confufion was great, but without ferious confequences.

M. de la Fayette arrived with his 15,000 commanders towards midnight. The time and the circumftances obliged all parties to remain inactive.

15,000

active. The national guards, inſtead of waiting in arms till morning, were diſtributed in the houſes of the citizens at Verſailles. The rabble, from want of any regular method of diſtribution, remained in groups, and ſome of them in the national hall, which they filled during the night, and ſpoke and voted along with the deputies, who affected to continue their deliberations in the midſt of the tumult.

Attack the Palace. No ſooner did day light begin to appear, than the unruly mob, which had firſt arrived from Paris, attacked the palace, forced the outer gates, and purſued the centinels to the inner apartments, where they thought they could make a better reſiſtance. The threats and imprecations uttered againſt the queen left no doubt of what was intended, but the brave reſiſtance of ſome of the life guards retarded their progreſs, ſufficiently for the king and queen to be appriſed of what was going on. Their firſt movement was to ſearch each other and their children. The queen *Queen* avoided death that day by eſcaping from her apartment only a few ſeconds before the door was broken open, and the aſſaſſins, who found themſelves deprived of their prey, exerciſed their rage by committing every ſort of exceſs that inanimate matter would permit. The banditti, though after a conſiderable loſs of time, were proceeding to ſearch out the king and queen, or at leaſt to follow the queen to his majeſty's apartments, when the Pariſian national guards being aſſembled put an end to their purſuit. Several of the brave life guards fell victims to their fidelity, and *two butchered.* two were inhumanly butchered before the king's windows by the mob.

The

The arrival of the Parifian guards, who were very numerous, though it prevented the perpetration of the horrid crime that was intended, not by any vigorous refiftance that they made, but merely by their occupying all the avenues and apartments, fo as to render a greater influx of the rabble impoffible, did by no means put an end to the diftubances without. The king, on purpofe to appeafe the mob, and prevent the longer continuance of murder amongft his faithful fervants, appeared at a balcony over the court where the *k. at a Balcony.* greateft crowd was affembled ; the queen and the two children accompanied him, and it was then for the firft time that a cry was heard of, *The king to Paris* " The king to Paris." His majefty promifed to go, provided his guards fhould be protected from farther deftruction. It was now that things changed their appearance, all was joy, goodnature, and peace.

It is beyond a doubt, then, that one of the objects was to bring the king to Paris, and it feems to be equally certain, that this object was only occafioned by the failure of fome other project, for in fuch a tumultuous and mixed an affembly, it was impoffible that the general intention could have been concealed. It cannot be credited, that the mob left Paris the day before with the intention of doing this, and that no figns of that intention fhould appear. If the leaders of the mob really imagined the court wifhed to go to Metz, they took a method more likely to produce a bad effect than a good one, by menacing the queen and filling the royal apartments in this manner. The national guards fhould have made

known

known their intention the night before on their
arrival, and all would have been peaceable.

It is poffible, that there might have been two
parties, as M. Rabaut fays, amongft the mob,
and that only one of them meant to murder the
royal family; but who was the leader of this
party, for it was not without a leader or leaders,
that they began fo precipitately at day-break to
put their plan in execution? A mob without leaders affembles irregularly, and commits irregular
diforders as this one did the night before; but
here, on the morning of the 5th, in one quarter
of an hour, that mob affembled from all the bye
ftreets, the courts, the alleys, and other places,
where, during a rainy night, they had taken
fhelter, and all prefs forward for one object, to
break into the palace and feize the royal family;
this was certainly not the work of chance, nor
fpontaneous movement, but of defign; and it
neither was to procure bread, to prevent the royal family from going to Metz, nor to bring the
king to Paris.

A fmall portion of the rabble returned to Paris,
carrying the heads of two of the life guards; and
thofe who remained threw all the infamy of the
maffacre and attack on the palace upon them;
but the fact was quite otherwife, for the women,
the French guards, and the far greater portion of
the rabble, only left Verfailles at the fame time
with the national guards and the king. The
whole of the mob was prefent at the attack on
the palace, and though only a fmall number
could penetrate into the interior, it is allowed by
every one, that till the national guards came, all
                                                    parties

parties operated to the fame end, though that end having failed, it was very natural, as well as convenient, to difavow it.

M. Rabaut fays, at this moment the national character was difplayed in all its candour : we muft be at a lofs to conceive what idea he entertained of candour, when he applies it to any part of what happened that day, which even the enemies of kings could only vindicate on the fuppofition, that by fuch infamies greater mifery was avoided to the nation. It would be abfurd to throw upon the people all the blame of fuch actions which were evidently conducted by a party, and which were vindicated by the affembly, and by all thofe perfons who had the power in their hands. Why, if only a fmall number were known to be guilty of thefe exceffes, was not that fmall number punifhed, or, at leaft, fought after ? If the rulers of the affembly did not approve of making the king prifoner in this manner, why did they not fhew their difpleafure ? On the contrary, to remove every difficulty in the way, they decreed, that they would not feparate from the king, and that a deputation of their members fhould accompany him to Paris ; to fome of the members of which deputation an order was given to feek out the moft commodicus place in Paris for holding the fittings of the affembly.

The proceffion of fallen majefty to Paris was one of the moft confufed, the moft humiliating, and the moft riotous that was ever exhibited. The candour of the nation might be perceptible to fome perfons, but its depravity and ferocity

of

of manners were evident to all. The king's carriages, preceded, and followed by the revolted
guards and citizens in insurrection, mixed with
the life guards, with whom, under the appearance of reconciliation, they had changed part of
their uniforms, men and women of the lowest
and most haggard appearance riding upon cannons, and carrying loaves upon the points of
pikes ; all this together filled the road for several
miles, and arrived at Paris in the evening of the
same day.

The Parisians, in general, seemed rejoiced to
possess their king within their walls; they were
taught to believe, that it would lower the price
of bread and restore plenty ; and there was
actually some foundation for this belief, for now
the assembly might be considered as the supreme
head of the nation, to whose will nobody could
any longer oppose resistance ; whereas before
they had the court, which still preserved some
power, and the assembly, which of consequence
was limited as to its authority, and as the two
were at variance, the confidence in government
could not be such as in the case of one supreme
will, or a concurrence of wills, tending towards
one purpose.

Confidence in government,

It would be improper and unfair, to say that
the party of the duke of Orleans actually aspired either at the regency or the throne, because
it has not been proved ; but then it is to be observed, the contrary was by no means established.
It would be equally unfair to acquit the duke
on account of the report of M. Chabrond
[*Note* I.] in which he was found not guilty, as it
would

Orleans not proved to have aspired at the regency.

would be to condemn him, becaufe the revolutionary tribunal condemned him as guilty. At no time has juftice been adminiftered in France fince the revolution, and every perfon who has been judged by any of the tribunals for political affairs, has fuffered, or been acquitted according to the power and influence of his party at the time.

The inquiry concerning the duke, though it ended in his favour, certainly tends much more to find him guilty than otherwife, though there was not any pofitive proof. It is certain, that during the Monday he was in the Bois de Boulogne on horfeback, and fending meffengers (jockies or ftable boys) with the greateft fpeed to Verfailles and Paris at different intervals; it is certain, that during the night he was not vifible, either at Paris or Verfailles; and different perfons gave evidence, that they faw two men, whom they fuppofed to be him and the duke de Biron in difguife, pointing out the paffage that led to the queen's apartments in the morning of the attack. A perfon was heard to fay in the crowd, when the queen had efcaped, and the national guards were arriving, " *Monfeigneur le coup a manqué*." No other perfon but himfelf, could be addreffed in this ftile, and about ten o'clock he arrived in his poft chaife and four from Paris, to affift in his place at the affembly as ufual. The duke had the beft horfes in France, and in three quarters of an hour could go from Paris to Verfailles, and he had at leaft three hours and an half to perform this journey, having from half paft fix to ten. It is true, fome of the duke's fervants fwore to his being at home and in bed all

Z   night;

an active Man

night; but this was the moſt improbable of all things. The duke was a very active man, and never went to bed when intereſt or ambition required him to be up. He was deeply concerned in the reſult of this buſineſs, whether it was his own plan or not, and as he was proved to have been very much employed the day before, his going to Paris and *ſleeping* was extremely improbable; and even his deliberate arrival at Verſailles at the uſual hour of going to the aſſembly, was a proof that he wanted to conceal ſomething; for it was like a man arriving who knew nothing of what was going on, which could not be the caſe. All this was a proof preſumptive, at leaſt, of his being guilty; and if any one feels a reluctance to find him ſo, let his conduct ſince voting for the death of the king be remembered, which puts his criminality of intention beyond a doubt.

Mounier
... of the Rights
of Man

To all theſe reaſons are to be added the conduct and opinion of M. Mounier, who was preſident at the time; who was far from being a friend to abſolute power (as he was, as has been ſaid, the author of the Rights of Man, ſuch as it was, adopted by the aſſembly), but who was a royaliſt, and who left the chair of the preſident, addreſſing himſelf to Mirabeau in theſe memorable words, " *Je ne veux etre, ni coupable, ni complice.*"* This was in anſwer to a demand made to him by Mirabeau, who had, during the whole day, been going backwards and forwards from the preſident to the mob, and making different propoſitions.

Mirabeau

* I will neither be principal nor accomplice in crimes.

Previous

Previous to this day, the laft of the liberty of
Louis XVI. numbers of meetings had been held
at Moufleaux, a feat of the duke's near Paris, *Moufseaux*
remarkable for its gardens in the Englifh ftyle,
and its arrangement as a place favourable for
pleafure and debauchery. Mirabeau and the Abbé *Mirabeau, Sieyes*
Seyes had affifted at thefe meetings, with feveral
other deputies; though, when the affair was
over, Mirabeau appeared as if he had quarrelled
with the duke, and is faid to have expreffed himfelf in a very forcible ftyle (which, however, it
would be indecent verbatim to repeat), fignifying,
that the duke was capable of plotting the black-
eft of crimes, but too great a coward to affift in
the execution.

Perhaps the thing that may the moft convince
impartial men of the exiftence of a criminal plot,
is, that the moderate party of the reformers in the
affembly, that is, thofe who were royalifts, but
had obtained popular favour by their eloquence
and love of liberty, were thofe whom the
party in power, the Lameths, Barnave, Mira- *Lameth, Barnave*
beau, &c. turned againft with the greateft fury. *Mirabeau*,
Mounier, the Count de Lally Tolendal, and up- *Mounier Tolendal*
wards of forty more of the moderate party, re-
ceived anonymous letters threatening their lives.
One of the minifters received the lift, and communicated it to the profcribed members, moft of
whom immediately difappeared; fome returned
afterwards, and others, amongft whom M. Mounier was one, never came back.

This was the more extraordinary, and leads
the more decidedly to a conclufion, that the Abbé
Maury, M. de Cazales, Malouet, and others, *Maury, Cazales*
who *Malouet*

who were at all times oppofed to the new fyftem,
were not menaced, but remained quiet.   This
would feem to be a proof that the reigning party
were more afraid of thofe men who were attached
to liberty than of the pure royalifts, as the perfonal
characters of the former left no hopes of leading
them over to the violent meafures in view.   It is
a fingular enough fact, that the perfon who laid
the firft foundation of the projected conftitution,
by the Rights of Man, fhould already be obliged
to fly; for, certainly, had nothing but liberty
been the object, he was one of the moft ufeful
men in the affembly.

Amongft fuch a complication of caufes and
events, we muft be contented to feize upon the
leading facts; and in viewing them, every thing
tends to prove that there was a plot, the object
of which was either to maffacre the royal family,
or to put them entirely into the power of the
leaders of the revolution.

There certainly can be no injuftice in laying
to the charge of the men who protected and vindicated their ^perpetrators, a part of the guilt of
thofe crimes, particularly as a great portion of
thefe fame men have been themfelves guilty of
fimilar ones fince then.

However the truth may be with regard to the
exact degree of culpability of the actors in this
affair, and the primitive movers, certain it is that
all parties, except, as may be fuppofed, that of
the court, feemed pleafed with the change, as in
times of calamity almoft any change is agreeable
that affords hope.

                                              There

There were, however, two great changes which no well-meaning man could approve of, that arofe out of this. The king became a prifoner, and, as fuch, was of no ufe as a king; and the affembly, by being in the midft of a large town, upon all occafions ready to revolt, and where the number of idle vagabonds who furrounded the hall amounted upon an average to eight or ten thoufand, and upon occafions to many more, became only the tool of the faction which governed the mob. By this change royalty was deftroyed, and the national reprefentation degraded. Paris became then the miftrefs of France, and the idle black-guards the rulers of the affembly.

10,000 idle Vaga bonds.

Paris Miftrifs of France & Blackguards rulers of Paris.

Such, from that time forward was the government of France, with the fame of which the whole of Europe has refounded; which men, pretending to love liberty, have exalted above whatever exifted either in ancient or modern times, and for refifting which, or even for cenfuring which, men who are true lovers and fupporters of liberty have been abufed and calumniated. The atrocities committed, the daily journals publifhed at the time, and the declaration of thofe leaders, who have fince then loft their popularity, are all proofs of the truth of what we are here faying; and without the gift of prophefy, we may announce, that the day will come when the yoke of Paris will become infupportable to France; when the odium it merits will fall upon the fyftem of infurrection and of affiliated clubs; the affembly will ceafe to inhabit a town where it never has been, is not, and never will be free. A period may then be expected to that excefs of anarchy, which we have feen take place under all

all the different factions ; for nothing is more certain than this, that even the dregs of the nation, if elected into an affembly and permitted to reign, without being the flave of infurrections, would govern better than the moft virtuous affembly under the power of the rabble.

Transfer the inhabitants of Botany Bay to France, and make them a free and independent affembly, they would enrich themfelves firft, but then they would eftablifh order ; whereas the principle of infurrection does not permit the rulers to become rich, becaufe thofe who compofe the mob rule, and that is always the portion of the people that has nothing to lofe.

The three powers actually exifting in France after the fifth of October were, the Affembly, the Municipality of Paris, and the Jacobin club. The balance of power between thefe three was, the people in infurrection ; which ever of the three could fucceed beft with the mob, was mafter of the field. During almoft all the time of the firft affembly, the Jacobins, the municipality, headed by M. Bailly and La Fayette, were oppofed to each other ; the rabble and the national guards were the foldiers of the two parties, and the affembly was in the Jacobin intereft. When Petion became mayor and Santerre commandant, then the municipality and the club were united and ruled the affembly, becaufe they commanded both the mob and the foldiers ; and from this formidable coalition arofe the power of Robefpierre and the committee, which with their coloffal weight deftroyed the energy of the municipality and the club, thereby preparing for themfelves

felves a fall, as foon as the national affembly fhould have an opportunity of exerting itfelf.

It is this perpetual conflict of powers that we are now going to follow, but which being depri-ved of that novelty that attended the firft tranf-actions of the revolution, we do not think it ne-ceffary to follow out very minutely, particularly as the great operations are already performed; and what followed, reduces itfelf to a variation in the forms of defpotifm and anarchy, attended, *Defpotifm Anarchy* however, with that gradual deftruction of prin-ciple and virtue amongft the people at large, that is always the confequence of diforder; we mean only from this time till the total deftruction of monarchy, when the revolution took a new form, the Jacobins getting entirely the better, and for fome time reigning alone, with the multitude at their command; for the municipality was then compofed of Jacobins, the affembly was compofed of Jacobins, and every public office filled through-out the kingdom with them.

There is a very unfortunate thing attends all ge-neral movements, when oppofed by no force. Men calculate perfonal fafety, and not perfonal intereft, fo that through fear, granaries of corn *Fear* and of flour are delivered up without any regard to price. This makes a momentary plenty, only in the end to increafe the want, and the populace is led into an error, and conceives that infurrec-tion and diforder create plenty. The Jacobin fociety has always alledged, that the ariftocrats made commodities of neceffity dear, and Rabaut *Rabaut* in his hiftory defcends fo low as to fay, that loaves were bought from the bakers and thrown

into

into the river. It would be defcending almoft as low as himfelf to condefcend to refute what was fo unnatural, fo ufelefs, fo dangerous, and one may almoft fay, fo impoffible. We fhould take no notice of this, if it were not that here we get a fair fpecimen of that gentleman's regard to truth, and of his refearch, for as to the thing itfelf it does not deferve refutation.

Firft of all, the flour that came to Paris daily, went all to one general hall or market, through which every perfon might pafs, and it is notorioufly certain, that the bakers who came there to buy, could not be fupplied with fo much as they wanted. That inftead of the building* being filled with facks, piled upon each other, it was almoft empty ; this therefore was an evident and well known caufe for the dearnefs and fcarcity of bread in Paris; therefore, as it is not neceffary to feek any farther, much lefs fuppofe that the ariftocrats† would go to the doors of the bakers, before day light in the morning, and wait till two or three in the afternoon to get a loaf to throw into the river ; obferving at the fame time, that the ftrange animal an ariftocrat, eats as well as a democrat, and had no other means of getting his provifions than other people. M. Rabaut wrote his hiftory long after the abfurdity and falfity of this report, which was only circulated to inflame the minds of the people, had been fully refuted

---

* The hall au Bled was a curious piece of architecture, being a high dome, not unlike that of St. Paul's and one half of it glafs.

† I ufe the word ariftocrat as it was ufed in Paris, and not according to its real meaning, for conveniency.

by

by a melancholy affair that took place a few days after the king had been brought prisoner to the capital.

The nation,* or rather about one hundred vagabonds, pretended to have difcovered an ariftocratic baker ; a woman who was before his door waiting for bread, had advanced that he threw his loaves into the river, and in a moment he was dragged from his wife and family was hanged, and the patriotic mob thinking the wife of an ariftocrat deferved little better treatment than her hufband, brought his bloody head and threw it down upon the table before the affrighted woman, who was in the laft month of her pregnancy. All Paris fhuddered at the deed, except thofe who frequented the popular focieties : it was foon difcovered that the baker was a very honeft and induftrious man, and not an ariftocrat. The pretended zeal of his murderers, for the public good, for the welfare of the people, mixed with feigned lamentations for their having miftaken their man was what the inftigators and protectors of infurrection fhewed as the only atonement made to infulted humanity. No body was ever punifhed for this crime, though its perpetrators were known, fo that the rulers of the time, the afien b'y, La Fayette, as commander, and Bailly, as chief of the municipality, were all culpable. M. Rabaut, as an active member of the affembly, perhaps thought he was pleading his caufe, when he afferted that the deftruction of the bread was actually known to be true. We defy any of his admirers, of his followers, or of his difciples, to prove that

The Nation 100 Vagabond

A mobish Mistake

---

* Every fmall body of the populace was called the nation.

one fingle perfon was ever difcovered throwing a
loaf into the river ; and we appeal to all the journals of the time, on both fides of the queftion,
to the facts we announce ; as for the conclufions
from thofe facts, they are clear to all men, and
we do not venture to affert one fingle thing for
which the journals and other publications at the
time are not vouchers.

It would be unneceffary to quote eternally the
papers and books from which the facts are taken.
At the end of the work there will be given a lift
of thofe publications, and fuch perfons as chufe
to examine them, may be convinced of the truth
of whatever in this hiftory we announce as a
fact.*

Before we entirely leave this 5th of October, it
will be neceffary to obferve, that there never was
any fort of proof offered in fupport of the fuppofed project of carrying off the king to Metz ;
that it is, however, not impoffible, that on the
Monday afternoon when all the banditti of Paris
arrived, carriages might be prepared in order to
fave the royal family from being maffacred, and
that thofe were the carriages flopt by the national
guard of Verfailles.

* The king flood godfather to the child of the baker, that
was born very foon after, and gave the widow fome pecuniary
aid ; the other *conflituted authorities,* as they termed themfelves,
were employed in works fuperior to that of juftice or charity.
It would have been unworthy of their dignity to ftoop from
the grand employment of making twenty-four millions of
people happy and free, by murdering and imprifoning a part,
and robbing others, in order to attend to the claims of juftice
and humanity, in favour of a widow and a child, whom their
own emiffaries had treated with fuch unjuft and barbarous
violence.   This,

This, in place of being a part of a long-concerted plot, has rather the appearance of being a momentary idea, occasioned by imminent danger, and certainly it was by no means an unnatural one. Those who pretend; for want of other proof to support their assertion, by the flight of the king two years after, do not certainly consider that the circumstances were then very different. Until the 5th of October the king had been free ; but on the 20th of June, 1791, he had already been, during twenty-one months a prisoner, mal-treated, insulted, and abused. On the 5th of October his party was yet strong within the kingdom; when he left Paris in June, they were dispersed entirely in the interior, and the only friends he supposed he had, were in other countries. At the first of these periods, his majesty had rather resisted, and having still concessions to make, might expect either to regain his former power, or at least by a sacrifice of what was left, purchase peace and confidence in a new order of things ; but at the time of his departure from the capital, he had no remnant of power left ; he had sacrificed every thing to his enemies, without purchasing peace, or acquiring confidence ; he was left almost without hope, and the journey which he so unfortunately took, was the result of necessity, and not of choice ; whereas at the time we now speak of, it must have been the result of choice, not of necessity. Besides this, all parties allow, that the king himself had never consented, nor even known of such a plan, and without his consent and knowledge, with what success could it be attended ? The enemies of a fallen king may call him what they please, but certain it is, that on all occasions he shewed the greatest desire for

the

the good of his people; if he was intractable in any thing, it was upon this subject; whenever any thing was likely to occasion the shedding of blood, the most determined assassin was never so resolute in doing it as Louis XVI. was in preventing its being done; that he had *charactere* and firmness where moral principle or religious opinion came in question, is beyond a doubt; he has even left proofs of a strong and vigorous mind, that will remain when the calumnies of his enemies will have been long consigned to oblivion; and it is no small consolation to those who have wished well to his cause, that though every action of his life was known from his early youth, that though many of those who had been brought up in his palace had become his enemies, and that though he had many millions of accusers, though rewards and honours, such as miscreants can give, were all certain, for whoever could accuse him, there was not found any person who could give the shadow of probability to any thing that had the appearance of a crime; of mistakes, he committed many, but he was a man and not an angel; of crimes he committed none, and even his errors did not originate in himself, any farther than the errors of good men generally do, when opposed to bad, and who being incapable of conceiving their wickedness, are not capable of avoiding the snares which are spread for them.

The massacre of the baker was the occasion of what they improperly called martial law being proclaimed, and which, in fact, was nothing more than our riot act in England. Our riot act is a standing law, and a very necessary one, but

in

in France it was not to be a standing law; on the contrary, it was to be the suspension of the sacred right of insurrection upon certain occasions. The manner was this: When the mayor and municipal officers found tumults were going to break out, or had broke out, they were to assemble and determine whether the public force might be applied to quell the insurrection; if they determined to do so, then a red flag was to be suspended from the window of their hall, and the commander of the armed force was to have a right to read the riot act as in England, and pretty nearly in the same manner.

Sacred Right of Insurrection

If, on the contrary, the mayor and council did not carry this point by a majority of voices, the riot act could not be read, and any resistance to the mob was unlawful, if it went any farther than pushing or pulling, that is to say, the swords or bayonets in the hands of the national guards, were not of so much use as clubs and stones, with which a mob can at any time arm itself.

This martial law, however, as they called it, which might be rather considered, in fact, as a law to prevent the military from acting, than for empowering them to act, was a sort of triumph of the moderate party over the violent Jacobins, and served during some time to preserve order. It was for having put this law in force, the only time that it ever was done, that M. Bailly was afterwards beheaded with all the marks of ignominy which his enemies could invent. La Fayette would have shared the same fate had he staid in France, and certainly the fathers of insurrection were culpable in decreeing two principles

Bailly

Fayette

ples fo oppofite to each other ; fo that thofe who
approved of M. Bailly for having by this martial
law fuppreffed an infurrection, and who therefore
were inclined to pity him, when they faw him
carried to the place of execution in a dung cart,
cloathed with a red fheet, and the red flag drag-
ging in the dirt by way of ignominy, may confole
themfelves by confidering that he and La Fayette
had been the firft protectors of infurrection, and
that they only wanted to oppofe it when it happened to be directed againft themfelves.

C H A P.

C H A P. VIII.

*The national affembly decrees that the poffeffions of
the clergy belong to the nation—Mobs around the
affembly are employed to enforce the decree—A baker murdered—Martial law—Paper money, or
affignats—The confequences upon all ranks—Divifion of France into departments—Affairs of
Avignon—Injuftice—Europe to be greatly blamed
for looking quietly on—M. Necker finks every
day lower—Nobility abolifhed—Generally fœderation on the 14th of July, 1790.*

THE national affembly having once obtained
poffeffion of the king's perfon, and of all his family, the royal treafury was, in fact, in their
hands. M. Necker had already loft a great part
of his reputation, and all his power; the diforder of the finances was attributed to him, and
the affembly now enjoyed over him that fame triumph which he formerly enjoyed over his enemies and the court. M. Necker formerly appealed to public opinion by means of the print-
ing prefs, againft a court which had no means
of employing the fame weapons, or, which if
they had employed it, would have been without
effect, as they were unpopular. The affembly
fwarmed with young orators, who declaimed
againft abufes in government and finance, and
who treated M. Necker with very little ceremony.
The whole nation now gave to them that attention which they formerly had fo willingly given

to

[handwritten marginalia: foederation. 14 July 1790]

[handwritten marginalia: Necker Sinks]

[handwritten marginalia: young Orators.]

to the financier himfelf; and any anfwer he could make, ferved only as a matter of ridicule and abufe. That pompous ftile which had fo long been liftened to like the fyrens fongs, excited mockery and laughter, and his attachment to principles fo much boafted, was an irreparable fault in the eyes of men whofe bufinefs it was to overturn every principle. M. Necker began to fhew his ill humour, and the laugh increafed; and perhaps few men have received more cutting mortification than he did during the latter part of the ftay which he made in France.

Mirabeau
Claviere

The partifans of Mirabeau, ftimulated by their own wants and ambition, and by the vengeance of Claviere, were determined to facrifice and difmifs Necker, to do which, the beft method was to render him ufelefs and contemptible.

The affair of finance occupied ftill the heads of all, and Mirabeau's party, which had oppofed itfelf fo firmly to a circulation of paper money, now laid the plan of one. The treafury was actually in their own hands, and it was now as convenient to have it filled, as it had hitherto been to keep it empty.

Clergy

As the clergy had renounced part of their rights on the fourth of Auguft, and that which remained did not feem much more facred than that which had already been given away, it was propofed to decree as a *principle*, that the property of the clergy belonged to the nation.

This

This decree was oppofed, however, by a vaft portion of the affembly, the debates were long and warm, but the mob of citizens without the *The Mob* walls of the affembly offered the moft convincing arguments. The members who oppofed this decree were given plainly to underftand, that the cafe was (juft as at Bagfhot or Blackheath), that their lives or property muft go. When there is no means of refiftance, this argument is one of the moft conclufive in the world, for even if there could be a comparifon between the prefervation of life and property, it would not alter the weight of the argument, as with the life the property muft go. Amidft threats and menaces of every kind, this important queftion was determined, and the affembly voted away all the property of the church, not, however, without determining to hire clergymen at fo much a year,* for the payment of which wages the different diftricts would provide.

It would be unneceffary to enter into arguments in order to fhew the injuftice of this tranfaction, becaufe, at all events, if the clergy were to be preferved at all, it would not only have been fair but wife to have left to themfelves the adminiftration of, at leaft, as much of their own lands as would have fecured the payment of their fervices. It was evident, that as they were to be paid. it was ufelefs to take all their lands away and fell them at a low price, in order afterwards to pay a yearly fum to a great amount,

* The word falaire, employed on this occafion, is equivalent to that of hire; and though not a term of reproach, is, at leaft, one of humiliation; it was intended as fuch, and felt as fuch at the time, in its fulleft force.

and by which, every calculation made, the nation
loft confiderably, while the clergy were left without any fecurity or certain term of payment.

Many people foretold at the time, that thofe
falaries would never be punctually nor long paid;
and that to get quit of that debt, the nation would
get quit of the clergy themfelves and of religion
too; and the end has but too completely juftified
the prediction.

This fecurity for iffuing a paper money was
no fooner decreed, than Mirabeau, who a few
months before had called paper money a tax
levied by the bayonet, became its moft zealous
fupporter. The contraft between his fpeeches
in the month of Auguft and thofe of the month
of January following, is one of the moft
ftriking that is to be met with; money was neceffary, to borrow was impracticable; no great
degree of eloquence was, therefore, required to
fupport this meafure. The famous affignats were
decreed, but as it would take fome time to make
them, and as the wants were urgent, it was ordered, that the Caiffe d'Efcompt, or bank of
Paris, fhould furnifh feventy-two millions in
their notes upon the faith of the decree of the
church lands; and as thofe notes had been difcredited, it was decreed, at the fame time, that
they fhould pafs current, like money, all through
the kingdom.

This was no fooner decreed than it was executed; and notes, red, blue, and green, were prefently fubftituted for hard cafh, which difappeared
almoft

Tax levied by the Bayonet.

almoſt every where, as the diſcredit of the paper was conſiderable even at its firſt outſet.

Though the aſſignats have ſuſtained the revolution, and their creation makes an epoch of great importance, yet we muſt avoid entering into all the details concering them, which alone would require a great portion of a volume. The aſſignats are, in this Hiſtory, to be conſidered as the means of ſupporting crimes, and as the cauſe that led to their continuation; they are, therefore, of the utmoſt importance, when viewed in the great ſtile, but they do not require any minute inveſtigation.

Of the aſſignats it is at preſent ſufficient to ſay, that being creatable at will, and the circulation forced, until they become totally uſeleſs, no diſcredit whatever can deprive the aſſembly of that reſource. Until it coſts a million to make a million in aſſignats, they will ſtill have a value, as a gold mine, which only ceaſes to be uſeful when the extraction of an ounce of gold coſts the value of an ounce of gold.

The national treaſury has accordingly never been empty ſince, although few taxes have been collected, and although the expenſes have been ſo enormous, that at preſent France expends more in one month than the Roman empire expended in a year in the time of Auguſtus.

The artfulneſs with which the aſſignats were decreed is actually a maſter-piece; they were to be forced in their circulation, and only to be reimburſed by purchaſing the lands of the clergy.
A double

A double purpose was thus anfwered, for the paper being difcredited, and of no value whatever if the lands of the clergy did not fell, every man who held affignats in his hand was interefted in their being fold; and to perfons who received great payments in that paper, thofe lands, became a defirable purchafe; fo that the fales went on rapidly, as the emiffion of paper increafed.

Levelling System

The operation of the affignats is the greateft of all the operations of the levelling fyftem, and it is fimilar to all their other plans, well combined, executed with energy, and fo contrived as to oblige even its enemies to fupport it.

The affignats made the low people friends to the revolution by freeing them from taxes; thofe who had money in the public funds, by paying up their arrears, and the whole nation, almoft by the feeling that if the revolution were overturned, this chimerical wealth, with which, however, people could eat and drink, would be deftroyed.

Revolutionary Gov.
Maximum.

It was the opinion of many people at the time, that this paper would finifh by being totally difcredited, and Mirabeau himfelf was heard to fay, that it would become in time the cheapeft book on which children could learn their letters. That period is not, however, yet come. Another invention, that of a revolutionary government and the maximum * has retarded its arrival; but

---

* It is impoffible to ufe other words than their own for fuch things as never exifted before. The revolutionary government, which is nothing elfe, but the will of the rulers being

but it is only retarded, the nature of things will bring it about; and it is more than probable, that since the guillotine has ceased to operate so actively, the assignats will also soon ceafe their operations.

Trade revived the moment that paper was created at will; the public treasury then paid its debts, and individuals hastened to acquit theirs also, with a money that loft confiderably against gold and filver, as well as in all tranfactions with other nations. This change fucceeding to the languid ftate of affairs before creation of the paper, completed the deception of the great mafs of the people; and it muft be confeffed, that without fome fuch invention the revolution could not have continued; for taxes muft have been levied, and that requires order and force in government, and obedience in the people; fo that it is, in fact, to this invention that we are to attribute the duration of diforder and anarchy in that country.

Had the other powers of Europe conceived the danger which menaced them from France at an early period, or had they with any energy or unanimity combined to deftroy its refources when they did difcover the danger, the crifis in which Europe is at this day involved would never have exifted.

Mirabeau and the Jacobins knew the courts of Europe, but the courts of Europe were not at

being fubftituted for law, and is what, in common language, is called complete defpotifm.

The maximum is a fixed price put upon all articles payable in affignats.

the

the pains to study Mirabeau and the Jacobins. The contempt for each other was mutual, too much attached to routine and ancient custom, and to those diplomatic arts which they practise against each other, the courts despised men who discussed all the secrets of state publicly, and who openly and boldly set about defying the whole world, and pulling down whatever was solid or sacred amongst themselves.

Mirabeau and his associates, on the other hand, feeling what hardiness and energy could do, feeling, above all, that the work of destruction is an easy one, and that destruction was their business, trusted to the rapidity of their progress for success; they knew that while the cabinets would only be corresponding upon the subject, they would totally overturn France, and with that the balance of power in Europe, and then each one might do his best.

In order the better to prevent any possibility of the ancient order of things from being restored, a new division of France was proposed by the Abbé Seyes. It was first proposed to divide it geometrically into squares, as the United States of America do their new lands; but the impracticability of this absurd plan produced a modification in the execution. As mankind had not been prepared for this effort of human genius in past ages, towns, villages, gardens, &c. would have been divided, and, as a wit in the assembly observed, the kitchen might, perhaps, be in one department and the dining-room in another; so that one could not punish the cook if he should spoil his dinner without a long proceeding between

Sieyes.

tween the two departments. It was, therefore, resolved to adopt another plan, and France was divided into eighty-three departments, which were named from the remarkable rivers or mountains to be found in each.

Departments named from Rivers and Mountains.

Navarre, Dauphiné, Lorrain, Alsace, and other portions of France, which were formerly separate principalities, and which still retained many laws, customs, and privileges, that were different from each other, were thus all amalgamated into one. This destroyed the pretensions of the parliaments, and laid the foundation for the whole kingdom becoming, at some future period, a single people, with the same laws, language, and manners.

The appearance of philosophy and genius, which was artfully given to all those new regulations, inspired the people with respect for the men who made them. If the appearance of religion served as a colour for the errors into which men were led some centuries ago, the appearance of virtue and philosophy have been no less used in this singular revolution. The preamble to every decree was composed with a design to inspire respect and blind confidence; the motives were represented as good, and the means as wise and just; and if there had been a disposition to inquire into the wisdom and justice, the rapidity with which the new regulations succeeded each other baffled all examination.

Show of Religion

Show of Philosophy

Although the general run of decrees were favourable to the majority, yet they were not always favourable. Besides this, La Fayette, Bailly, and

and fome others, who, by having got the advantage in point of time of their colleagues, had got into places of power or profit, were not ready to fupport every change. They were well, and they wanted to continue fo ; this created a fort of fchifm or divifion in the affembly, and the moderate party retired from the Jacobin club. This divifion might, perhaps, have rendered the revolution tolerable, had not the club, by means of its affiliations, regulated the whole kingdom ; and had it not, by its members difperfed through Paris, contrived, whenever they thought proper to ftir up a tumult, to furround the affembly, and fo to make any difficult decree pafs.

Affiliations

The friends of the French revolution cannot deny that this was the conftant practice ; we are not fpeaking of things that paffed a thoufand years ago, but for which there are thoufands of living witneffes, befides the papers publifhed at the time. Neither can it be faid, that this was liberty ; fo that they muft confefs, that if they have not been the affociates in the deception, they have, at leaft, been the dupes of it.

It was now that the leaders of the affembly, feeling themfelves powerful, begun to fhew openly what they afpired at. Univerfal dominion was their theme ; not, however, as they pretended, a dominion acquired by the fword, but by reafon and by wifdom ; and in the mean time they begun by feizing upon the fmall territory of Avignon, which had been ceded formerly to the Pope, and the ceffion of which had been repeatedly ratified.

Univerfal Dominion.

Avignon

The

The arguments by which they endeavoured to support this invasion were too weak to deserve the name of reasons; they accordingly imposed upon no person whatever; but force, which is stronger than argument, was all on the side of the assembly.

Such a violation of the rights of nations should not have been overlooked by the powers of Europe, because it was a beginning of that system by which the assembly intended to aggrandise France at the expense of other sovereigns. It was opening one of those doors which lead to the destruction of the political state of society; and, in fact, when careless, slothful Europe saw the defenceless head of the Church of Rome robbed of his rights, it aided and abetted that system by which its own future destruction was planned. *When the peaceable inhabitants of a town stand by, and see one man shed another's blood, or pillage his property, without defending him, the bonds of that society are broken, and the foundation of its ruin laid.* The discord, the want of plan and want of energy, which we have since witnessed amongst the nations leagued against France, are only a continuation of that same conduct. Selfishness has taken place of the love of the general interest; when men, or nations are old, they become indifferent to every thing but ease or profit.

Age seeks ease or Profit.

In individuals, the selfish passions are the only ones that increase with age, and they increase from natural feelings, and not from reason and calculation. Thus at seventy, we see selfish misers and gluttons; and as love, generosity, and

C c ambition

ambition of glory ceafe, the individual becomes felfifh and groveling. Something the fame, it would appear, is the cafe with kingdoms. What energy has the Empire fhewn, that ufed to fhew fo much; or Spain, or Italy, or Holland? They all faw the evil approach, and, like the frightened traveller who waits for the ferpent, they made no effort equal to their power, or worthy of their former greatnefs. But if they will not prepare ferioufly to refift, they muft prepare ferioufly to fuffer; for France will give law to Europe if fhe once gets the better, and then adieu to thofe principalities and powers who have quarrelled about ufelefs etiquette, when they fhould have rivalled each other in manly courage, and who will continue, in all likelihood, to difpute about their rights and privileges, till there will none remain for them to difpute about.

The revolution of Avignon was conducted upon the fame principle with the other manœuvres of the Jacobins. At the fame time that the affembly was debating whether they fhould take poffeffion of it or not, a chofen band of affaffins, with a man of the name of Jourdan at their head, who by way of pre-eminence was diftinguifhed by the title of Cut-throat *(coup tête)*, which is the fame thing, were difpatched to that beautiful fpot, where the peaceable nature of the inhabitants was equal to the excellence of the climate. Thofe banditti emiffaries began by inftituting a club and gaining partifans amongft the people, and they finifhed by maffacreing a part of the moft refpectable and peaceable inhabitants, and forcing the remainder to meet in an affembly, and vote their union with the kingdom of France.
The

Jourdan

The affembly by this fort of management had the appearance of only acceding to the will of the majority of the inhabitants, when they afterwards declared that Avignon was an integrant part of the kingdom.

The horrors committed in Avignon were fhocking; nothing but the greater horrors that have fince been committed all over France, could diminifh the fenfation which they infpired. Long did men repeat with difmay the name of the glaciere under the walls of Avignon, which was filled up with the dead bodies of its flaughtered inhabitants. Every fort of outrage that is committed upon the inhabitants of a city taken by ftorm by an enraged and lawlefs foldiery, was committed on this miferable town. Murder, pillage, and women violated in the moft brutal manner, were the works of Jourdan and his affociates, while their mafters of the affembly and the Jacobin club named commiffaries to go and fettle differences which they pretended had arifen amongft the inhabitants, and between Avignon and Carpentras. Whether the villainy or the impudence of fuch conduct were the greater, pofterity muft judge, as the prefent age does not *Prefent age not alive.* feem fufficiently alive to what is going on, and, by its filence, feems not entirely to difapprove of thefe acts of injuftice and ferocity.

Ye men of feeling, of humanity, of refearch, *Very good!* and ye who employ volumes to defcribe a ceremony in Hindoftan, who feem to be penetrated with the defire of difcovering truth in Africa, the wilds of America, and the fartheft Indies, what have you been about? Is the track of a fhip, or the

the form of a rock, or are the manners of a favage nation, either fo curious or fo important, as
the change that the human mind has undergone
in Europe fince the beginning of the French revolution ? We may grant that fuch refearches are
more entertaining, but they are much lefs ufeful ;
for deftruction advances, and fooner or later will
arrive, unlefs we make as great an effort to ward
it off as others do to bring it on.

The commiffaries who went to Avignon were
loaded with decrees and affignats ; for it was too
important a point to make good, and fecure their
firft conqueft, not to make every effort to do fo.
The attempts of the Sovereign Pontiff to regain
the loft territory were only fubjects for mirth and
ridicule at Paris ; and as the whole nation participated in what was done, it was a fort of fepa-
ration already declared between the French and
the Church of Rome.

The affembly was aftonifhed that other powers
did not meddle ferioufly in this affair ; and it was
even believed by many that certain of its leaders
actually intended to ftir up a foreign war, and
thereby give fcope to the ambitious and idle, who
in France began by this time to be too numerous
for thofe who were already at the top of the tree.
This opinion, however, does not feem to be well
founded ; it is, no doubt, certain, that Avignon
was feized with a hardy hand at the rifque of going to war, and there can be little doubt that
they would have infifted on maintaining the poffeffion of it at all rifques ; but ftill that is very
different from its being attacked on purpofe to
create a foreign war, which at that time would
have

have been attended with great danger ; the old fyftem had not been long enough deftroyed, nor was the new one fufficiently eftablifhed, to run fo great a rifk with intention.

The character of the leading deputies was rather that of bravadoes than of brave men ; they acted like themfelves when they robbed the defencelefs, feeble Pope, and when they braved all Europe ; but it is far from probable that they did it with a defign to engage in hoftilities ; particularly as they might have found a better occafion by affifting the people of Flanders and Brabant againft the Emperor Jofeph the Second, who was then on his death-bed.

The nature of the Jacobins is to bully and intimidate by hardinefs, but not to fight, till it becomes unavoidable : as long as they can gain their ends by infurrections, or by ftirring up diffenfions, they will prefer that to arms ; neverthelefs, when arms are neceffary they are ready. They cannot be called brave in the true fenfe of the word, but they are hardy and determined, and do not want courage, when pufhed, as they have fhewn to all Europe fince that time.

Jacobins want not Courage

The means which a people has of becoming formidable to its neighbours are very great, when they liften to the ideas of all who have any to propofe, when they take the beft, or what feem to them to be the beft, and when they are never at a lofs for money to put them in execution, and when they never let a principle of right or juftice ftand in their way ; and fuch advantages the Jacobins

cobins enjoyed even from the commencement of the revolution.

When the affembly had divided the kingdom into eighty-three departments, and forty-feven thoufand municipalities, each of which had the command of the armed force within itfelf, the executive power was no longer formidable, and, of confequence, it was but of little importance to the leaders of the affembly whether their decrees met with approbation from that quarter or not. The executive power was only, as they termed it *un hochet d'enfant* (a child's rattle). When great legiflators have fubdivided nations, with an intention of promoting the caufe of order or the diftribution of juftice, it has always been done with an attention to fubordination, and that gradation of power, that connection, which renders the whole capable of energy *as a whole*, though the parts can act feparately for particular purpofes.

Hochet.

The departments were regulated by twenty-four members, who deliberated and gave their orders collectively, and who were, therefore, in a certain degree independent of fuperior orders. At any rate it would have been wife, in cafes of fuperior orders, to have not only difpenfed with the deliberations of the department, but even to have ftrictly forbidden all fuch deliberations, and to have made the prefident of the department, or his fubftitue, tranfmit or execute the order without formality or delay. This, however, was carefully avoided, and the orders of the king were liable to be canvaffed and examined in every department; and, upon the leaft pretext of not

agreeing

agreeing amongſt themſelves, or of not comprehending the order, a delay might be obtained
without incurring any degree of cenſure.

This was extremely unfavourable to the kingly
government, but extremely favourable for that of
the Jacobins, who had many friends amongſt the
members of all the departments, and who, if that
failed, could, and did, call to their aid the clubs
in the department, who either by menaces or
intrigues defeated every meaſure which was not
agreeable to the prime movers at Paris.

The obedience which the nation had given to
the will of its deputies did not, however, ſo far
ſatisfy the leaders, as to put them at their eaſe
with reſpect to the chicane by which they had
placed themſelves actually upon the throne of
France. They were by no means ſatisfied with
the negative approbation of their conſtituents,
who might at a future day call to mind their cahiers of inſtructions, and aſk by what authority *Metamorphosis*
they had metamorphoſed the States General into
a National Aſſembly. Such a thing might, in
ſome future time, be aſked ; it was, therefore,
propoſed to celebrate the anniverſary of the
taking of the Baſtile by a public ſolemnity, at
which the whole nation ſhould aſſiſt by deputies
choſen from amongſt the national guards of each
department. This fête was called a fœderation, *Fœderation.*
and was to ſerve as a teſtimony of the approbation of the whole national guards of, France in
favour of the revolution. They were to ſwear,
as military men, to obey the king and the aſſembly, and to be faithful to the cauſe of liberty.
Such was the project ; it was repreſented as a
meeting

meeting of brothers and friends, assembled from all parts of the same country, with one intention and one mind.

In this fœderation, that at its first appearance seemed only a sort of military parade, much more was meant than empty form, and merely an exchange of good wishes and good will. The national guards consisted of all the voters in the kingdom; so that the nation might with greater propriety be said to be represented by the deputies called fœderates, whom those guards sent to Paris, than by the National Assembly itself. It was, therefore, by no means an ill-concerted scheme to jocky the nation out of its approbation of their conduct, and no pains were spared upon this great occasion to raise enthusiasm to its highest pitch.

Previous to so sublime a spectacle, it was proposed by the leading members of the assembly to abolish all titles of nobility, all coats of arms or other signs of feudal times, " that," as they emphatically expressed themselves, " neither the " eyes nor the ears of their virtuous fellow citi- " zens might be offended by the remains of des- " potism."

A decree had been passed after the 4th of August, which forbid the assembly, in an evening sitting, making any constitutional law; for which they, with great propriety, assigned this good reason, that, after having deliberated all the morning, and till three o'clock, and then dining copiously, the mind was not in a state fit for such weighty affairs. The abolition of nobility was

an

an act of this fort, and, therefore, fhould have been deliberated in the fitting of the morning; it ought alfo to have been given notice of before it was brought on; but as both thefe formalities might have been very injurious to the fuccefs of the defign, it was thought proper to difpenfe with them.

Amongft the violent Jacobins of Paris was a Pruffian, known firft by the name of Clootz the Pruffian, under which name he ufed to write in the public papers; he next took the name of the fection in which he lived;* and laftly named himfelf Anacharfis Clootz orator of the human race. This man, with an exalted brain, and not without learning and imagination, but without any folidity of judgement, appeared at the bar of the national affembly on a Saturday evening, when nothing material was expected to be debated. Clootz was at the head of a group of people dreffed all in different forts of dreffes, Africans, Chinefe, Americans, Poles, Turks, Siberians, &c. as well as Englifh, Dutch, Germans, and Spaniards, were there, that is to fay, the dreffes of the inhabitants of thofe countries were there. Clootz made a fpeech, in which he declared himfelf to be the orator of the whole human race: he affirmed, that all men were his conftituents, and that thofe who followed him came from their different nations to teftify their joy and approbation at the labours of fo wife an affembly. The wifdom of the affembly was fuch, that its orator, or prefident, returned the compliment of the human race in a fimilar ftile.

* Val de Grace.

D d   The

The enthufiafm of the human race, of the affembly, and of the gallery, was complete ; and as
a facrifice to fuch generous feelings, a defcendant
of the ancient family of Montmorency* propofed
abolifhing all titles and infignia of nobility, as
being emblems of pride, folly, and defpotifm.
The Jacobin fide of the affembly was all there,
and amongft others La Fayette, though of late
he had been but feldom permitted to attend by his
duty as commander of the national guards.

Thus was the old order of nobility in France
deftroyed in about two hours, in a fit of frenzy
rather than of cool reafoning, and attended with
a mock farce, that will always be confidered as
a difgrace to the conftituent affembly. †

It has always been obferved, that when the affembly paffed a decree to deftroy any thing,
it was immediately put in execution ; but when
it paffed a decree to eftablifh any thing new,
conducive to order, or the obfervance of law,
it was flowly, and often never executed. This
decree about armorial figns was foon put in execution, and that fort of deftruction to which they
Vandalism. have fince given the name *vandalifme*, was begun by mutilating the famous monument in
the Place des Victoires at Paris ; not that it had
any particular connection with nobility, but that

* The family of Montmorency produced a man named
Mathieu, who was the mover of this decree.

† The reprefentatives of England, Italy, Germany, &c.
were chiefly teachers of languages, who were induced to go
by being promifed a place of honour at the approaching fête.
The dreffes of the Chinefe, &c. came from the wardrobe of
the opera.

probably,

probably, it was a part of their plan, by degrading monuments of kingly power, to prepare the minds of people for deftroying the thing itfelf.

This decree, tho' paffed only three weeks before the fœderation, was put in full force all over the kingdom before that meeting took place. The Jacobin club had not been idle all this time, it had written to all its affiliated clubs or popular focieties (as they began to be called), to imprefs them with the neceffity of fending good ftaunch patriots to the fœderation. This was accordingly done, and afforded an excellent opportunity for judging between the Jacobins of the country and thofe of Paris. The former, although the cream of the provinces, were very different men from thofe of the latter; they were many degrees below them in violence and patriotic zeal, and as many above them in cool firmnefs and good intention.

The royalift party conceived hopes of yet triumphing, when they faw that the bulk of the nation was compofed of men fo different from thofe who conducted every thing at Paris; but they reckoned too haftily. As it cofts confiderable fums to come to Paris, and the fyftem of fans-culottifm was not yet in vogue, the federés were all men of fome property, who came at their own expenfe, and who though they were the beft Jacobins that could be got of that defcription, yet they were by no means the fame men that conducted the clubs. Both parties were deceived for the moment by this circumftance; the Jacobins entertained ufelefs fears and the rayalift ufelefs hopes; for in going back into their provinces, the

the fœderates carried with them a little of the en-thufiafm of Paris and their own infignificance.

Delirium

Every art was employed to work up the public mind to a pitch of delirium for the fœderation, and thereby attach the whole people more firmly to the new order of things.*

Fayette

This fœderation was held in the Field of Mars, where a fort of theatre was formed of earth, with wooden feats, and an altar, or mound of earth furmounted with an altar in the middle. Here the whole of the fœderates, with La Fayette at their head, and in prefence of the royal family, fwore to be faithful to the king, the nation, and the law, TO PRESERVE THE CONSTITUTION.

It was not to take any oath to the conftitu-tion that they had been deputed there, becaufe the conftitution was not yet half formed ; but it did not ferve the lefs to bind them on that ac-count. It is one of the many imperfections of hu-man nature to perfift in an abfurdity with greater obftinacy than in a thing that is reafonable; and when any of the ariftocratic party endea-voured to fhew them the ridicule attached to an oath of fidelity to a non-entity, they vindicated themfelves with all the warmth of wounded pride, by faying, that the fpirit of the conftitution was

Oath to a Non-Entity.

* A plan was made for removing fo much earth, that no ordinary exertion could accomplifh it in the time ; all the peo-ple of Paris, therefore, affifted, and the king, to fhew his willingnefs to pleafe the people, went there one day to wheel a few barrowfuls of earth. The people fang, laughed, danc-ed, and worked, till they had converted a beautiful green field into an ugly unmeaning mafs of mud. If it was meant to be as a theatre, it was not half elevated enough.

known,

known, though the conflitution itfelf did not
then exift; befides, that they ran no rifk in committing themfelves by adopting the work of the
philofophical reprefentatives of the nation.

This was a very great point accomplifhed; and
by it the new order of things had acquired a greater degree of folidity. The fœderates had
been feafted by the Parifians, and all of them
were charmed with the eloquence and patriotifm
of the leading deputies of the affembly; thefe
carried back to their provinces enthufiafm and
adoration for the new fyftem, but the Parifian
Jacobins failed in infpiring either hatred or contempt for the king and royal family. They had
made many attempts before the fœderation to fee
whether a part of the ceremonies of that day
fhould not be contrived fo as to humiliate the
king; they had publicly, though not formally,
fpoke of abolifhing the title of king, and eftablifhing fome other in its place more confiftent
with his limited power, and with the philofophy
of the nation.

The public prints, particularly that of Briffot,
propofed, at all events, placing the prefident of
the affembly upon a fort of throne, as the reprefentative of the nation, and the king upon a feat
immediately before the prefident, a few fteps
lower; but thefe plans were abandoned as foon
as the moderation of the fœderates from the departments was perceived; for it was hinted by
the royalifts to the party of republicans, that the
king might, perhaps, employ that occafion to
make an appeal to the nation in his own favour,
and fo the tables effectually be turned againft
                                                    them;

them ; and it is certain, that the national guards
and Jacobins of Paris were during the ftay of
the fœderates, extremely moderate, and much
more modeft in their deportment, than either before or after that period. The projects of humiliating the king were adjourned till another
year, and this moderation was very lucky for the
Jacobins themfelves, for it produced an appearance of harmony and peace that was well calculated to make individuals think, that the people
at large approved completely of the revolution ;
fo that the firft end which the fœderation was intended to bring about was pretty nearly accom-
plifhed.

The affembly occupied itfelf without intermif-
fion during the ftay of the fœderates in the capital, in difcuffing the moft popular laws, fo that
an impreffion was conveyed to the provinces of
the candour, philofophy, and patriotifm, of the
majority of the reprefentatives.

As the plan during the whole of the revolution
had uniformly been to lead the people into meafures which they did not properly comprehend,
and to bind them to fupport whatever was done ;
it is unneceffary to difcufs ferioufly the queftion of,
whether the oath taken by men who were not appointed either to make or confirm laws, was
binding upon their fellow citizens, who had only
fent them to partake of a public rejoicing, and to
teftify their pleafure at the profpect of being happy
and free ? and this inquiry is the lefs neceffary,
that infurrection being a right, and the people
having the power of changing the laws and conftitution at will, oaths of obedience and attachment

ment to any particular order of things were inconfiftent with the fundamental creed of the revolutionifts.

We have not yet confidered a main article in
the conftitution, which conferred upon the king
what they called a *fufpenfive véto*, or a right of refufing his fanction to any legiflative act, until
two fuccellive affemblies fhould have infifted upon the fanction, which then could be no longer
withheld. A *fufpenfive véto* was of no importance to an imprifoned king, nor would an abfolute *véto* have been of any greater utility. Had
the reformers of France paid any regard to example, they would have allowed the king the
liberty of refufing his fanction altogether as in
England ; or had they confidered, that a king
who has no fhare of legiflative authority, is nothing more than a fimple agent, and that therefore their fucceffors would be left without controul, they certainly would not have arranged the
matter as they did ; but whether it was done
from ignorance, or with a defign to render the
king unpopular, they put the ufelefs and dangerous fufpenfive power in his hand ; it would
have been much better to have given him no
power at all, becaufe this might be very badly
employed by a bad king, and opened evidently a
door for a mifunderftanding between him and the
affembly, in which the nation could not fail to
take part with one or the other.

The king, on his fide, was extremely ill advifed, when he made ufe of this mock power,
which was employed as the chief means of rendering him odious to the people. It was the ufe

of

of this power that in the end afforded a pretext
for the people to enter the palace with violence.
The *véto,* a word that the people did not underftand, was ufed as a fort of term of reproach and
contempt ; the king was contemptuoufly called
Monfieur Vêto, the queen Madame Vêto, thereby giving it to be underftood, that they two alone
ftood between the people and that happinefs
which the reprefentatives intended for them.

The fœderation had been looked upon by a
great number of perfons who now began to wifh
for the reftoration of law and order, as a fort of
term to the revolution, or at leaft as preceding
the term of it a little time ; and when they found
that it was by no means advanced, but that the
reign of diforder and confufion increafed, they began to lofe patience, and the affembly turned the
anger, which naturally attends impatience, perpetually againft the king and his minifters.   It is
perhaps one of the greateft obftacles to the happinefs of a people, who are governed by large
affemblies, that the attention is in general all
given to one fide of the queftion, and refufed to
the other.   The minifters could never obtain any
attention to their remonftrances and complaints,
when they alledged their want of power to do
good, and to put the law in force.   The nation
and the affembly were equally deaf to all their
complaints, and it required but very little fore-
fight to be perfuaded that neither king nor vêto
would long exift among fuch a people, and with
fuch reprefentatives.

The affembly was now regularly divided into
a right fide and a left fide, taking their names
from

from being on the right and left of the prefident ;
the right fide was compofed of ariftocrats, as they
called them, and the left of democrats ; there
were a number of perfons who called themfelves
impartials, or moderates, who placed themfelves
in general between the two, but who were confidered as being ariftocrats.

Thofe who were on the left fide, were almoft
all members of the Jacobin club, and were by
far the moft numerous, as well as the moft vigorous and energetic.

This vigour and energy of character, fo remarkable in the Jacobins, deferves to be examined ; it probably arofe from a combination of
caufes, one of which was, that they were perpetually employed in attacking, and their enemies
in defending. That men who go to extremes in
their opinions, are never retarded in their operations by reafoning, which makes men balance,
hefitate, and delay ; but, above all, as deftruction was their work, and anarchy their means,
expedition and promptitude were eafy and neceffary. The new men who had nothing before
the revolution, had all one object, which was to
get fomething ; but thofe who had the property
to protect, had not all the fame fort of property
to take care of ; and hence naturally arofe delay,
and want of unity and action.

The clergy, proprietors of land, and monied
men drawing their revenues from the employment of capital, had all different interefts to a
certain degree ; and the Jacobin faction divided
them ftill more, by making the one believe it

might

might be faved at the expenfe of the other two.
It is certain the two latter expected, as they expreffed themfelves, that the clergy would pay for
the broken pots, and thus the fenfation of felf-
intereft was rendered predominant ; in the place
of which, men of property fhould all have made
one common caufe of it, and then they might
very probably have made fuch a ftand as would
have kept their invaders within fome fort of
reafonable bounds.

The affembly decreed, that all places, fuch as
that of members in the ancient parliament, no-
taries,* money-brokers, &c. &c. fhould be re-
imburfed in affignats, the prices which had, upon
an avarage, been given for them ; thus a whole
phalanx of enemies were converted, if not into
friends, at leaft into neutral powers, by having
their whole, or the greateft part of their fortunes
in a paper, that derived its whole value from the
continuance of the revolution, and the fale of
church lands.   This was a.very great ftroke to
the ariftocratic party, and from that time the decline of its power became more rapid than ever,
and the new government acquired a degree of folidity that fecured it againft all attacks from its
open enemies.

The Jacobins were now proof againft every
thing but their own fyftem, which carried with
it the revolutionary principle, or in orther words,
the principle of felf-deftruction ; for as it rendered
every thing that poffibly could be done, liable to
be undone by violence ; and as in a violent ftrug-

---

* Conveyancing attornies.

gle,

gle, chance often determines the refult, it was probable that fome time or other, a party would arife who fhould explode this principle, and with it Jacobinifm.

The remainder of the year 1790 was em- *1790* ployed in fpreading affignats more widely, in abolifhing the traces of ancient government, humiliating the king, and perfecuting the nobility in the provinces, moft of whom, for fear of being deftroyed, reforted to Paris, and fome few began already to leave the kingdom, and join the Prince of Condé, who was on the oppofite banks of the Rhine, on the frontier of Alface.

M. Necker had been teazed and ill treated by thofe deputies, who were chofen by the affembly to infpect the national accounts, and particularly by that fame M. Camus who was fince then delivered up by Dumourier, whom he came to arreft; fo that being tired with writing perpetually to the affembly for more affignats, and of being taken rudely to tafk for their employment, he thought proper to refign and leave the kingdom. His refignation coft the king, whom he had ruined, fome regret, but occafioned great joy to the affembly, which he had fo greatly contributed to raife up, and the people, of whom he had fo long been the idol, were not at the pains either to teftify pleafure or concern at his departure; though if there was any general emotion, it was rather that of fatisfaction than of regret.*

                                        Thus

* M. Necker had a regular paffport, but the Jacobin club, who wifhed to humiliate and torment him once more, fent orders to have him ftopped and fearched at the fmall municipality
                                        of

Thus departed the principal caufe of all the troubles that had for fourteen months defolated France; it is equally impoffible to pity him, or to excufe his enemies. He had fully fhewn by his conduct, that his motives for changing the form of government in the kingdom, were perfonal and not patriotic; and they, on the other hand, muft have been very fenfible that the revolution had obligations to him of the moft ferious nature, and that they would have acted only as gratitude dictated in fhewing fome fort of regret, and paying fome honourable tribute to the father of the revolution.

During the fummer of 1790, the king had been permitted to fpend the greateft portion of his time at St. Cloud, a fmall palace about fix miles from Paris, where he was guarded by the national troops as ufual, and this contributed not a little to alleviate the perfonal inconveniency refulting to him and his family from being prifoners; it likewife prevented the affembly from having occafion to torment and infult him fo frequently as during his ftay in Paris.

In the courfe of proceeding in framing the conftitution, at which a M. Target, an advocate

of Darcy-fur-Aube, were the mob wanted to put him and his wife to the lantern. The fcene was very curious. The people on the outfide of the inn were calling out, to the lamp-poft, to the lamp-poft; while thofe within who were employed in fearching his trunks were crying out, ftop a little, we have not yet found any fufpected papers, when we do, we fhall let you know. Long live the nation! long live liberty! This fcene continued almoft all night, and it was not until exprefs orders came from the affembly that he was allowed to proceed.

of but fmall merit in Paris, worked indefatigably, it was propofed to alienate the royal domains, and allow the king a certain fum as a civil lift.   The affembly defired the king to name a fum himfelf, but he was for once aware of the fnare that was laid, and refufed to do it.   The affembly then fixed it at twenty-four millions, or a million fter-ling,* with which, had other arrangements been folid and durable, and the people happy, the king certainly would have found himfelf more con-tented than when he had an unlimited power of difpofing of all the revenues of the kingdom.

During the operations of this year, that of re-imburfing fuch perfons as had places, was one of the moft advantageous to the members who had ruled in the affembly.   Mirabeau on account of his known abilities, and his no lefs notorious pri-vate character, was applied to without hefitation by thofe who had protection to folicit ; it was faid, but not proved, that the civil lift paid him a large fum monthly, and that the directors of the bank paid him a very large fum, when their affairs were in a ftate of liquidation.†   Though thefe

* That it was only a fnare laid, is evident, by the future conduct of the affembly, which repeatedly, and without any ceremony, reduced the fum by affigning payment of guards, taxes, and many other expenfes out of it, from all which by the firft grant it was free.

† In November 1789, bills of Mirabeau's were handed about to be difcounted among money-lenders ; there were four on Le Fay, the bookfeller, of 4000 livres each, making in all about 700l. fterling.   In 1790, he bought a great part of his father's library, which was one of the beft in France ; he bought almoft all the library of the celebrated Buffon ; and befides that, the houfe of M. de Fleffeles, who had been behended

Mirabeau's Patriotism

thefe affertions want proof, it is not neceffary to
refult to any to be convinced that Mirabeau accepted bribes ; as from being in a ftate of abject
want, he had become a wealthy man, living in
great ftyle, and purchafing property of every
fort. M. d'André, the Lameths, Barnave, and
numbers of others, grew rich alfo. The Jacobin
agents who were not in the affembly, imitated
the fame example ; fo that on all hands property
was veering about from one fide to the other.

Patriots grow suddenly rich.

Mirabeau began to be lefs decided and lefs defperate as he grew rich ; the more violent Jacobins began then to accufe him of being a moderate
man ; it would have been much lefs dangerous
for him to have been accufed of murder and robbery, and it was upon the firft appearance of popular opinion turning againft him, that he ex-
claimed with his ufual commanding tone of voice,
*I know that it is but one ftep from the capitol to the
Tarpeian rock.** As the idle people, who called themfelves the nation, and who attended
round the hall of the affembly, to fway the decrees and mal-treat the members who did not vote

Mirabeau begins to be suspected.

beheaded the firft day of the revolution. He had likewife
agents at all the fales of books, or rarities at the hotel de
Buillion, and muft have laid out at leaft 50,000l. fterling,
befides his expenfes, which were not of the moft economical
nature. His falary was fifteen fhillings per day during this
period ! ! Let thofe who admire fuch patriots think of this.

　* So much were people of that party perfuaded by this time
of the nature of popular favour, that Mirabeau's friends
would tell him in jeft that he would certainly be hanged. He
is faid once to have anfwered, *oui, je fai q'uil faut ou que
j'etouffe la revolution, ou la revolution m'etouffera.* But it is
not certain that he did fay fo.

as

as they wifhed, began to diflike the falling off
that was perceivable in their favourite, it was no
wonder if he began to think of the Tarpeian
rock, and it was no wonder if his enemies began
to be more bold.*

Mirabeau, whofe penetration and audacity
were equal, perceiving that the faction of the
Lameths, Barnave, Petion, Robefpierre, &c.
were going farther than he wifhed, fignified,
without naming any names however, that he
would, with a relentlefs feverity, purfue the
factious, whoever they might be; he was taken
ill a few days after very fuddenly, and in a manner that induced many people to fufpect that he
was poifoned.

The people of Paris are fufficiently apt to
teftify immoderate joy at events, but here they
teftified very evident marks of anxiety and grief.
At the end of the fourth day, Mirabeau was no
more, and the whole of that immenfe city feemed
to mourn like a family that had loft its father;
even the royalifts were forry,† and many of them
enter-

* Marat had long been the enemy of Mirabeau; he had
propofed in his paper to hang one third of the affembly, and
to broil Mirabeau on a gridiron, as being the greateft traitor
amongft them. It is impoffible to conceive the various interefts and plans of thefe revolutionifts; they were all friends
when it was to pull down any part of the old government, but
that done, they all wifhed each other hanged.

† There are many reafons for thinking that Mirabeau was
poifoned, and though fixty furgeons were chofen from the
different fections of Paris, and declared that he died a natural
death, yet that by no means is any evidence; few of thofe
furgeons approached the body to examine it minutely, as they
themfelves

entertained the belief long after, that if Mirabeau had lived, the revolution would have taken
a more mild and favourable turn.

There is not a doubt but that the king and the
court had more confidence in Mirabeau's intentions and conduct, than in that of the popular
leaders. The affembly evidently loft in energy
and in weight with the public when this extraordinary man was no more; they had ftiled him the
coachman of the affembly, and a few members
excepted, all confeffed his fuperior talents for
guiding the deliberations. The funeral of Mirabeau was fuch as have feldom been feen, the
whole affembly, the king's minifters, every public
man, and the whole of the national guard, affifted in the ceremony, at which all the inhabitants of Paris were prefent.

It is certainly a miftake to think that Mirabeau,
or any other man, could have ftemmed the tide
of infurrection and revolution which had been let
loofe by the invafion of power and property. To
the men who had let it loofe may with great propriety and truth be applied the fublime defcription
given by the immortal Milton in his Paradife Loft:

—————————— She open'd, but to fhut
Excell'd her power; the gates wide open ftood,
That with extended wings a banner'd hoft
Under. fpread enfigns marching might pafs through
                                        .   With

themfelves confeffed, and there was a mob of above one
hundred thoufand perfons affembled in the neighbouring ftreets
to know the refult, and vowing vengeance if he was found
to have been carried off by unfair means. Againft whom
this vengeance was meant, nobody knew, it was not therefore
to be expected that the furgeons would venture to declare
their opinion, even if they had found marks of a violent death.

With horfe and chariots rank'd in loofe array ;
So wide they ftood, and like a furnace mouth
Caft forth rebounding fmoke and ruddy flame,
Before their eyes in fudden view appear,
The fecrets of the hoary deep, a dark
Illimitable ocean, without bound,
Withoutdimenfion,where length, breadth and height,
And time and place are loft ; where eldeft night,
And chaos, anceftors of nature, hold
Eternal anarchy, amidft the noife
Of endlefs wars, and by confufion ftand.

The different parties (the leaders excepted)
began now to look around and to obferve into
what an immenfe ocean of anarchy they had
launched the kingdom. Diforder increafed faft,
and the conftitution advanced but flowly, and it
already became pretty evident, that there would
be ftill greater difficulty in putting it in execution
than in making it. The French nation, extremely impatient, began to demand and expect
that happinefs which had been fo often promifed
and always delayed.

Two methods of averting the ftorm were ufed;
the one, to torment the king, and render him
odious ; the other, to make a new facrifice to the
people of Paris.

The Jacobin club determined not to permit
his Majefty to go to St. Cloud this fummer, under
pretext of his wanting to efcape ; and the affembly decreed that all goods, and in particular the
neceffaries of life, fuch as wine, poultry, and
garden-ftuffs, which hitherto paid a very high
duty on entering Paris, fhould pay no duty after
the firft of May following.

F f   The

The king, wishing to pass the Easter holidays
in the country, was stopped by a furious mob
after he got into his carriage ; and, after being
detained more than an hour, and hearing every
insulting expression applied to himself and the
queen, in the presence of an armed guard and
Monf. la Fayette at their head, was obliged to
return to the palace. This seems to have been
the beginning of that hard treatment by which his
enemies forced him shortly after to abandon his
capital, from a conviction, that, as he did neither
possess their affection nor confidence, nor power
to have himself respected, he could never fulfil
the duties, or preserve the dignity of a king.
We shall have occasion to shew that, whatever,
or whoever, may have actually been the immediate cause of his departure, there are many reasons for thinking that it was rather the project of
his enemies than of his friends.

During the latter part of the year 1790 the
revolution had marched with a more peaceable
step than either before or after. The new mafters of France were occupied with confolidating
their fabric, and the people had been tolerably
peaceable, as their patience was not quite exhaufted, for it had been induftrioufly spread
abroad that two years were neceffary for a revolution, and that in two years the affembly fhould
be renewed.

The emiffaries of the Jacobins on their part
had been very actively employed in feducing to
their party the remainder of the regular troops
that had continued faithful, not to their king,
for there was no queftion of that, but to their
officers,

officers, and to their duty as foldiers. They had been almoft every where fuccefsful, and it is fcarcely worth while to mention the obftacles they had met with, nor the difturbances which they occafioned. When fo great a nation is let loofe from obedience to the laws, tumults and diforders are the natural confequences, and it is not of any particular importance to examine them. The general outlines of anarchy, and the actions of the main actors, are all that can be traced ; for every town in France having become an executing and deliberating government, there is no poffibility of entering into any details of the particulars. The riot at Nancy, the difturbances at Montauban, at Marfeilles and Bourdeaux, were only repetitions of the fame things that were paffing fo often in Paris ; for, though the circumftances of time and place were different, the caufes and the confequences were the fame. They arofe every where, from the general fpirit of infurrection excited by the clubs, which were now called popular focieties, and they all forwarded the caufe of anarchy, and the deftruction of whatever yet remained of order.

The moderate party had long endeavoured to eftablifh focieties to counteract that of the Jacobins ; and they had held meetings at a convent of Fuillants, fo that they, as well as the Jacobins, were named after the place of their affembly. M. La Fayette was fome time a Fuillant, the Count de Clermont Tonnere, and many of thofe perfons who in the beginning had been very active in the infurrection ; but thefe Fuillants were but a bad copy of a bold original : they conftituted themfelves into a club in imitation of

their

their rivals, but they wanted the affiliations which was the great thing in which its importance confifted. They reafoned calmly and coldly, and infpired no intereft any where, or on any occafion. Men of fenfe were at a lofs to conceive, as they had patronized infurrection, and maintained the perpetual rights of the people to change the government, what reafon they could have for differing with the Jacobins ; and every frank royalift owned that the Jacobin was the more refpectable and moft confiftent character of the two. Ambition and the defire of reigning, which all could not do in one fociety, was confidered by fome as the caufe ; others faid that the Fuillants had repented ; and others again that they approved of the principles of the Jacobins, but difapproved of their confequences ; and certain it is, that the Fuillants themfelves could never give any fatisfactory caufe for their feceffion from the mother club.

The Jacobins defpifed fuch milk and water rivals too much to fet ferioufly about crufhing them, for there was little danger from men who had neither been faithful to their king, nor to the bill of rights which they had themfelves decreed.

Amongft thofe who never let pafs an occafion of defending the throne, the altar, and the nobility, there were two men particularly diftinguifhed ; M. l'Abbé Maury and M. de Cazalés ; and, perhaps, the circumftance that is the moft honourable to the Parifians is, that during the whole of the two years that they remained amongft them, though they had been perpetually blamed, and fometimes infulted, they never received

ceived any ferious injury ; they even were efteemed perfonally by vaft numbers of the oppofite
party, while thofe who were perpetually balanc-
ing from fide to fide were almoft univerfally defpifed.

In revolutions nothing is fo ufeful as a decided *Decided Character.*
character, and a firm mode of action ; thofe who
want that, never will fucceed, the others fometimes may, *Boldnefs, firmnefs, and energy*—Thefe
are the qualifications for a revolutionift : thofe
who want to crufh revolutions, muft to thefe
three join *a love of juftice and of their country,* and
the victory will be decided in favour of him who
has the firft blow. It is impoffible to fucceed in
revolting if the rulers of a country have the qualities above mentioned, where the government is
already regularly eftablifhed ; accordingly, we
never read in hiftory of any revolt being effectually made, except under weak, undecifive, or
bad rulers.

The Jacobins amufed themfelves with raifing
the populace, and making them torment the
Fuillants, who were at laft obliged to abandon
their meetings ; and neither any party, nor the
public caufe, fuffered any thing by the difperfion
of fuch feeble, undetermined, non-defcript fort
of men, who were incapable either of infpiring
any intereft or doing any fervice to their fellow
citizens.

When the affembly had recovered a little from
that ftupid inactivity in which it remained feveral
weeks, or, rather, when it had began to adopt a
plan of action, which with Mirabeau it had entirely

tirely loft, it turned with fury upon the clergy. It would have been natural to fuppofe that, having abolifhed tythes, and reduced their livings to the fums which the greateft enemy of the clergy would not regard as too great,* it was to be confidered as an affair finifhed; but now it began to appear that the *perfecution* of that order was in view; the fales of church lands went on rapidly, and the ancient poffeffors fubmitted with more refignation than could have been in fuch a cafe expected; but, under the plaufible, though infidious name of organifing the evil ftate of the clergy, they made it one condition, that all who enjoyed livings in the church, fhould take an oath that was thought to be inconfiftent with the fupremacy of the Church of Rome.

However men who had no religion might laugh at this, as the fupremacy of the Roman Pontiff is one of the tenets of the Roman Catholic faith, every reafonable man, let his own perfuafion be what it may, will confider it as the moft unexampled degree of barbarity and injuftice to propofe fuch a facrifice: it feems to be equivalent to the ceremony of trampling upon the crofs, fubmitted to by thofe who wifh to trade with the inhabitants of Japan, and which Britifh merchants have never confented to do. It is in vain in fuch cafes to remark, that to trample on a piece of wood is an indifferent matter, if the confcience of the man who is to trample on it is not reconciled to the action; but the inhabitant of Japan only propofes this condition to thofe

* A Bifhop had 12,000 livres, or 500l. a year; the country curates had 50l. thofe in towns fomething more, and other clergy in proportion.

who

who want to gain by dealing with him, he does not infift upon any perfon either doing it or ftarving; for fuch was the alternative left to the clergy of France—one of the moft cruel and moft unjuft that ever was propofed to any fet of men.

The confequence of this was, that the clergy who had abandoned their temporal affairs to the tide of things, made here a pofitive ftand and refufed obedience, as the king alfo refufed his fanction to the decree. This ended, like all the other contefts, by a forced fanction being exacted from his Majefty, and the decree being ordered to be put rigoroufly in execution.

Greatly to the honour of the clergy of France, a very fmall number took the oath required, and were therefore obliged to quit their livings and their parifhes, and to retire upon penfions which every one, even at the time, was fully perfuaded would never be paid.

M. Rabaut, a Calvinift and writer of a hiftory of this period, treats the fcruples of the clergy as being merely on purpofe to excite a fchifm in the church and confufion in the nation; we cannot, in juftice, let this affertion pafs without refutation. Without entering into the queftion as Roman Catholics, let us enter into it as men, and we fhall at once be convinced, that this oath muft have appeared a matter of great importance to the members of the church, otherwife they would not have abandoned every thing in order to avoid taking it. The enemies of the clergy themfelves, who accufe that body of too great

an

an attachment to its temporal welfare, muſt allow the force of this argument in its whole extent. As to the faƈt, that penury and want ſtared the nonjurors in the face, the circumſtance is yet recent, and many perſons living who remember that it was the general opinion at the time in France, that they never would be punƈtually paid, and that they ſoon would ceaſe to be paid at all.

There was even a ſtrong reaſon for thinking, that to pay the nonjuring clergy would be impoſſible, and this was no other, than that there exiſted no fund from which they could be paid, as the ſales of the church lands went to pay debts, and the ſalaries of the officiating clergy amounted to more than the intereſt of the money ariſing from thoſe ſales.*

If any thing can add to theſe arguments, in themſelves ſufficiently concluſive, it is the abſurd rumour ſpread abroad by the Jacobins at the time, that the clergy wiſhed to make a counterrevolution, and that they wiſhed to gain over the people to their ſide. Now, if this was the caſe, the clergy ſhould have remained in their pariſhes where they had the means of operating upon the minds of the people at large, and not have condemned themſelves to inaƈtivity, and to a total incapacity of doing any thing of the ſort, by abandoning their funƈtions.

* The ſeizing the lands of the clergy only ſerved as a pretext for creating the aſſignats, for, in faƈt, the nation loſt money by ſelling thoſe lands, and giving the clergy the ſalaries which they had decreed. This matter has been ſufficiently examined and proved by different writers at the time.

This

This allegation of the levelling party was exactly of a piece with those accusations brought against the nobility in the Jacobin club, and even in the assembly, where they were said to have burned their own castles in order to excite counter-revolution. It is difficult to suppose men capable of accusing others of such ridiculous improbabilities, but it is altogether inconceivable, that any people should be so depraved, or so ignorant, as to give any credit to such assertions.

The people, in many parts of France, saw their conscientious curates depart with regret; in others, the Jacobin emissaries chased them from their parishes with much mockery and insult; but through the whole kingdom, all classes of men, from the highest to the lowest, who retained any sentiment of religion and justice, approved of the conduct, and lamented the lot of those men who from attachment to their duty (even if that attachment should be founded on mistake) laid themselves open to all the inconveniences of indigence and want.

Lot of the Curates lamented

We cannot leave this subject without observing, that the regular plan laid for degrading religion, and by degrees abolishing it altogether, was a quite new thing in the history of mankind; we have never read of one mode of faith being pulled down, except for the purpose of establishing another: but here the plan seems to have been to destroy all religion, and leave the people without any; and if we have any doubt of its being then intended, we may clear that up by examining the conduct of the Abbé Seyes, of Petion, of Robespierre, &c. since that time.

Plan to destroy all Religion

G g   The

The firmnefs of the high clergy was fuch in this cafe, that none of the bifhops could be found to ordain the new intruders, and that two men who were bifhops *in partibus*, that is, who had no bifhoprics, and were a fort of penfioners on the Church of Rome, were employed for that purpofe.

It is fome confolation to reafonable men, whatever their mode of faith may be, to think, that the lot of thofe who rendered this cruel and unjuft decree, and of the unprincipled intruders who occupied the place of thofe who were thus difmiffed, has been ftill more difaftrous than that of the men whom they had facrificed. Many of the intruders finifhed by revoking the oath they had taken, and all of them were defpifed. Numbers have, on various pretexts, been put to death, or fent out of the country, and not one of them has had the fatisfaction of approving of his own conduct.

From the time that this decree was rendered, even the appearance of unity and concord that had been preferved hitherto was at an end ; it was evident to every one, that this fevere and unjuft order tended to ftir up diffenfion, and did not, like other decrees, put any money into the treafury of the nation ; on the contrary, it took a great deal out, by the penfions that were to be paid to the nonjurors ; or if thofe penfions fhould ceafe to be paid, it would be a breach of faith that could not but be attended with difgrace.

The nation (that is to fay, the populace, which went by that name, and which actually ruled,
though

though cloathed in rags and filth) confidered itfelf as being extremely rich, and was become fo
œconomical and avaricious, that * if this regulation about the clergy had offered any profit, it
would have had many advocates. but it offered
none, and, of confequence, was the moſt unpopular act the aſſembly had yet paſſed.

During this time a divifion manufactured itfelf
amongſt the national guards of Paris.   Santerre, *Santerre*
a brewer in the Fauxbourg St. Antoine, and who
commanded a divifion in that quarter, had endeavoured to fupplant La Fayette in the good graces
of the people.   This was a matter of no fmall
importance, for it was from the Fauxbourg St.
Antoine, which was peopled only with poor workmen, that thofe mobs had come that were fo formidable to the ariftocrats, and as the revolution
advanced, the effeminate manners of La Fayette
ceafed to be fo popular as formerly ; a coarfe,
rough brewer feemed more fit for the confidence
of men, whofe profeffed aim was to level all dif-

* One of the king's fervants, or carriages, could not pafs
without *the nation* faying, that it was a pity and a fhame
that their blood and treafure fhould fupport fuch luxury.
It was propofed, that M. Bailly, the once favourite of the
people, and ftill the mayor, fhould not be allowed appoint-
ments fufficient to keep a carriage, but that he fhould walk on
foot.   In the public papers it was propofed to abolifh all
carriages in towns, and to oblige people either to walk or to
go on horfe-back.   The order of proceffion propofed was,
that thofe on horfes fhould walk at a flow pace and follow in a
ftraight line ; nobody but a doctor or a furgeon was to be
permitted to trot their horfes in the ftreet.   We may eafily
judge, when fuch plans were ferioufly propofed and difcuffed,
though not adopted, to what an extravagant pitch the ignorance and folly of a people ftyling themfelves free was
carried.

tinctions ;

tinctions; add to this, that Santerre was the abler of the two, he was hearty in the caufe of anarchy; whereas La Fayette was become moderate, and, to complete his nothingnefs, was a Feuillant.

A riot, occafioned under the pretext of de-ftroying what remained of the Palace of Vin-cennes, which, being uninhabitable on account of its ruinous ftate, had been employed for keep-ing ftate prifoners, in the fame manner as the Baftile, ferved to fhew the two parties in their true colours. La Fayette, the fuperior officer, oppofed himfelf to the demolition, and Santerre oppofed himfelf to La Fayette, until feeing that he had only a fmall party to fupport him, he was prudent enough to give way. La Fayette re-turned to Paris,* and being told, that a number of gentlemen were in the palace of the Thuille-ries (where they had actually gone, thinking that the mob might come there), and gentlemen whofe attachment to the perfon of his majefty was not equivocal, he haftened to vent his fpleen upon them. The few friends that yet remained attached to the king were beat and kicked, and a few of them imprifoned, without any appear-ance of their having committed any fault. The common report was, that they were armed with poignards of a particular form,† but that was

never

* Vincennes is but about a mile diftant.

† The fear of poignards was fo great about this time, that a fword cutler came to the municipality in order to declare, that he had orders to make a dagger, the handle of which was to be ornamented with falfe diamonds; that it was for a

lady

never credited for a moment, though it ferved as an opportunity for diftinguifhing the king's friends in future by the title of knights of the dagger, the word ariftocrat having loft fomething of its force.

It was now become a fufficient reafon for being fufpected and ill treated, if any one feemed to have a connection with a nonjuring prieft; and the king had great odium thrown upon him on this account.

The departure of the two aunts of the king, who were too old to conform to the new regulations in point of religion, and who went fuddenly off to Rome, afforded great matter of complaint againft his majefty who was literally in the fituation of the lamb in the fable, when accufed by a wolf for troubling the water : it was the fame thing to his accufers, whether this unfortunate prince had a good reafon to give for his conduct or not, the blame was laid to him all the fame, and certainly without confidering, whether a king, who was accuftomed to rule, feels more than another man or not, his fituation was fuch

lady, and that, probably it might be for the queen. This was a very grave affair. He was told to finifh the dagger, and give notice to have the perfon who came for it arrefted. All this was done in the moft ferious manner, for the poignard was no common weapon, it had a contrivance in the handle to receive the fteel, which flipped back the moment the point was preffed againft any thing, and this was thought a very dangerous contrivance. The lady who had commanded it was a lover of the theatre, and was to perform on a private ftage, a part in which felf-murder was to be perpetrated. The conftruction of the dagger might have unriddled all this, but fear is the blindeft of all leaders.

as no man that had not crimes to reproach himfelf with could have envied.

To add to the pain which daily mortification
muft have occafioned, the conftitution, fo far as
it was advanced, offered only a bizar jumble of
principles and regulations, which promifed nothing but more anarchy and more confufion.

As it was then generally believed, that the
king was a carelefs, eafy, and ill-informed man,
it was fuppofed, that he was either ignorant of
or indifferent to the profpect before him ; but his
conduct fince, when in prifon and alone, where
there could be no deception, has proved, that he
was by no means the man they thought.   Having fo completely cleared up this point himfelf, it
would be unneceffary to enter upon it ; and we
muft remain convinced, that few men in his
kingdom had ftudied the decrees rendered by the
affembly more profoundly than himfelf, nor forefaw the evil confequences more clearly.*   He
begun, therefore, to be convinced, that there
was no hope of a good iffue to the affairs, and
through the intreaties of his friends and ill-treatment of his enemies, was at laft induced to endeavour to make his efcape.   The circumftances
with which this unfortunate journey were attended are univerfally known, but the particular
caufes of it are concealed, and probably will
continue fo till an end is put to the prefent war,
when the truth may perhaps come out.

* After the conftitution was accepted, the king had always by him a copy of the whole, and it frequently fell to
his lot to explain to the affembly that fucceeded, decrees
which they did not properly underftand.

There

There are three opinions on the subject respecting its cause; one is, that the royal family and the emigrants without the kingdom had imagined this mode of raising a civil war. Another is, that the moderate party, with La Fayette at their head, let the king go with an intention to stop him on his journey, and by getting him entirely under their power, be able thereby to triumph over the more violent Jacobins. The third is, that the more violent Jacobins had persecuted him by hindering him from going to the country that summer, and perpetually harrassing him with messages, on purpose to induce him to depart, with a design to convert France into a republic.

It would be wasting time uselessly to attempt settling this point, because the different facts on which the different opinions are supported, are not proved. La Fayette's enemies maintain that it was his plan, that he knew of their departure, and had determined beforehand where they were to be stopped. La Fayette had many faults, and was guilty of many inexcusable pieces of cool deceit; but without pretending to determine the point positively, we may safely acquit him of this until some real proof is brought against him, as it is very improbable; he run personally a great risk, as his plan might have failed, and even the first moment of popular fury might have been fatal to the man who had answered with his life for the king's person. It is still more unlikely that the violent Jacobins could have laid the plan, for the nation was by no means ready for such an experiment; besides, it was impossible for them to calculate at all about its success, as they had no means of approaching his person to give him council,

council, as none of their party guarded him, and
as the circumftance of the king's being abfent,
would be the fignal for all the royalifts in the
nation affembling round his perfon, and occafioning a civil and foreign war both at once.

Upon the whole, it feems moft probable that
this journey was the plan of the royalifts, and
that it failed through mifmanagement. On the
morning of the 21ft of June, the royal family
was found to be miffing from the palace of the
Thuilleries, and Monfieur, the king's elder brother, from the palace of the Luxemburg. Nothing could equal the aftonifhment and ftupid
fort of wonder difplayed by the Parifians in the
firft part of that day. They had affected fuch
a fovereign contempt for the king's underftand-
ing, that their pride was prodigioufly mortified
by an efcape, of which nobody could give the
leaft information. The total ignorance of the
manner, as well as of the courfe which he had
taken, mixed with the anxiety as to what might
be the confequences, produced a ftupid ftate of
inactivity, which was afterwards reprefented as
majeftic filence and refolution.

The affembly, however, acted upon this occafion with more than their ufual moderation and
wifdom. The minifters were fent for, and it was
determined to keep things peaceable till the event
of the efcape fhould become known.

Towards evening, the people began to recover
a little from the blow, and employed themfelves
in effacing the name and arms of the king, and
the word royal from all the fign pofts and public
buildings

buildings where it yet remained. The people were so little prepared for a republic, that the conversation amongst the groups in the Palais Royal, and round the assembly, ran upon the propriety of offering the throne to the Duke of York; that, said they, would change the dynasty, and unite France to England, which would be exchanging the family compact with Spain, for a far better one with England.* Paris continued in a kind of sullen but impatient silence till the fourth day, when news came that the king was stopt at Varennes, it was then that all countenances changed, and that the people began to vent themselves in abusive language. The chief movement seemed to be occasioned by the pleasure which they expected from seeing a king, who had outwitted them, humbled and brought back a captive.

The enemies of royalty had now another triumph, which they did not long delay turning to advantage. The king had unequivocally shewn himself to be the enemy of the constitution; and it is certain, after what had passed, no man who had common sense could ever expect a happy issue to the affairs. The step which the king had taken, was of itself a proof that he did not give his consent to the change of government that had taken place; but that there might be no doubt on that head, he had left a long declaration, all written with his own hand, in which he criticised very severely, and disapproved very decidedly of the plan of government. People were now convinced that the king was capable

* As soon as any new word was employed by the members of the assembly, it was repeated perpetually in the groups.

H h of

of profound diffimulation, and from that day
forward little difcernment was neceffary to fee
that either the king or the new order of things
muft fall before any very diftant period.

This flight of the royal family muft be allowed
to have been contrary to many profeffions which
the king had made, and as fuch blameable, but
it muft at the fame time be allowed that his enemies were to be blamed in a much greater degree.
Long before the time of the king's flight, he had
only acted a paffive part; it was for the great,
majeftic affembly therefore (as a king was a part
of their conftitution) to have rendered him its
friend by good ufage, and by allowing him fome
degree of perfonal eafe and comfort; but like
thofe favages who amufe themfelves in mutilating and degrading a fallen enemy, this affembly,
which profeffed virtue and philofophy, was perpetually employed in vexing and humiliating the
king; all the democratic journalifts, the democratic groups, and all the clubs in the kingdom,
were employed in rendering the king and kingly power odious and contemptible, for which
conduct it will be very difficult to affign a good
reafon, or to furnifh a good excufe.

The king, fuppofing him only to have been
the firft public functionary, as they affected to
call him, ftill he ought to have met with great
refpect and implicit obedience, when he did not
exceed his powers, and the affembly ought to
have fet the firft example of honouring and refpecting the chief magiftrate of the nation. As
it fo happened that the king never exceeded the
authority given to him, it is hard to fay whether
the

the injuftice or the imprudence of this conduct
towards him was the greater, particularly as a
fort of refpect, bordering upon idolatry,* was
fhewn to every other of the conftituted authorities.

This circumftance, which fo naturally attracts
our attention upon the prefent occafion, may
perhaps juftly be confidered as a proof that the
reigning party of that time wifhed to prepare the
French people for a republic ; and if they did fo,
it is certain the method they took was the moft
likely to fucceed of any that could be adopted.
The king had been allowed, as we before faid, a
fufpenfive veto, which gave him a privilege more
invidious than ufeful, and he was obliged, when
he did fanction a law, to do it without making
any obfervation or requefting any alteration. The
power granted to all kings, and which is fo neceffary to refide fomewhere, of pardoning crimi-
nals in particular cafes, was refufed to this unfortunate fovereign, upon whom all the refponfi-
bility and odium of executive government was
thrown, without his being permitted to enjoy

---

* In a new piece produced on one of the theatres, a municipal officer was made to appear with the three-coloured
echarpe over his fhoulders, and the people were offended that
the facred and conftitutional colours fhould be degraded by
decorating an actor on the ftage. This happened among a
people who had often feen the Saviour, and fometimes the
Creator of the world, reprefented by an actor on a public
ftage, and who never, during the times of the moft violent
royalifm, nor when religion had its greateft power, thought
there was any impropriety in reprefenting kings and priefts
on the theatre. Kings and priefts have often too been turned into ridicule on the ftage, but the municipal officer only
appeared as fuch, without the leaft attempt to expofe him,
either as an object of hatred or of contempt.

either

either the honours or the privileges that are equally neceſſary for the governor and the governed.

The philoſophers of the revolution talked much of the rights of man, and of liberty ; did they think then that they had a power to deprive their king of all his rights as an individual ? They might claim, perhaps, with ſome appearance of right, the power of caſhiering him, as they expreſſed it ; but they ſhould have ſaid in this caſe, as they ſaid on ſo many others, that though he was a king, he was likewiſe *a man*, and that nothing but crimes committed by himſelf could take away from him any of his natural rights ; as being a man, he ſhould therefore have had his free choice of being king, or refuſing to be ſo ; or at all events, if public good required that he ſhould abſolutely be king, he merited every ſort of reſpect and good treatment as an individual, devoted innocently and againſt his will to be the ſlave of the nation.

If juſtice required this, policy required alſo that the chi f magiſtrate, entruſted with the execution of the laws, ſhould be loved and reſpected by thoſe who were to obey, and it was even very eſſential to have him execute willingly, and with comfort to himſelf, the duties of the office in which he had been placed. It did not certainly require any great degree of juſtice, common ſenſe, or acuteneſs, to have ſeen all this, and as the aſſembly cannot be accuſed of wanting that laſt quality, it is more than probable that its real intention was to have a republic as ſoon as the people ſhould fully have got over their ancient

prejudice

prejudice in favour of kings. This feems to be the more probable, that the men who at that time ruled, have been very active fince royalty was abolifhed, and have never concealed their preference to a republican form of government.

It is beyond a doubt, that fince the affembly and the other authorities had no power to make the law refpected, by fecuring to the king that perfonal liberty which they had fo formally decreed, he had a right to feek means of abdicating the throne by whatever method he could;* and this was the more lawful, as it had been decreed, that if the king abfented himfelf without leave, and did not return when fummoned, he by that act abdicated his crown. Now by taking this decree in the fenfe that the king had a right to take it, if he chofe, it implies fairly, that if the king thinks proper to abdicate, he may do fo by going away out of the kingdom, or to any diftance farther than fixty miles, and refufing to return.

Such, as to the right of the matter, muft be the reafonings of every one, but it muft be confeffed, that nothing could be fo unfortunate as the difpofition of the king to go away, and that of the affembly to force him to return, as it rendered confidence in future impoffible to be maintained, and without that a king can never be ufeful in any free country.

* The king was permitted to travel to any diftance, not exceeding fixty miles from the capital, or the national affembly, and this decree was previous to his being forced by the populace to return to his palace, when he only intended going to St. Cloud, fix miles diftant, and that under a guard of armed citizens.

The

The circumſtances of the king's return are well known to all, we ſhall therefore paſs over them to the conſequences of this unfortunate journey.

The career of the democrats was impeded by this flight, although it might naturally have been expected to be accelerated. A momentary union took place between the royaliſts and the moderate party, who diſcovered their intereſts not to be very oppoſite to each other; and even many of the Jacobin club, and its admirers, having been ſtruck with amazement and fear at the proſpect of a decided civil war, which they had ſo narrowly eſcaped, determined to avoid thoſe extremes which might be the occaſion of bringing one on; even the ferocious Barnave was ſenſible of the neceſſity of adopting meaſures of greater moderation in future.* Petion, Robeſpierre, and the Abbé Gregoire, as well as ſome other leaders of the Jacobin club, amongſt whom Briſſot muſt be mentioned, and Danton, wiſhed to have embraced that opportunity of depoſing the king, by trying him and finding him guilty; however, the committee appointed for examining into the affair, declared that the king himſelf could not be tried, as he was inviolable, but that the authors and abettors of the project ſhould be ſearched out and puniſhed.

As it had been the ancient uſage in France, that the declaration of the king or queen were to be

* Beſides Barnave, Rabaut de St. Etienne, d'André, Thouret, Chapelier, and even the Abbé Seyes, were for moderation; every body knows that it was neither from reſpect nor attachment to the king that this could ariſe, it muſt, therefore, probably have been from an idea of neceſſity.

receìved

received in the courts of juftice, but that they could not be *interrogated*, the affembly and the king both were inclined to adopt this mode ; accordingly the king declared to a deputation that waited upon him for the purpofe of receiving it, that having been continually infulted in Paris, without any redrefs being obtained, he had been under apprehenfions for the lives of himfelf and his family ; that his intention had been to avoid danger by going to Montmedy, where he meant to have ftopt to learn the real difpofition and will of the nation, which he could not do as a prifoner in fo turbulent a city as Paris. To this he added, that during the latter part of his journey he had been convinced of the unanimity of the people, and their defire to fupport the conftitution, which he therefore would confider as the national will, but upon which he could not give his own opinion until it fhould be completed.

With regard to the guilt of thofe who co-operated in the flight, he declared with firmnefs that it was his own action, that no one had prompted him to it, that they had only obeyed, and that therefore no perfon could be guilty on that head.

While the affembly was endeavouring to take moderate meafures, the violent party in the clubs, both of the Jacobins and of another called the Cordeliers, where Marat and Danton were *Cordeliers* members (and which was more violent than even that of the Jacobins) were making every effort to carry things to extremities. The groups in the Palais Royal were the fame, and hand bills were

were circulated and pofted up, demanding the
trial of the king.   All the men who had
fuffered by the firft revolution, and were afraid
of a fecond, joined the moderate party ; but the
dregs of the people were firmly attached, as
ufual, to the caufe of anarchy and revolt, fo that
there was every appearance of things being
brought fpeedily to a ferious conteft.

17. July

Briffot.

Paris had been continually in a ftate of com-
motion from the 20th of June, till the middle of
July, while thefe queftions had been agitated ;
and on the 17th of July, which happened to be
a Sunday, a great crowd of people went to the
altar of the fœderation, there to fign a paper
(compofed by Briffot, as it was generally believed) which they called a petition, but which was
a remonftrance, followed by a declaration that
they never would fubmit to be governed by
Louis the Sixteenth.

This patriotic mob of petitioners began by
hanging an invalid who had loft his leg, together
with a hair dreffer whom they found lying drunk
or afleep under the altar.   This was done upon the
pretence of their being fpies (for the *good populace*
pay much more regard to feverity than to juftice
in punifhing), but more probably, as has fo often
been done fince, in order to ftir up the ferocious
paffions of the multitude, by the crime of murder recently committed.*

Bailly Fayette

M. Bailly, La Fayette, and the national
guards, were inclined to the moderate fide, and

* The fame thing was done on the morning of the 10th
of Auguft.

they

they embraced this opportunity of attacking their enemies; martial law was proclaimed, and they marched in force againſt the mob. When arrived at the Champ de Mars, where they were aſſembled, upon ordering the mob to diſperſe, the mayor and commandant were aſſailed with a volley of ſtones, which was returned by a diſcharge of muſketry, without ball, only to intimidate the aſſailants, but without effect: the ſhower of ſtones continued, and was anſwered by a ſhower *Diſcharge of Ball* of bullets. The mob now run off in all directions, leaving about a dozen dead upon the field. The ring-leaders all eſcaped, and diſappeared for a conſiderable time; Danton, for one, had been *Danton* ſeen there on a white horſe, and was one of the firſt to make his eſcape.

The aſſembly approved completely and heartily of the conduct of Bailly and La Fayette; and for once the aſſembly and the municipality of Paris joined in one intereſt, and had one triumph over the promoters of diſorder. The Jacobins were *Jacobins at Paris* humbled in Paris, at Birmingham, and in Swit- *Birmingham & Switzer-* zerland, almoſt at the ſame moment;* and *land.* though their fall was but for a ſhort period in France, it is to be attributed to this, that thoſe who cruſhed the revolt, were the ſame men who had formerly headed it themſelves, and who had been the firſt to preach up the ſacredneſs of the duty of inſurrection.

* This was the ſame week with the riots, occaſioned at Bir- *Riots at Birmingham* mingham by the celebration of the glorious revolution, and in the Pays de Vaud, where it had been celebrated likewiſe, and where ſome of the celebrators who had circulated incendiary hand bills, were taken into cuſtody and carried to Berne to be tried.

I i   We

We fee here one of the beft occafions that the revolution has furnifhed for proving the falfity of the principles, and the villainy of the men who had themfelves led the people to revolt two years before, and who now fired upon them for practifing it, becaufe it had continued too long. So thought Bailly and La Fayette now, but they did not think fo when Berthier and Foulon were maffacred ; and fo thought Briffot, two years after, when he found that infurrection was likely to be turned againft his party. It is thus that the leaders of different factions confider what is right, to confift in what fuits themfelves ; and infurrection may be added to infurrection, without a complaint, till it becomes inconvenient, and then it becomes a crime.

If men are too blind to fee into the manoeuvres and villainy of fuch practices, then we may bid adieu to all that inftruction which hiftory and experience can give. Never was conduct more uniformly felfifh and villainous, than that of the leaders of French democracy ; we fee them perpetually holding up the general good as the main object in view, as the great end of fociety, and we as uniformly fee them employing the multitude to advance their own private ends. We muft pity the multitudes which they miflead, and we muft condemn in the moft decided and unequivocal terms all thofe cruel, felfifh, ambitious, and hypocritical men, who ruined their own country before their deceit was found out, but whofe practices and whofe principles, it is to be hoped, are now fufficiently known, that other nations may be fecure from a fimilar error. The

The national affembly and the nation itfelf
feemed to be frightened at the danger from which
they had efcaped, and it was determined to go on
with and finifh the whole conftitutional act, and
thereby fecure the country from a fimilar rifk on
any future day.

CHAP. IX.

Retrospect of what had been passing in the interior—Mobs, cruelties, and burning of castles—Industry flies when there is no security for persons and property—Affairs of St. Domingo—That island a prey to the different opinions of two factions—Contradictory decrees of the assembly concerning the men of colour, the blacks and the whites—Poverty and want of commerce in France—Efforts of the Jacobin emissaries in other countries—In England—At Liege—Brabant, Switzerland, Germany, and Italy—Emigration and appearance of hostilities—The general confusion determines the assembly to finish the constitution, which they resolve to do, and then to separate.

BEFORE we enter upon the conclusion of the constitutional act, it will be necessary to turn back to take a view of the different manœuvres that had been practised in the provinces of France, in the colonies in the West Indies, and in other countries of Europe; which, for the sake of not interrupting the relation of what was passing amongst the chiefs themselves, have been left behind.

The

The firſt perſecution of the prieſts and nobles had begun in order to procure an exemption from tythes and feudal rights, as the oppoſition to the crown had been begun to procure liberty, but tythes were long ago aboliſhed, and the noble, far from exacting obedience or money, was obliged to obey, and to ſubmit to arbitrary contributions.   A new mode muſt now be adopted of ſtirring up the people againſt them, and this was not neglected.   Stories totally void of foundation were ſpread every where about the plans and plots of ariſtocrats, which word was ſubſtituted for that of royaliſt.   The dearneſs of bread was attributed to them, and, however improbable it might be, there were not wanting thouſands to give credit to that report.

Ariſtocrats ſubſtituted for Royaliſts

It has been too evident, from the reports of the aſſembly ever ſince the beginning of the revolution to the preſent day, that order has never been eſtabliſhed in the finances, nor in the diſtribution of juſtice.   How far the country muſt fall back in ſo long a period, and how great the ſhare of individual miſery muſt be on that account, is not difficult to conceive.   As the decree of the aſſembly ſeemed calculated to render the people richer and more happy, and that they had, in fact, become poorer and more miſerable, it was natural to attribute it to ſome other cauſe than the popular decrees of the aſſembly.   As, however, there was no other cauſe, none could be perceived, and therefore one was imagined.   The nobles and the clergy, who could not be expected to be friends of a revolution by which they were ruined, were fixed upon as the latent cauſe of the public misfortunes, and this belief, like
many

many others, became general, not becaufe it was
well fupported by facts, but, becaufe it became
general feemed to need no facts to fupport it.   In
the national affembly, in all the democratical
papers and clubs, the nobles and clergy were accufed without any proofs, as being a matter of
courfe, and that needed none ; at the fame time,
when any circumftance that could be conftrued
unfavourably for them took place, it was employed to augment the general fury ; of this fpecies
was an unfortunate explofion of powder at the
houfe of a member of the parliament of Befançon
while he was giving a feaft to a number of his
neighbours ; it was reported immediately, that
this unfortunate man had blown up his houfe
with defign,* and a banditti, moftly compofed
of peafants in Franch-Compté, vented their revenge for this fuppofed treafon, by actually burning and pillaging a number of gentlemen's country feats, not one of whom met with either protection or with indemnification from the governors of France ; from the leaders of that happy,
that glorious revolution, which Dr. Prieftley and
his friends prefer to that of England, under
which they obtained both.

Though the barbarities at that time exercifed
are now almoft forgotten, on account of that terrible feries of crimes with which they have been
followed ; yet they are, neverthelefs, good fpeci-
mens of democracy in its moderate moments, and
as it has become fo fafhionable to expofe the
crimes and follies of kings, a few of the firft

---

* The falfity of this was immediately after recognifed, and
the whole let fleep when its fabricators began to find its effects too ferious and likely to affect themfelves.

essays

eſſays of the common people may not be uſeleſs. They are taken from newſpapers publiſhed at the time, and ſome of them from reports laid before the national aſſembly, and they are all of them to be found in the Memoire de M. Lally Tollendal, who was himſelf a friend to liberty at the beginning, but who, ſooner than moſt others, ſaw and repented of the manner in which he and his colleagues in the aſſembly had ſought after that ineſtimable bleſſing.

" In Languedoc, M. de Barras was cut to " pieces in the preſence of his wife, who was far " advanced in her pregnancy, and died with the " fright.

Barras

" At Mans, M. de Monteſſon was ſhot, after " witneſſing the murder of his father-in-law.

Monteſſon

" Madame de Battenay was forced to give up " the title deeds of her eſtates by an enraged " mob, who menaced her with immediate death, " and held an ax over her head.

" The title deeds of a gentleman were de- " manded of his ſteward, who refuſing to de- " liver them, was carried to a fire, and his feet " were burnt off to oblige him to give them up."

We almoſt think, that we are recounting the cruelties of the Spaniards upon the inhabitants of Mexico and Peru; but no, the caſe was worſe ſtill. The followers of Cortez were but a ſet of adventuring freebooters, and had left their country to ſeek gold at any price. The diſciples of modern philoſophers acted thus with their neighbours,

bours, and in their own country, not from the
hope of enriching themfelves with gold but from
revenge, which is certainly a ftill more deteftable
paffion than avarice.

Revenge

Such are a few of the inftances of popular fury
and injuftice which France exhibited in a great
number of different parts during the two firft
years of the revolution, and which the democratic
writers do not attempt to deny, but which, they
affert, were the acts of the ariftocrats themfelves,
in order to bring on a counter-revolution.   This
affertion, though it gained credit amongft the
people of Paris, it would be an infult to the reader to offer to refute.*

two first years.

On account of thefe exceffes many of the ancient families faved themfelves in Paris, and be-

* On the banks of the Soane, where the country is in general fertile, a country attorney forged an order from the
king to deftroy gentlemen's feats.   He affembled a mob of
about five thoufand men, and, in the courfe of fix or feven
days, above feventy gentlemen's feats were burnt down, and
the churches and fmall towns were plundered.   This armed
mob was at laft attacked and defeated by a fort of army raifed by the gentlemen of the country with a confiderable
flaughter.   Some of the banditti were legally tried and punifhed.

The mifchiefs in other parts did not ftop, and no attempts
were made to punifh them.   The Chevalier d'Ambli was
taken from his houfe, dragged naked through the village, his
hair and eye-brows were then torn off; he was thrown
upon a dunghill, whilft his tormentors, like Indian favages,
were dancing round. M. de Monjuftin, who had, with
twenty-three other gentlemed, figned voluntarily a declaration very favourable to the people, was fufpended for more
than an hour over a well, while his enemies were difputing
which fort of death he fhould fuffer.

ing

ing almoft deprived of revenues from their lands, the proprietors found themfelves in a ftate little better than the clergy, and were induced from neceffity, as well as from finding things perpetually get worfe, to encourage that emigration which has fince been fo fatal to their interefts. It will be neceffary, farther on, to examine into this emigration, and fhew, that it was not a meafure either of loyalty or prudence, as it was at firft reprefented, nor a meafure of blameable neglect and cowardice, as another party has fince reprefented it. The emigration originated in the burnings and cruelties of which we have been fpeaking, and it was continued by caufes of which we fhall hereafter fpeak.

Emigration originated in the cruelties,

From thofe injuftices and cruelties with which the people began, at a very early period of the revolution, the bad effect of fuddenly overturning eftablifhed government was eafily to be difcovered. It might have been expected, that the affembly would, in confequence, have retarded the work of deftruction, and have attempted to accelerate the inftitution and organization of the new government, but no fuch thing was attempted; and though the fame horrors could not all the time continue, the deftruction of forefts where the wood was cut and burned, the non-payment of rents, and a very lawlefs and pillaging manner of living introduced and maintained itfelf in the whole of France, a few provinces excepted. This ruined the country, and rendered its inhabitants more poor and miferable than ever, while the towns were reduced by the expenfes of guards, contributions of plate, under the name of patriotic gifts, the voluntary contribution *exacted by*

K k *force*

force of one quarter of every one's revenue, but above all, by the immenſe circulation of aſſignats ſubſtituted for ſpecie without any limit or meaſure. This gave the inhabitants the means of consuming without creating,* and not only did it do ſo, but, by the variation of the price of articles, gave room to that moſt ruinous ſort of ſtock-jobbing, and ſo encouraged every kind of perſonal extravagance. Miſery and the appearance of wealth increaſed at the ſame time ; for though the prejudice againſt paper money was very ſtrong and very general at firſt, the people began by degrees to conſider as a real value a ſign which procured them bread as eaſily as gold had formerly done; and the longer this continued the more did their confidence increaſe.

As property was not ſecure in France, where there was no law, and where every ſort of value was repreſented by a ſign that was perpetually

consuming, without creating.

Miſery & appearance of Wealth.

Value repreſented by a varying Sign

* One of the greateſt evils of the aſſignats has been, that as they ſupplied the place of taxes, the nation has all this time been conſuming its capital and not its revenue. When a man pays a ſum to government, he expends and conſumes leſs than his income amounts to by that ſum, the expenſes of government are therefore the ſavings of individuals, and the balance is kept up between the productive and conſuming power of the nation ; but when a nation contrives to ſubſtitute ſomething elſe for taxes, then the conſumption of the individual is equal to his production (this is only ſpeaking in a general ſenſe, without conſidering ſuch perſons as are getting in debt or hoarding up money), and the conſumption of the nation in its public capacity is added to this, ſo that the total conſumption exceeds the total production by a ſum equal to the public expenſes. It was thus that the influx of gold ruined Spain, and that whatever the device may be, a ſubſtitute from taxation will in the end ruin any country.

varying,

varying, induſtry ſuffered greatly, and therefore
the poverty and wretchedneſs of the country became greater than in the time of the farmers-
general. Every article increaſed in price, and
this to ſuch a degree, that the abolition of duties
paid on entering Paris did not ſenſibly diminiſh
the price of the neceſſary articles of life. Formerly a bottle of wine, which coſt 5d. Engliſh
money in Paris, could be purchaſed without the
gates at the low price of 2d ; when the duty was
taken of, it was expected that the capital would
enjoy a great advantage in the reduction of price;
but it was only reduced from 6d. to which it had
riſen, to 5d. as it had originally been, and was
ſoon after augmented to 7d.

If the French reformers were miſtaken in the
manner of rendering the people happy by good
laws, they were no leſs ſo in the way of making
them rich ; ſecurity and order are the baſis of
induſtry, and induſtry of riches, without which
there can be none.

At the ſame time that the true ſource of riches
in the interior of the kingdom was ſtopped, its
reſources from foreign trade were greatly diminiſhed ; aſſignats did not paſs current in other
countries ; ſo that the courſe of exchange which
had formerly been in favour of France two or
three per cent. was now eighteen or twenty per
cent. againſt it, which is a moſt ruinous circumſtance for any country when it continues long.
The trade with the colonies was a ſo in a manner annihilated by the fooliſh and contradictory
decrees which had been rendered concerning the
ſlaves and people of colour, or mulattoes.

M. Briſſot,

Brissot

M. Briffot, in particular, but not without the aid of fome others of his Society of Friends of the Blacks, never loft any opportunity of exciting the colonies to infurrection; and the revolution was no fooner known of in St. Domingo, which is the principal of the French Weft-India iflands, than a glorious infurrection took place, of the planters againft the governor, and of the foldiers againft their officers. This in the caufe of liberty was applauded by the National Affembly, into which fix deputies from St. Domingo had been admitted.*

As in St. Domingo and the other iflands there are three different claffes of men, white men, mulattoes, and blacks; and the two laft are divided again into free mulattoes and mulattoes who are flaves, as well as into free blacks and black flaves, there was an ample field for the operation of the rights of man; but a fort of compofition was entered into between philofophy

* The admiffion of fix deputies was not an act of the affembly itfelf, but of the king, or his minifter, before the meeting of the ftates. Though this feems to be founded on equity, it does not, in reality, anfwer any purpofe; for a fmall number of members from a portion of an empire that is not fimilarly fituated with a country itfelf, only ferves to augment difcord, or to legalize oppreffion. As regulations for St. Domingo different from thofe for France were neceffary, if the fix reprefentatives did not agree to fuch regulations, it only ferved to render the colony difcontented; and if they did agree, it gave an appearance of legality to what is only founded on policy, and not in juftice. Small rich colonies will always be fubject to arbitrary laws—not, perhaps, unjuft ones, nor hard ones, but depending on the will of the mother country. It is in vain to deceive ourfelves on this point, and it is unworthy of a great country to infult a fmall one, by giving it the appearance of a free government, when it is under an arbitrary one.

and

and interest. Mulattoes born of free parents, and who therefore were themselves free, were considered as men, and admitted to enjoy all their rights. But no good could be expected from a decree that changed the old system and did not conform to the new one. " All men," says the Declaration of Rights, " are born and " remain equal in rights ;" the blacks, therefore, might with reason complain, and the whites were inclined to look with a very jealous and discontented eye on the new power conferred on a very numerous body of the inhabitants of the island, and which tended to derange entirely the internal government. When men find their interest sacrificed to a principle that seems just, they may repine a little, but still they cannot refuse giving it some degree of approbation ; but, when every thing is deranged by arbitrary will, as in this case, the discontents occasioned are without any allay. The consequence of this was, that the assembly which had passed this decree in the month of May 1791, repealed it the September following ; thereby satisfying the white planters at the risk of displeasing and rendering desperate the other inhabitants of the islands.

Such a foundation for civil war and discord being laid in the colonies, and fomented by the defeated party which had obtained the first decree in France, it is not to be wondered at, if the blacks and mulattoes making one common cause, have since desolated that miserable island,* which seemed,

* The insurrections, massacres, and cruelties, of St. Domingo would make a large volume, were they to be detailed. The Abbè Gregoire and Brissot were two of the most active instigators

feemed, by a fatality hitherto unexampled, neither to partake of any of the bleffings of freedom
nor of that fecurity which an arbitrary government generally affords.

The affembly, in repealing the law in favour
of mulattoes, in which they gave to the colonial
affemblies the rights of internal legiflation, re-
ferred the rights of the whites to the fucceeding
national affembly. Such conduct was neither
firm, politically good, nor conformable to their
own principles. The French themfelves now
found, that, inftead of making a general declaration of the rights of man, they fhould have
contented themfelves with declaring what were
the rights of Frenchmen ; or, as they were vain
enough to give the general declaration, they
fhould have maintained it in its full force, and,
as far as refpected French dominions, have eftablifhed and protected it.

The trade to the colonies was the chief foreign
trade of France, it was computed to have given
fupport to feveral millions of people; and therefore the internal miferies of that country were
greatly increafed by the colonial difturbances.

inftigators of the revolt of the negroes and mulattoes. Gregoire, who was a member of the affembly, when he heard
of a terrible maffacre, in which the negroes had for their
bloody ftandard a white infant impaled on a fpear, declared
it was the *plus beau jour de fa vie*. This philofophic cannibal
was at fupper when the news was brought, and he and his
friends finifhed the evening with mutual congratulations and
joy on the fuccefs of their plans. Human nature, whether
white or black, muft fhudder at fuch barbarity, and blame
the cool inftigators much more than the ferocious people
who revolted.

                                                    Whilft

Whilst the Jacobin faction had thus destroyed government and law, and while the capital and fources of wealth and industry were every day diminishing under their government, they had not been inactive in endeavouring to induce other nations to follow their example.

The leaders of the violent party, and those of the more moderate, however much they differed with respect to regulations in which they were personally concerned, agreed all nearly in their views with respect to other countries. As they imagined that people were free in proportion as government was feeble, they well knew, that France by acquiring liberty lost a great deal of that vigour which the other governments of Europe poffefs. The general opinion, therefore, of the reformers at the first outfet was, to establish the same system all over Europe. The violent democrats and the moderates had at first taken America for a model; but it had been argued, that if the Thirteen United States were upon the same continent with European kingdoms, their government would be found unequal to the tafk of protection from its enemies: they had all, therefore, originally formed one plan as to the neighbours of France, and their quarrels amongst themselves did not alter their opinion in this refpect. There are numberlefs proofs of this, but the chief one is founded on the rights of man which was drawn up by Mounier, La Fayette, and the moderates. This declaration of rights is evidently worded as if they were legislating for the human race, and not for their own country alone.

The

Moderates abolished Titles.

The same moderate party was present, when the ridiculous embassy of the representatives of all the nations of the world appeared at the bar 'a year after, and when titles of nobility were abolished; and it was the principles of the moderate party that were trusted to for the conversion of mankind.

Paine agent of the moderates

Thomas Paine was the agent in England of the moderate party, and considered La Fayette as his patron and protector in Paris; yet La Fayette and his party pretended to be attached to a monarchical form of government, which clearly proves that, though they differed from Petion and Robespierre in point of the application of principles, they did not differ much in the principles themselves.

Before other nations were fairly aware of what was meant by the French reformers, agents were sent into different countries; and these agents were known by the name of the Propagande, which implies perfectly the intention of propagating their opinions.

Propagande

Philosophy and good-will to men were the avowed principles of the members of the Propagande, but it was unfortunate for these missionaries, that they had not more modesty or more address.

Those who preach philanthropy and humanity are naturally to be expected to do it with some degree of meekness and patience, to offer their good advice, and to pity those who are too ignorant or wilful to follow their precepts; but as the Jacobin Propagande pursued another mode, it is clear they had another intention.

It

It is very true that the laws of this nation are fuch, that men dare not openly revolt; and it is equally true, that thofe who favour the French fyftem confider nothing fhort of open treafon and rebellion as a proof of treafonable and rebellious practices; fo that, until the mifchief is done, they will not allow that it is intended.

Moft people in England who are well difpofed, and wifh to fupport the prefent conftitution, are inclined to believe that efforts have been making ever fince the year 1790 to create diforder by an imitation of the French revolution. As for thofe who kept up the clamours about liberty and re-form, THEY KNOW that fuch manœuvres have exifted; they know that the law of England is in criminal matters fo attentive to the rights of indi-viduals, that in all cafes where there is not a di-rect crime proved, no punifhment follows; and that it is very difficult to apply the law to a new fpecies of an attack made upon the peace of the community at large, and which can be carried on under the appearance of patriotifm and good intention.

Of thefe manœuvres in England we fhall fay more hereafter, but as far as they relate directly to the French, it is a fufficient proof of their exiftence, that at Paris the club publicly boafted of propagating its principles in all nations. That the name of the Propagande was given to its emif-faries by the club itfelf, and that correfpondences in a fraternal way were actually commenced between

L l

tween some Englifh focieties and the French
club.*

If a number of circumftances have concurred
to prevent the flame of reform from breaking
forth, in all its Parifian fplendor, in England,
that is no proof that it was not attempted, although *its not having fucceeded* is the only argument that is offered by thofe who deny its exiftence, while there are, on the other fide of the
queftion, numerous and incontrovertible facts,
which convince us that great numbers of perfons
admired, or affected to admire, the French revolution; and as the firft way to bring on revolution is to excite difcontent with the prefent ftate
of things, the celebration of French liberty and
infurrection was the natural beginning of revolution in England.

We firft admire, then love, and then embrace.

The celebration of French liberty, which was
called French emancipation and happinefs, feemed

* The affembly was as defirous of foreign importance and
fame as the club. A poftmafter's fon at Louvain, of the
name of Wolfe, whofe intellects were deranged, had for
many years imagined himfelf to be a prince; as his madnefs
was harmlefs, his friends did not confine him, and he ufed
to fign his name the Prince de Wolfe, and to wear ftars and
ribands of different orders. This prince wrote a letter to the
affembly, teftifying his admiration of the wifdom and philofophy of their decrees, and promifing to imitate fo great and
good an example in his own territories. The letter was received and read with enthufiafm in the affembly, and the
prefident was ordered to write an anfwer to the Prince de
Wolfe. One would be apt to think, the ignorance of the
twelfth century was returned, when the geography of Brabant was unknown ni France.

to

to the unfufpecting as an act merely occafioned
by a benevolent principle ; and there exifted no
law to prevent fuch celebrations, although it was
clear, that men who in this manner approved of
the revolution of France, were actually holding
up all the exceffes and extravagances of that revolution to our admiration ; it tended directly to
make the common people in England difcontented with their fituation, by artfully reprefenting
France as the freeft country in the world ; and
whatever the theory of the French revolution
might be, it led the ignorant to conceive, that
murder, maffacre, and deftruction of all diftinction and order in fociety, were the methods of
obtaining the happy fyftem which they were employed in celebrating.

The friends of the French fyftem had, at the
beginning, motives to fupport it, which they have
not now, and they had arguments in its favour
which they can never have again. The principles
of the revolutionifts had not been tried, and
therefore its admirers might imagine that they
could be reduced to practice ; they did not,
then, perhaps, know, that the revolution would
deftroy its own founders, nor had experience
then proved what it has done fo completely fince,
that wherever revolt againft the ruling powers is
admitted as a fundamental law, it muft deftroy
every other law, and that the real term of the
French revolution will only be when this principle fhall be completely exploded, and when
thofe clubs which, though felf-created, interfere
in executive government, fhall be confidered as
inimical to the real liberties of mankind.

The

The democratic exertions of the Propagande, when the revolution was in its infancy, when the theory was promulgated with oftentation, but before experiment had fealed its condemnation, were as fuccefsful as they were energetic; and if the revolutionifts had been able to preferve even the appearance of liberty and happinefs, without really enjoying them, there would not probably be at this time any kingdom in Europe which would not have followed their example.

The infular fituation of England, its language, and the peculiar advantage long enjoyed by its inhabitants, of living under a free government, and of comprehending better than moft other nations in what freedom confifts; together with the fpirit of moderation which, upon almoft all occafions, they have fhewn, protected us againft fo violent and metaphyfical a reform as our Gallic neighbours wifhed to introduce amongft us; but other countries, that were not fo well fecured from the attacks of their fraternity and philofophy, foon felt the effects of a fyftem which offered plunder to the needy, equality to the vain, and promifed liberty to all.*

Liege

Liege, governed by an ecclefiaftical prince, had revolted againft its bifhop, in imitation of the French, and mutual congratulations had pafled between the chiefs of the parties; and if the principality of Liege had not formed a part of the German empire, it is very probable that the revolutionifts would have continued to be an imi-

* It is ftrange enough, that in the French language there is no word for freedom—liberty and freedom are not abfolutely fynonimous terms in Englifh.

tation

tation of France, which was profeſſedly taken as a model. The emperor's interference put an end to this revolt, and thereby prevented ſimilar acts of violence to thoſe to which the territory of Avignon has ſince been a prey.

A revolt in Flanders and Brabant was excited *Flanders Brabant* at the ſame time, but that taking a bad turn, did not meet with the full approbation of the French. Religion was not baniſhed from the Flemiſh provinces as it was from France, and the conteſt was not abſolutely for the deſtruction of order and property, but was directed againſt the houſe of Auſtria. When the power of the emperor over theſe fertile provinces was deſtroyed, the parties who had hitherto been united quarrelled amongſt themſelves, and the democratic party ſunk in the ſtruggle. The Flemiſh and Brabanters were then treated by the French as undeſerving of liberty, and thoſe who were exiled from it received from one of the French clubs the following letter of condolence upon the event of the revolt, and of congratulation as to their intentions, with a ſort of hint, that if there ſhould arrive a better occaſion, they might expect ſome aſſiſtance. The letter runs thus:

" Gentlemen,

" You know how to appreciate liberty, you
" wiſh for it, but unfortunate events have hin-
" dered you from conquering it. The friends of
" the French conſtitution* *embrace the whole world* *embrace the World*

* Which did not till long after exiſt.

" *in*

" *in their system of philanthropy*, and it is on that
" principle that they hope, that you will, Gen-
" tlemen, on returning to your country, sow the
" seeds of. OUR BENEFICENT PROJECTS, that
" they may produce a plentiful harvest."

Rochambeau

1791

This letter, signed Rochambeau, president of
the club of Maubeuge, in the month of September, 1791, shews plainly enough the disposition of the clubs with respect to Brabant and
Flanders, as well as their pretensions to the character of being the philanthropists of the whole
human race.

Switzerland

Switzerland, which has the misfortune of being contiguous to France, was worked upon in
the same way.

Mirabeau had instituted at Paris, in conjuncti-
on with several Swifs malcontents, a club, called
The Friends of Swifs Liberty, which club carried on its correspondences with its partisans in
Switzerland, and was so far patronised by the
national assembly, that a deputation from the
club was received at its bar, as if this club had
been a legal body. The Swifs magistrates, however, remonstrated against this, without any attention being paid to their complaints.

Papers distributed

Papers had been distributed in great numbers
in Switzerland amongst the country people in all
the aristocratic cantons, informing them of the
grievances they laboured under. Whether the
villany, the impudence, or the imprudence of
this conduct were the greater, would be difficult
to say, but the fact is certain.

A M.

A M. de Perigny was arrested in the Pays de *Perigny*
Vaud for difperfing feditious pamphlets, which
plainly excited the peafants to rebellion, and the
courts of juftice in Berne, where the fact was
proved, were fo well convinced that if they punifhed this man as the law directed by imprifon-
ment, they would offend the French nation, that
they did not venture to do fo, but were obliged
to fatisfy themfelves with banifhing him from
Switzerland. This fame M. de Perigny was a
Frenchman, and not a Swifs, therefore he could
not allege that patriotifm was his motive, as
moft of the Propagande gentlemen do. He was
active in exciting the peafants of Lower Valais
to infurrection, where he alfo efcaped without
punifhment.

Mirabeau had his fellow-labourers in litera-
ture, who were, as already has been faid, refu-
gees from Geneva, worked hard to create a revolution there upon principles of pure democra-
cy, fuch as reigned in France after the 10th of *10 Aug. 1792*
Auguft, 1792. This revolution was to be com-
menced when a fignal was given, by finging the
revolutionary air of *ça ira*, under the windows
of the magiftrates, in which the patriotic wifh,
of feeing all the ariftocrats hanged, was rendered
more complete, by wifhing that all the *burgeffes*
might fhare the fame fate.* The infurgents,
not finding themfelves fupported by the French
peafants in the neighbouring Pays de **Gex** as
they expected, difperfed after a few days of trouble and confufion.

* Tous les ariftocrats à la lanterne,
Et tous les bourgeois auffi.

That

That all thefe movements originated in Paris is clear from the circumftance, that the journalifts who were devoted to the Jacobin club celebrated this attempt to revolt, as well as all the other infurrections that happened in different places, and declared, that Geneva would very foon, like Avignon, beg to be incorporated in the French empire.

The Genevefe, far from begging to be incorporated, took the alarm, and begged to be excufed, fo that from that time the revolt was ftified, and the government of Geneva rather gained ftrength by this abortive attempt.

The revolution of the 14th of July was celebrated in the Pays de Vaud with fomewhat more eclat than at Birmingham, and was attended with a plot to give up that country, and even Geneva, and a part of Savoy, to the French, as Avignon had been given up. This confpiracy was carried on by the patriotic clubs in that country, which correfponded with the patriotic clubs in France; the ringleaders were arrefted, but the fenate of Berne was afraid to punifh manœuvres, in which the democratic leaders of fo powerful a neighbouring nation bore the chief part.

Even M. Necker was enraged at the attempts made to ruin the peace of his country, and complains that thofe little ftates had the *weaknefs to think themfelves happy* till the French revolutionifts fent their emiffaries amongft them.

Such were the efforts of the French clubs amongft their neighbours. It was impoffible to

do

do the fame things in what is called High Germany, but at Mentz and Frankfort there were clubs, and at Vienna and Berlin emiffaries, who did all that they durft venture in propagating their levelling fyftem.

Clubs at Mentz Vienna Berlin

During all this time, the emigration from the interior of France had been going on. Fear had fent off many of the proprietors of lands, and the infubordination in the army had fent away a great number of the military officers. The clergy, too, had begun to fly from perfecution and their native land; fo that in proportion as the revolution advanced, the two obnoxious orders quitted France; and one of the things that vexed the general bulk of the people moft, and excited the greateft difquiet and anxiety with refpect to the event of the revolution was, that though the nobility and clergy now exifted no more within the kingdom, mifery and difcontent increafed at a rapid rate. The burgeffes and the low people* began now to eye each other with jealoufly, and to fufpect that the exiftence of the privileged orders had not been the only caufe of former grievances.

Proprietors

Officers to Clergy

Mifery increafed.

This writer traces things very well. The fame thing has been feen in America, and produced the Conftitution of U. S.

In entering upon the famous fubject of emigration, refpecting which all Europe is fo much divided in opinion, and for which the emigrants are fo much blamed, it will be proper to examine with fome degree of attention into the caufes which firft led the proprietors of land in France to abandon their property, and royalifts to abandon their king.

It is always a difficult, and often an ufelefs tafk to plead the caufe of the unfuccefsful ; but let not thofe to whom fortune has been more favourable, judge with too great rigour the motives of the unfortunate emigrants. We truft, that though they have been miftaken, they have not been guilty, and we fhall fee that even their miftake in emigrating was a very natural one.

migrants report No body fo heartily laments the emigration as the emigrants themfelves do ; they are now per-fectly fatisfied that it might have been better to have ftaid in the country, and in this every one will agree ; but it by no means follows, that though it has had an unfortunate iffue, the origin was either wicked or foolifh.

To thofe who accufe the emigrants of having abandoned their king, and thereby having fhewn that they were not fteady royalifts, it will be fair to put the queftion, whether they think thofe fame emigrants were indifferent as to the lofs of their lands and property ? When thofe men abandoned their king, they likewife abandoned their all ; their feelings as proprietors cannot be doubted, and it will readily be believed that they did not mean to lofe the property that they abandoned. Finding, then, that thofe men did abandon, by leaving France, property which they did not mean to lofe, it is but fair to grant that they might have abandoned their king without any intention of hurting his caufe.

But we may go much farther, and prove that the emigrants abandoned their lands with an in-tention of preferving them, and their king with

the

the intention of supporting him; and that they are no more blameable for the unfortunate fate of their master, than they are for the decree that alienates their estates.

We have seen how on the 14th of July and the following days, France became a sort of camp, and shortly after how all the cities and towns were filled with clubs, and administrative bodies, who were all regulated by popular assemblies.

We have seen how instantaneously this change was operated, as well as the direction which it took. The nobles not only were deprived of all importance, and of all means of consulting together, but they were suspected, persecuted, and oppressed, so that there was no possibility for them to make any effort in their own favour.

Although the personal danger to the nobles was full as great, and even perhaps greater during the first year of the revolution than afterwards, yet the emigration did not begin then; for though personal danger might operate on some individuals, it by no means appears to have been the principal cause of emigration, which only became great in proportion as all hope of restoring peace and order was lost.

The uniform system of persecution towards the ancient proprietors, and the gradual incroachments upon their rights and titles, together with the system of equality which was openly proclaimed by the journalists, left no hope of justice but from an appeal to force; and any thing of the

fort

fort in the interior of the kingdom was, as we plainly perceive, abfolutely impoffible.

It may be very natural for proprietors in other countries to look with a fort of contempt on men who they fuppofe abandoned their king, their country, and their eftates, through fear; but if fuch perfons will examine the matter, they will find that fear of perfonal fafety was not fo much the caufe, as a confcioufnefs of the impoffibility of making any effort in a country where the re-union of a dozen of proprietors was confidered as a dangerous plot, and where, therefore, any co-operation in a general caufe was impoffible.

The conduct of the king, too, had left the no-bility without hope; they faw virtue and good intention in all he did, but they faw that nothing but conceffion added to conceffion were to be ex-pected from a king, who, together with his fa-mily, were under the perpetual danger of being maffacred by the mob, in cafe of any refiftance to the decrees of the affembly. If we muft be per-mitted to call things by their real names, Louis XVI. was not now a king; *he was a prifoner*, and the paffive inftrument of the Jacobin club, which governed the affembly, to whom the king was no more than the great feal of England is to the Chancellor; an inftrument that gives for-mality to decrees, and nothing more.

Louis a Prisoner.

The activity of the French nation is well enough known to every one, and though the court was ftupidly inactive, the whole of the pro-prietors in the kingdom were not; they had con-fidered very ferioufly, whether by force, by con-ceffion,

cefiion, or by firmnefs, they could protect themfelves, and, as the hiftory of the revolution plainly
fhews, they found them all equally ufelefs, the
king, their mafter, was a prifoner, and all power
was in the hands of the members of the clubs,
who were indefatigable in purfuing, denounc-
ing, and perfecuting the proprietors throughout
the whole kingdom.

The Count d'Artois had emigrated in the beginning, with all his family, as we have already
faid, as well as the Prince of Condé. A fmall
number of nobles attached to their perfons, from
various motives, had followed, and this infpired
into the unfortunate and profcribed nobility within
the kingdom, an idea, that as they could not find
any means of making a ftand, and of propofing
conditions to their oppreffors whilft they remained
where they were, they might fucceed better were
they to rally around the unfortunate princes of
the houfe of Bourbon, who were in a land where
men were permitted the liberty of affembling and
confulting for their mutual intereft and fafety.

Thus the emigration began under the conviction, that whilft they remained in the interior of
France, the nobles could do nothing but fubmit
to every injuftice and every indignity; and that
were they to re-unite in another country, they
might have fome chance of treating with their
oppreffors: it is not therefore fair to attribute to
folly or ill intention a meafure which, however
unfortunate it may have been, did at the
time that it was adopted offer a better profpect
than any exertion that could be made whilft they
remained in the kingdom.

Unfor-

Unfortunate as the emigrants are, have thofe proprietors that remained been more happy? or had they all remained, is it certain that they would have been better? nay, is it probable? No; the revolution was begun, and was determined upon. The affignats were neceffary to fupport the revolution, and the lands of the clergy were an infufficient pledge for their payment. The crown lands and the *appannage* of the princes were likewife infufficient, and it was perfectly evident that the foil of France alone could anfwer as fecurity for a fpecies of money which had no intrinfic value, and which was employed with unexampled profufion.

The nobles had but two things to rifk, a general profcription of their property in cafe of their emigration, or a continued fyftem of attacking their lives and properties individually if they remained. If an imprudence was committed, it was only in chufing the former rather than the latter. Many perfons will no doubt fay, that if the whole body of the nobles had remained within the kingdom, it would have prevented the feizing of their property. This is poffible, and it would be abfurd to attempt proving the contrary; but it muft be allowed, that though we admit the poffibility, the probability is liable to be greatly queftioned. The nobles compofed but a fmall portion of the kingdom, and they were all in it when fo many caftles were burned, when the peafants cut down their woods, and perfecuted them in every way that fuited their intereft or their inclination, fo that it is difficult to fee by what means men reduced to this fituation could have protected themfelves. One clafs of proprietors, the monied

ed men, who, on account of their democracy and their pecuniary refources, might have expected good treatment, did not emigrate, and they have been little better treated than the nobles that remained ; there does not therefore appear to be any great reafon for imputing to the emigration alone the misfortunes of the emigrants.

But when all is confidered, we muft allow that as the revolution has taken fuch a violent turn, and that the Jacobins never fhewed at any time a difpofition to accommodate matters, it would be highly unfair to lay to the account of the emigration the violence and injuftice of that terrible faction, and even if we do, what is the conclufion? Why, that the proprietors who emigrated were timid and unfortunate, and that the Jacobins were audacious and unjuft.

That thofe who began the emigration had no hoftile intentions to their country, is probable ; but even if they did wifh to appeal to arms for the prefervation of their rights, that was only doing what thofe who cenfure them fay they ought to have done in the heart of the country ; for nobody has gone fo far as to fay that they ought to have tamely fubmitted to robbery, and far lefs has any one ventured to deny the exiftence of the robbery.*

* The difference between the ariftocratic and democratic hiftories of the revolution, does not confift fo much in a difference with regard to actions committed, as the fuppofed motives of the actors. The democrats, to a man, allow the perfecution of the nobles, but then it was upon the *good grounds* of a fufpicion of their counter revolutionary intentions.

The

Emigrants deft prated

The firſt year of the aſſemblage of nobles beyond the limits of their country, had been ſpent in pleaſures and expenſes, for which they have very juſtly been reproached; but we muſt admit, that in charging them with levity and folly on that account, we muſt acquit them of the charge of bad intention. They appear to have truſted that the revolution was too violent in its principles, and too ill combined to laſt long; and many of them ſeem to have emigrated with an intention of waiting for the moment when, tired out with its exceſſes and miſeries, the nation ſhould become more juſt and reaſonable, or, when the conſtitution being finiſhed, ſecurity for property and perſons might be expected. It is not to our purpoſe to give a hiſtory of the conduct of the emigrants when out of their country, but the firſt cauſes of that emigration are ſo intimately connected with the Jacobin conduct, that it would have been improper, if not impoſſible, not to enter into an examination of it.

The aſſembling of the mal-content proprietors near the frontiers excited great alarm and uneaſineſs in France; and long before there was the leaſt appearance of any hoſtile attempt, the alarm was general, and fear magnified the reports ſpread abroad, without foundation of a formidable invaſion.

France being covered with armed men, the ancient regiments were of little uſe in the country: it was therefore propoſed by the aſſembly to take ſome ſteps to prevent invaſion, by forming camps upon the frontiers. M. Duportail, a friend of La Fayette's, who was war miniſter, being called to the

the bar, explained to the affembly, that though
it might be very prudent, and perhaps neceffary
to augment the garrifons in the frontier towns,
yet that as no movements of a hoftile nature
exifted amongft neighbouring nations, it would
be imprudent to *eftablifh camps* ; that fuch a thing
would be, as it always had been, confidered as a
hoftile meafure, and would furnifh the enemies of
France with a good pretext for making hoftile
preparations. This is a proof that the fears of the
affembly, and its accufation againft the Emperor
as being the firft to menace war, were ill founded, for the arguments of Duportail, who never
was a popular man, were fo far confidered as
good, that the meafure of eftablifhing camps was
for that time given up.

The anxiety and uneafinefs with which the
emigration was attended from the firft beginning,
was a proof that the democratic party conceived
that danger would ultimately arife from its little
regard to juftice, and from the defpair which its
conduct infpired to the party oppreffed. Injus- *Injustice afraid*
tice is perpetually attended with fear and fufpici-
on ; and furely, though this truth has always
been allowed, it never was before exemplified
upon fo large a fcale as in the prefent inftance.

Amongft the feudal rights which had been abo- *Alsace*
lifhed, were feveral in Alface, belonging to
German princes (as being formerly a part of the
German empire). The haughty reformers had
treated thefe foreign princes with as little ceremony as they did the fubjects of France, and
to all remonftrances made on this occafion, they
had

N n

had never given but either an evasive or inso-
lent answer.

Perhaps the emigrating nobility conceived
hopes, that as their cause was a common one
with that of many of the German princes themselves, they might expect the more readily support; and it is also not improbable that the level-
ing faction in France found its fears augmented
from the same reason; but certain it is, that it
was a general opinion in France so early as the
month of August, 1791, that a war with the
empire would take place, and it is equally certain, that at that time the Emperor had not even
the complement of troops that by the treaty of
peace he was allowed to have on the German
frontiers.

Things were in this state of inquietude as to
foreign nations, and of anarchy and misery at
home, when the moderate party got the better of
the enragées, as they were called, or outrageous
republicans, by the fusilliad of the petitioners in
the Champs de Mars, and when the general impatience called out for a constitution, and the return of peace and order.

The conclusion of the constitution was therefore resolved upon, and its revision, the proper
arrangement of the decrees, and the addition of
such as were yet wanting to render it complete,
were hastened by every means that could be
thought of.

Many people imagined that the impatience
and haste of the assembly on this occasion
arose

arofe from being fenfible of the critical fituation
in which they were. The patience of the people
was exhaufted; an enemy, it was thought,
menaced on the frontiers, and there were innu-
merable enemies within; the king too had fhewn
in an unequivocal manner his difapprobation of
what the affembly had done; the laws were without force, the finances in diforder, and no taxes
were collected; fo that without a change that
might give hope of a fpeedy end to thofe numerous evils, there was an impoffibility of going on
at all. It is generally believed that the affembly
was very fenfible of this impoffibility, and knew
that the approach of winter would be fatal to
their authority and to the conftitution itfelf, if it
were not fpeedily complete.

It was now that the talents of the deputies and
the couftitution itfelf were to be put to a trial;
they had the difficult tafk to perform of making
one whole of their work, and of giving fome folidity and durability to a fyftem, of which one of
the leading principles was, that it ought to have
no affured ftability, nor any fixed duration.

A complete criticifm on this conftitution would
require a whole volume to itfelf, therefore would
be inconfiftent with our plan; but it is neceffary
to enter a little into it, becaufe the manner in
which it is drawn up is remarkably favourable to
the Jacobin focieties.

When any two principles are placed in oppo-
fition to each other, the weaker is fure to fink *The weather of two*
under the ftronger, whatever the juftice of the *opposite Principles*
cafe may be; and if any legiflature, in laying *finks.*
down

down conftitutional principles, or in a code of
laws, falls into the error of inferting principles or
rules which are oppofite in their nature to each
other, that which favours the views of the people
to be governed the moft, will occafion the other
to be fet afide.

The conftitution included many articles in
direct oppofition to each other.   Infurrection was
declared a duty, and fecurity of property a right;
but where there is to be infurrection, there can
be no fecurity: this laft, therefore, falls to the
ground.   The Jacobins, it is true, have faid, that
their meaning was, that infurrection was only to
be employed in cafes of oppreffion ; but who was
to be the judge of thefe acts of oppreffion, and
did the Jacobins themfelves ever attend to this ?
Did they ever determine beforehand whether
they were oppreffed or not ? It would at any
rate have been very ufeful to have given a definition of oppreffion ; for, after they had conquered
their rights, it is not eafy to conceive how oppreffion was to take place.   According to themfelves the will of the majority made the law, and
therefore no law could be oppreffive ; as long as
the minifters of juftice confined themfelves to
the application of the law, refiftance was certainly not permitted, and when they went beyond it,
it is fo evident that refiftance may and ought to
take place, that to make a decree for that purpofe
is like making a decree to allow a man to defend
himfelf againft a robber and a murderer on the
highway.

It is well known, that when in any nation the
great majority becomes difcontented with the

form

form of government, it will be changed; but it is absurd to make this a right, and it was villainous to word the decree in such a manner as to lead the people into the error of considering opposition by violence to the governors as being a duty, or a right, because such a principle is destructive of every law or regulation that can be made.

This is too nice.

The article which, by way of making men free and independent, prevents the present race from binding their children, and frees us from whatever was done by our forefathers, is, if possible, worse than the decree of insurrection, because it leads men perpetually to think that the existing state of this, whatever it may be, is founded upon injustice. As a nation does not change its identity, like a single line of individuals, in what manner, and during how long a time, are laws, once made, to be in force? When are they to be revised and revived? Is it to be at the end of an age, or as soon as the majority of those who decreed them are no more? or is it to be at any stated period?* This question presented

Present Generation cannot bind the future.

---

* A full examination of this would be curious enough, if the absurdity of the principle did not render such a thing unnecessary. Suppose there are five millons of electors in a country, then 2,600,000 makes a majority; but as the whole five millions are renewed in the course of things, in twenty-five years, it follows, that there would be 100,000 new voters in six months. So that a new majority might exist without any change of opinion in any individual; in such a case the constitution should be revised every six months; and the rule to find the duration of a constitution would be (supposing men were not to be allowed to change their minds) found thus, the total number of voters divided by twenty-five would give the yearly renewals, and the number of the majority

fented itfelf to the affembly, and was debated
with great ferioufnefs, but all to no purpofe ; it
was found impoffible to reconcile the conftitution itfelf with any regulation for its duration.
The errors of wild, impracticable theory, and
the danger of paffing decrees in a half a minute
and without reflection, began now to appear ;
but it was too late to remedy the mifchief which
was already done ; the affembly was, therefore,
under the neceffity of finifhing the conftitutional
work with faying, that, though the right of the
people to change the conftitution at will was facred and inviolable, yet that it was the opinion
of the majority of the members of the prefent
affembly that it would not be prudent for the
nation to change it for thirty years to come.
So far they faid tolerably well, but the members who were now going to become private citizens were afraid, that this would not fecure
them from the arbitrary changes which their
fucceffors might probably think proper to make,
and of which they themfelves might not approve;* and, therefore, under pretence of directing the form in which the conftitution might
be changed, they ordained—That the two legiflative affemblies immediately fucceeding fhould
have no right to propofe any alteration ; that the
third affembly might propofe a change, and if a
majority of two other affemblies after are of the
fame opinion, then the fixth affembly might be

majority in favour of the conftitution, divided by the yearly
renewals, would give in years, or the fractions of a year,
the time that the conftitution ought to laft.

* A true democrat in the French way is a defpot when in
office and a rebel when out ; and in private life, oppreffive
to inferiors and infolent to fuperiors.

au

an affembly of revifion;* which laft, after all, fhould only have the right of altering fuch parts of the conftitution as the majority of *the three* preceding affemblies fhall have pointed out fpecifically.

If volumes were to be written on the abfurdity of the conftitution, nothing could fo completely fhew it, as this awkward manner of launching it into the world. The inutility of finifhing, and making the king accept a conftitution, which was not, perhaps, to laft a day, was evident to every one; and the ridicule of declaring the unlimited rights of the people to change the conftitution, and then endeavouring to fetter it with thofe arbitray conditions, is inconceiveable. The conftitution became a mon- *A Monfter* ftrous production, of which the parts were at variance amongft themfelves, and whatever credit it might have obtained in advance, ought to have been now withdrawn, for no party could defend it.†

The moft inexcufable of the miftakes committed by the conftituent affembly, was in the arrangement of the decrees, and not making any diftinction between laws that originate in natural juftice, that are immutable as juftice, and which,

* This affembly of revifion was to be compofed of 249 members more than the ufual affemblies. What ftrange combinations errors lead to, that men are too vain to acknowledge!

† Mr. Paine, for inftance, could not defend this latter part, and his opponents difpute the former, in which the perpetual right of changing is fuppofed to exift; fo that, as the conftitution ftood, it was exceptionable to all.

there-

therefore, never can admit of being changed; and thofe articles which are framed upon convenience and expediency, and which are liable to be changed with circumftances, and for which changes, therefore a provifion ought to be made.

In England, where we are not fo fond of abftract principles, and where we have contented ourfelves with laying down practical laws, and eftablifhing our rights as Englifhmen, without inveigling ourfelves in the labyrinths of theory, our forefathers by means of ftrong common fenfe made the diftinction, and refolved this difficulty that was infurmountable to the acute French lawgivers. The three powers in England of king, lords, and commons, cannot alter the original bill of rights; they cannot make an act of parliament that will infringe upon any article contained in that; but they have full authority and power to regulate every thing elfe belonging to the laws and government of the country.

what does he mean? Magna Gharta: or the Petition of Right. or the Bill of Right?

Thus, for inftance, the legiflative power in England could not make a law to enable the king to lay on new taxes merely by his own authority, becaufe fuch a change would deprive us of our rights as Englifhmen; neither could they make a law to fet afide the king's authority, as to the fanction of its acts, for that would be deftroying the convention made between the people and the king; nor can all the three powers united give effect to any law before the date of its paffing, becaufe that would be contrary to natural juftice. We have no need, therefore, for a revifionary parliament on that head; and, as to all other fort of acts, they can be either laid on, or laid afide,

afide, as kings, lords, and commons pleafe. Thus, without any *form being organized for change and infurrection*, or any theories which might lead to conclufions of which the refult would be dangerous to our peace and fecurity, we are happily governed.

It would be endlefs to point out the errors and contradictions of this conftitutional act, in which, after giving equal rights to all, a great number of articles exift, that deprive certain perfons of a part of their rights without their having committed any crime, by which men alone ought to be deprived of the natural rights of citizens; * and one very material regulation is that which deprives poor citizens, who do not pay three livres, or half a crown, a year in taxes, from the right of voting.

In one refpect the national affembly took from the people a part of their original rights as Frenchmen, who, when they chofe reprefentatives for themfelves in the ftates-general, had a right to give them, as we have feen, cahiers of inftruc- *Instructions,* tions; this right the affembly took away, and declared that the electoral affemblies only met to chufe reprefentatives, but not to debate on any fubject of legiflation. They likewife forbid any petition from being prefented by any portion of the people as an incorporated body, and it will appear that, though in the abftract declaration of rights they had been very lavifh towards MAN,

* To be a voter, a man muft be a national guard, and take the civic oath. The rights of man fhould, therefore, have its title changed for that of the rights of men who have enrolled themfelves in the guards, &c.

O o

yet

yet in his individual capacity as a citizen, they did not allow him any great fhare of importance.

It would, as has already been obferved, require much time to enter into all the inconfiftencies of the conftitution which is long ago thrown afide, as might have been expected; but it is worth remarking that the general defign apparent in the whole is to deceive the people by the pompous declaration of rights, which, when applied to practice, vanifh into air;* and which it is not to be wondered at if the deluded people fpurned from them in difdain, when, after the tenth of Auguft, they had by a new infurrection thrown off the thirty years fetters which the affembly attempted to put upon their fovereign will.

Defign to deceive the People.

It is an undoubted fact, that the affembly fucceeded much better in deceiving ftrangers and even thofe who confidered themfelves as men of knowledge and fcience in other countries, than they did in deceiving their own countrymen; for even the loweft clafs of the people foon perceived that the conftitutional act was made to deceive

* As for inftance, that all men are eligible to all employments in the ftate.—What is the fignification of fuch an article? Muft not a man have the talents fitted for the place, and muft not the choice fall amongft thofe who are fo fitted? and is it not the man who can make the beft intereft that will be chofen, whether that choice lays with an individual or a number of electors? So that this right which men in fact enjoy in England, and in moft countries, is a mere tub thrown out to the whale.

by

by aftonifhing, but was in fact a ridiculous combination contrary to common fenfe.*

Perhaps, after all, the greateft error confifted in
obliging the king, who was confined a clofe prifoner, to accept the conftitution : this was an inexcufable act, as it was oppreffion towards one,
who, if we only confider him as an individual,
had a right to refufe being king, and to retire
where he pleafed ; and it was great injuftice to
the nation, for no good could arife out of a
tranfaction, where there was neither confidence
nor good-will, and where both were fo indif-
penfably neceffary.

[handwritten: K. compelled to sign the Constitution.]

The king accepted the conftitution, fuch as
it was, with only making fome fevere but juft remarks. He obferved, that many acts which had
been paffed as fimple legiflative decrees, were in
the revifal placed amongft the articles of the
conftitution ; that he was afraid the power given
to him would not be fufficient to enable him to
render his people happy ; but hoping that time
and experience might bring things to a better
ftate, he would do whatever lay in his power to
make things go on well and happily.

The affembly, during the latter period of its
feffion, had been more free than either before or
fince. The fufillade of the 17th of July had not
yet loft its effect, and, during this period, fome
fymptoms of returning moderation and calm were
apparent. The laws againft emigration and the
formality of paffports for travellers were abolifh-

* Fait pour eblouir, mais un tas des cuchonries qui nont
pas du fens commune.

Fayette for a general Amnesty.

ed; and it is but juftice to M. de la Fayette to fay, that with him originated a motion for a general amnefty, and a ftop being put to all proceedings againft people fufpected of revolutionary crimes.

It is difficult to fay, whether this amnefty was moft favourable to the democratic or the ariftocratic faction : it is certain, that if law and regular government had been immediately to take place, the turbulent democrats had moft to fear ; the meafure muft, therefore, be confidered as being equally defirable to both parties, and as a very proper one to take place at the finifhing of the national regeneration.

The furrender of power made by the affembly, as well as the cordiality which appeared between the different parties at the time, has been held up as a matter of admiration, but without any juft caufe ;* for it is certain, the firft affembly had wearied out the patience of the people, that the power could not have been continued much longer, and that the members had all of them fufficient reafon to wifh for fome moderation in the method of governing. The violent members, who were now going to quit their public and inviolable character, were willing to avert the effects of private vengeance ; and the moderate members were equally defirous of averting that public perfecution which they had all along oppofed

* The term of the duration of an affembly had been regulated for two years only, and the conftituent affembly had already fat near two and a half.

and

and feared, and which was now more to be feared by them than ever, fhould it continue.*

The conftitutional affembly will never be ex-cufed for the deception it practifed in the latter part of its reign, and for the pufillanimity it dif-played in not venturing to inquire into any of the evils which were fo evidently exifting at the time ; and it is even a queftion, whether it would not have been better for France, if the violent party of the Jacobins had triumphed, for along with the moderate party came thofe half-meafures which are generally fo ruinous.

A king, who was known to be diffatisfied with the conftitution, was impofed upon the people as a king who approved it, and who, probably, would have approved of it heartily, had a few modifications been made to fatisfy his confcience with refpect to religious matters, and his feelings with refpect to himfelf, his family, and the nobles.

The French nation and the affembly boafted of magnanimity in paffing over the flight of the royal family ; but was there any thing like true courage, or greatnefs of mind, in keeping a

---

* It is certain that M. d'André, and feveral other members of the Jacobin party, accepted bribes from the court to in-duce them to be a little moderate towards the end of the con-ftituent affembly. Louis XVI. having always been the friend of moderation, had a right to purchafe it with money, as well as he always had done by perfonal fervices ; but what are we to think of violent patriots who receive fuch bribes !

king

king amongſt them by force,* and obliging him to accept a conſtitution which he himſelf was to put in execution, without attempting to render it agreeable to him by any modifications, or without, at leaſt, hearing what he had to propoſe, and reaſoning over the matter ſo as to convince his mind that it was well and wiſely arranged ? It is difficult to conceive what ideas of liberty that aſſembly could have ; they talked of giving liberty to the ſlaves in America, and there is no ſlave ſet to perform ſo ſlaviſh a taſk as that which they aſſigned to their king.

The deſpotiſm, with reſpect to their ſucceſſors, who muſt alter nothing of their conſtitutional code, which unanointed and unanealed was thrown out into the world as a perfect work ; but, above all, the want of courage to inquire into the real ſtate of France with reſpect to its neighbours, that it might be known whether war or peace was to be brought upon the nation by the invaſion of Avignon, by the invaſion of German property in Alſace, and by the attempts made and avowed of overturning all the governments of Europe.

The maker of a machine ought to keep it in his poſſeſſion till he has tried whether it will work, or it ought to be put into the hand of

* A pretended offer was made to let the king retire from Paris, and accept the conſtitution ; but this was only to blind the people. The perſons who had aided in the king's eſcape were yet in priſon, and it was not conſiſtent either with his honour or known character, to abandon them ; beſides, would he have been more free while he remained in France ? The king declined accepting this offer.

ſome

some one capable of rectifying any errors that may be, or of supplying what may be wanting; this is the practice that experience and common sense have dictated, and from which it follows evidently, that the constituent assembly should have either remained at its post, and made a trial of the constitution, or left a power with their successors to make such changes, as on trial might be found to be necessary. It was very evident, that by leaving the constitution in this untried state, in the midst of broils and discontents, that were but little short of civil war* within the kingdom, and the danger of an attack from without, it could not be expected that the constitution would long stand its ground. There seems to be only three ways of explaining this extraordinary conduct in the constituent assembly.

It has already been observed, that the impatience of the nation was become so great, that it was absolutely necessary to finish the constitution, and to afford hopes of returning repose and tranquillity to a fatigued and miserable people. To have produced it as an imperfect work would not have answered this purpose,† and would have been

* In a letter addressed to the people of England, and printed in Paris in the beginning of 1792, to warn them of the efforts of the Propagande, and against admiring the French constitution, it was clearly proved, that an insurrection must be made from necessity, in order to give the assembly the power of modifying the constitution.

† It is one grand part of the Jacobin system to give hope of better times; thus the 5th of October, when the king was brought to Paris, was one æra for the commencement of happiness. The fœderation on the 14th of July, 1790, was another

been even dangerous to the affembly itfelf, for they had promifed to the people happinefs, and they had taught the loweft of the rabble to con- fider themfelves as fractions of the fovereign, and had thereby rendered them very wilful, impatient, and imperious.

Rabble witful.

The theoretical principles by which the affem- bly had all along been guided led to fo many in- confiftencies, that it would be very difficult for the fucceeding affembly to make a complete and durable work, even if powers were left them fuf- ficient ; and it was beyond a doubt, that if fuch powers had been left, the firft ufe made of them would have been to expofe all the inconfiftences and miftakes, and thereby throw odium and dif- grace on the firft affembly. It has, therefore, been imagined, that to avoid fuch confequences, and knowing that the revolution was not finifhed, and that they could not finifh it, they deter- mined * on this method as the fafeft and the beft for themfelves, and perhaps as good as any other for the nation ; becaufe, if another revolution muft come, the manner of its coming was not of much importance.

Another motive has been affigned to the af- fembly ; it has been fuppofed by many, that the

another. The deftroying the cuftoms at the entrance of towns in May, 1791, was a third, and now there only remained the completion of the conftitution.

* During the whole of the revolution affignats did not di- minifh in value fo rapidly as while the conftitution was re- ceiving the *laft degree of perfection and folidity*, which is a plain proof of the general opinion.

repub-

republican party, finding itfelf unable to maintain its ground by force (fince the fufillade of the
17th of July) was determined to undermine by
ftratagem the monarchy, and affifted with pleafure and alacrity in fetting the new monarchical
conftitution agoing in fo imperfect a ftate, that it
could not continue to go long. One thing is
certain, that the apparent moderation of this
party, which broke out in all its force on the 10th.
of Auguft in the year following, gives a great
degree of probability to this belief; and certain
it is, that if the greateft enemy to monarchical
government in France had been confulted, he
could not have advifed a more infallible method
of bringing it to an end than by finifhing the
conftitution in the manner which we have feen.
As we have yet to follow the manœuvres of that
fame party during the ten months that the conftitution exifted, we fhall have many occafions of
proving the probability of this opinion.

The conftituent affembly was divided as we
have already faid, into three parties, royalifts,
moderates, and democrats; but that of the royalifts was now reduced to filence and infignificance, therefore, the opinion or the will of thofe
few who remained is of little importance, though
it is certain they never expected the conftitution
would ftand long and perhaps they had fome
expectation, that at its fall the ancient form of
government might revive.

The moderates were divided, not by difpofition but by their talents, into two claffes; the ambitious theorifts, and the dupes, or as they were

P p

called

Imbeciles

called, *les imbeciles.** The firſt of theſe were afraid of the work of their own hands, and wanted to get quietly out of the danger ; the ſecond, ignorant of the imperfections of the work, and thinking to decree an equality of rights and liberty was all that was neceſſary to render men free and happy, thought, that in concurring in ſealing the conſtitution, they were inſuring happineſs to the nation ; it is not therefore aſtoniſhing, under this view of the matter, if the whole of the moderate party joined cordially in finiſhing the work which it had begun.

Democrats

That the republican party was not ſincere on this occaſion is very certain ; but it was impoſſible, as we have already ſaid, for them to change matters immediately by force, and therefore they concurred with pleaſure in putting the French monarchy upon a footing that was certain to end in its deſtruction before long.

It muſt alſo be conſidered, that the violent party, in quitting their public ſtation, did not quit their power ; they were members of the Jacobin club, and, therefore, counted upon preſerving that importance which would enable them the firſt moment of criſis that ſhould arrive, to realiſe the plans which Bailly and La Fayette had deranged on the 17th of July.

* *Les Gens de bonne foi—les nigauds de la revolution,* were alſo terms applied to theſe dupes. All the converts to French principles amongſt men of rank in England were of this claſs, according to the opinion of the French, and hence the repeated declarations, that they deſpiſe Mr. Fox as much as they hate Mr. Pitt.

If

If the conduct of the individuals in a private
capacity is to us any rule for judging, we fhall
find it confirms what we have been faying. The
royalifts for the moft part endeavoured to leave
the kingdom under the law about emigration.
The *imbeciles* continued to preach up in Paris,
and in their provinces, in a public manner, the
conftitution, all the conftitution, and nothing
but the conftitution.* The ambitious conftitutionalifts, fuch as La Fayette, endeavoured to
retire from public affairs, and to hide themfelves
in the provinces, but the republican members remained almoft all in Paris, or took the lead in
the Jacobin clubs in the provinces, and were the
firft to attack the conftitution which they had affifted in making.

One of the reproaches juftly made to the conftituent affembly, is its having feparated without
making any attempt to arrange and put in order
the finances, which were in the moft confufed and
ruinous ftate poffible. As the affembly had been
called together exprefsly to arrange the finances,
this negleA is the more inexcufable ; but when it
is confidered that it had augmented beyond all
fort of calculation, and beyond any thing of
which hiftory gives an example, that diforder we
muft not fpeak of as inexcufable, we muft fay
that it was unpardonable.

Aftronomers tell us that the moon, which appears fo polifhed and clear, is made of earth, but
that the diftance produces the deception. Thofe

* Thefe were their words, *La conftitution, toute la conftitution, et rien que la conftitution.*

who

who have had a good opportunity of minutely examining the conduct of the French constituent assembly, which viewed from a distance appeared to be composed of great men and philosophers, may tell its admirers likewise, that it is the distance that occasions the deception, for that it was composed of ambitious intriguers, and ignorant dupes; and at the present day, there is not a character so completely detested and despised, by all parties, as that of a constitutionalist, whose business, whose pleasure, and whose pride was to pull down and destroy, who ruined every thing and established nothing, and whose whole exertion evaporated in attempting to appear what he never was, the friend of his fellow citizens, and of the liberty and peace of mankind.

Intriguers

Dupes

Constitutionalists are Said to be growing popular 1796 97.

CHAP. X.

New assembly called legislative—Its conduct and temper—The king tormented and ill treated as formerly—His guard dismissed—Jacobins triumph—Red bonnet adopted—Jacobins fill all offices—Republican spirit begins to break out afresh—War declared against the Emperor—Jacobin ministers—The banishment of the non-juring clergy, and a camp of twenty thousand men decreed—The king refuses the sanction—Ministry dismissed—Insurrection of the 20th of June, when the king is insulted—Petion's conduct; he is suspended from the functions of mayor—Petion reinstated—The fœderation—Marsellois arrive in Paris—Pusillanimity of the Parisians—Review of affairs, of the assembly, and of the nation, previous to the fall of the constitution—Fermentation previous to the 10th of August.

T H E new assembly, which is distinguished from the former by the name of legislative, was composed of seven hundred and forty-nine members, two thirds of whom were lawyers, a few clergymen, and still fewer proprietors of lands. The remainder was composed of men who lived as they could, without any fettled profeffion or employment.

As thefe members were elected by the new method, which gave a vote to every man who paid three livres, or half a crown a year; it is in this place that we ought properly to examine this part of the conftitution.

It is very evident that as men muft delegate their power to others, as all cannot be employed in governing, the end in view in elections is to choofe fuch men as are moft capable of making a proper ufe of the power with which they are intrufted; or in other words, every nation which has a conftitution, is interefted in having the parliament or affembly of reprefentatives, by which ever name it may be called, compofed of men who are interefted in the prefervation of the conftitution and the general welfare of the ftate.

With all due fubmiffion to theoretical reformers, it is to be prefumed that the method which is the moft calculated for this end, is the beft, whether it happens to correfpond with their theories or not; for as in natural philofophy it is a rule to abandon theory the moment that it is contradicted by experiment, fo it ought to be in political matters, and experience ought to be the guide as much as poffible; and if neceffity obliges us to have recourfe in any unforefeen cafe to theory, we fhould endeavour to correct or confirm that theory by experience as fpeedily as poffible.

Experience the Guide

The

The people who had a right to vote in elections, were called active citizens, but they had carefully avoided giving any title to the inferior clafs of people, who, however, foon took to themfelves that of paffive citizens, aud renewed the game of the third eftate upon the nobility and clergy.

[margin: active & paffive citizens.]

[margin: Game renewed of the 3° Eftate.]

The rule of determining the right of elections was altogether an arbitrary one, without being either wife or ufeful, or fanctioned by long habit, as many arbitrary rules are. It left the elections entirely in the hands of the working clafs of citizens, who greatly outnumbered the proprietors, farmers, and burgeffes. One of the firft confequences of this was, that the working clafs infulted and mal-treated the others in the electoral affemblies ; and it foon after followed, that thefe latter entirely withdrew themfelves from affemblies, where their prefence was of no ufe to any one, and extremely difagreeable to themfelves.* The elections therefore fell entirely into the hands of the petit peuple, affifted by thofe intriguing fpirits who were willing to ftoop to take the means of pleafing them. In large towns, the leading members of the clubs were chofen, and in the country fuch perfons as made their court to the populace, but in no inftances were men of landed property chofen, and in the legiflative affembly there was not one man of independent fortune.

[margin: Working Clafs all powerful.]

[margin: Elections in the hands of the Petit Peuple.]

* The working people took delight in fhewing their equality with their mafters, and the proprietors of lands in the primary affemblies ; and this defire of fhewing equality ended always in demonftrating their fuperiority in point of numbers, and frequently in force.

[margin: This is Montefquieu's Love of Equality, That great villain was not Mafter of this Subject.]

One

One of the greateſt dangers incurred in chuſ-
ing men who are not in a capacity of living without induſtry, for repreſentatives, is, that all ſuch
by leaving their daily occupations, are ruined,
unleſs during their attendance on the affairs of
the nation they can gain what will ſufficiently
indemnify them for the loſs of their buſineſs.——
Such men are not only to be conſidered as hav-
This is of great Im- ing a temptation to fill their pockets placed be-
portance. fore them, but they may be laid with truth to
be under the neceſſity of doing it ; accordingly
we find they have generally been very careful to
do ſo ; and the electors who choſe them, cannot
complain, or at leaſt do not deſerve to be pitied,
if they find them more attentive to their own intereſt than to the intereſts of the nation.*   The
pay of eighteen livres a day, given to the deputies, was ſcarcely ſufficient to defray the ex-
penſeſ† of ſuch as meant to appear with decency ;
and as the greateſt part of them had families to
maintain, either which they had left in the country, or brought to Paris with them, there was no
other alternative but to ſtarve or rob the public.

* All municipal officers, as well as judges of the courts of
juſtice, were choſen by the people in the ſame manner, and
were all choſen for a limited time, ſo that it was juſt like
letting loofe fo many privileged harpies to prey upon the public.   With reſpect to the judges it was worſt of all ; they
were for fix years.   Now what man capable of adminiſtering
impartial juſtice, would accept of ſuch a place for ſo long a
time, in order to be a beggar afterwards, or at leaſt to have
the world to begin again ?

† There were ſome deputies, however, that ſaved money
out of this ; theſe lodged in garrets at five livres a week, and
dined at ordinaries at thirty ſous a head, that is, they lived
like common workmen or inferior clerks.

In

In such a case, a reformer particularly is at no great loss to decide which of the two he ought to do, and accordingly there are very few examples in the three assemblies, which have taken place of deputies who have neglected their own interests.

From the first meeting of the new assembly, the hopes of the nation that had for a moment been raised, when the constitution was signed, were damped by the captious manner in which the king was treated, and which plainly indicated that there was neither mutual affection nor confidence.

This new assembly, with much more circumscribed powers than the last, had a far more difficult task to perform ; they were to establish order and make things go regularly and well ; they were not now to put off the happiness of the nation from week to week, and from month to month, when the constitution should be finished ; that great last object of hope was already accomplished, and if happiness did not follow, there was nothing for it but to confess that the constitution was a bad one, and to wish for another revolution.

This new assembly, limited in power, and employed in doing what was impossible to be done in France, that is, in establishing order and subordination, was very soon regarded with contempt by the Parisians, who could not find in it any thing of that bold hardy manner for which the former had been so much admired. Novelty and astonishment now no longer diverted the at-

Astonishment gave place to a sense of suffering

Q q

attention from prefent fufferings ; and as we
have faid before, the time for expecting enjoyment and tranquility was come, therefore hope
alfo was wanting, and of confequence the decline of public credit, and the increafe of malcontents, was at no period of the revolution
more rapid than during the firft months of the
legiflative affembly.

There was now nothing to be faid in order to
appeafe the people, but that the executive power was to blame, and ftood in the way of their
happinefs.   The king was accordingly the perpetual object of complaint and reproach, but
without the affembly being able to produce any
well-fupported, or even probable caufe of complaint.   As nothing does better for the populace
of Paris than fufpicion and imaginary crimes,
the executive power was foon rendered more obnoxious than ever.   The clubs had began to
affume their wonted vigour ;* Petion had been
chofen mayor of Paris, and the violent fyftem
revived with great rapidity, and now without
any counterpoife as formerly.

La Fayette had quitted his command of the
Parifian guard, and as it had been found fo inconvenient to the club to have a national guard
to oppofe infurrection, which guard might be

* Befides the Jacobin club, there was a club ftill more violent, that of the cordeliers ; it was in this latter that the plan
originated for fending a band of affaffins into every country
of Europe, called king-killers, on purpofe to difpatch the
different monarchs. Courage, however, being wanting for
fuch an undertaking, the propofition was applauded but not
adopted.

head-

headed by a moderate man, a decree had been passed that the commandant of the guard should be renewed every two months, so that there would be no time for any* commander to gain a dangerous ascendancy over the minds of the soldiers and officers. Another fusillade was not now to be dreaded, and therefore fœderalists of the 17th of July began to appear and to hold up their heads.

The constituent assembly had decreed that the king should have a life guard to be paid from the civil list, and wearing an uniform different from the national soldiers. This guard was forming and completing with rapidity, and soon became an object of fear and suspicion to the inhabitants of Paris, who considered them as aristocrats in disguise; and such was the bravery and courage of the Parisians, that a body of only eighteen hundred men was sufficient to cause great alarm and uneasiness; but the assembly had not now the power of destroying what the constitution had made, and therefore, it was thought necessary to have recourse to artifice. Early in 1792, suspicions were thrown out, and circulated against the intentions of the king, and against the civism of his guards, whom it was not difficult to render odious to the populace, and to the national guards of Paris. When unexplained accusations and rumours, of which no person could trace the origin, had worked up the minds of the Parisians to a state of anger and inquietude, the assembly declared itself permanent,

* The commanders of divisions were to command by turns.

under pretence of a plot which menaced its exiftence and the fafety of the country. The
guards of the king were pointed at as being the
guilty, and under pretext of punifhing them for
a crime, the exiftence of which was never proved, nor attempted to be proved, the life guards
were licenciated, and the Duke de Briffac, their
Briffac. commander, fent to prifon at Orleans. This
gentleman was known to be unalterably attached
to his majefty, and it was a double advantage to
fend him to a diftance, and by keeping him in
prifon to be tried on a future day, have the appearance as if fome charges could be actually
brought againft him.

At the fame time that this plan was carrying
on to deprive the king of the only defenders
whom the conftitution had allowed his perfon,
M. Briffot, who had fo long fhewn his hatred to
Briffot royalty, and who was a member of the affembly,
denounced M. de Leffart, the minifter of the
interior, and had him imprifoned and fent to
Orleans; the affembly rendering the decree, and
ordering its execution without the conftitutional
intermediation of the executive power.

It was now that the king was literally obliged
to take his enemies into his bofom, by chufing
his minifters from the Jacobin club. Dumourier,
Dumourier Roland, Servan, and Claviere, were made the
Roland, Servan counfellors of their fovereign and every man who
Claviere was attached to the royal caufe, and who was not
blind, forefaw that a new revolution was foon to
be expected.

During

During five months which had elapfed fince the clofing of the conftituent affembly, emigration had become more frequent than ever; there remained few of the nobles or proprietors within the kingdom, and the officers of the army and navy had for the moft part followed their example.*

France was now become more wretched than at any former period of the revolution—the nobility were gone, the conftitution exifted, and want and diforder were increafing every day. It was difficult to find any grounds for hope in this ftate of things, and accordingly men had none, and were now prepared for thofe defperate meafures, to which defpair alone reconciles the human mind.

In this ftate of things the Jacobins ruled; but they had one thing ftill to fear: they found from experience that the proprietors who remained, the mafter tradefmen, the merchants, and manufacturers of all kinds, were enemies to any new commotions; they had become the firft clafs of men in the prefent order of things, and, having already gratified their vanity and their vengeance, had nothing to defire fo much as to remain and enjoy their victory with permanent tranquility. To defire peace and prefervation of order is to be, according to the French meaning, an ariftocrat. So that the democrats of

* The common foldiers and failors frequented the Jacobin clubs, and were regularly infcribed in the regifters like the other members; fo that the commander who would have been hardy enough to have punifhed any of them, could not long expect to efcape a fevere vengeance.

1789,

The Democrats of 1789 the Aristocrats of 1792

1789, thofe fame men who had exerted themfelves fo violently to bring down their fuperiors,
were become the ariftocrats of 1792, and employed in ftudying to preferve order which they
had formerly ftruggled to overturn.

The guards of citizens fo highly refpected, and
fo proud of their honours and their epaulets, in
the beginning of the revolution, began to be
looked upon with a jealous eye, and even to be
defpifed. The fufillade of laft year was not to be
forgotten, and the ragged emiffaries of the Jacobins begun to arm themfelves with pikes, and to
form pretenfions which evidently tended to the
deftruction of their ariftocratical fuperiors.

*Paſsive Citi-
zens equal
rights with Active.*

It was hinted to the populace that the paffive
citizens had equal rights by nature with thofe to
whom the abfurd conftitution had given the
rights of voters and of active citizens; and certainly there was no poffibility of contradicting the
fact, that if all men were born and remained
free and equal, there was an abfurdity in giving
a full exercife of his rights to the perfon who
paid fixty fols of taxes and refufed all his rights
to another, becaufe he only paid fifty-nine.

*I have ſeen more
of this than I
for ſaw.*

A material confideration is here held up to
reformers. Let them beware how they throw out
abftract rules, and then vainly think to modify
them in the execution, for fuch a thing never can
be done. We might as well think to make a
coalition between ornament and mathematics, as
between abftract rules and arbitrary regulations.

After the declaration of rights, it was abfurd
to think that any portion of the inhabitants of
the

the country would be excluded from a full and free participation. If the nobility could not defend the ancient abfurdities of the feudal fyftem two years before, it was not to be expected that the new-made ariftocrats could now defend the recent abfurdities of the conftitution. The Jacobins ftill had in their hands the fame arms by which they had pulled down the nobility; they had the non-proprietors, the people who had nothing to lofe, at their fervice,* and it was, as hitherto, the rafh audacity of the latter againft the cautious timidity of the former.

* It was about this time that the populace adopted the title of Sans Culottes, which had been given by the Ariftocrats, at firft by way of derifion. As they found it impoffible to get quit of the name, their leaders thought it better to adopt it, and make it honourable, as had been practifed at Avignon with the plunderers, whom they called the Brave Brigands of Avignon. A favourite amufement of the Sans Culottes had been for a long time to go into the convents or churches where religious women or nuns were affembled, and drag them into the ftreets, and there, after expofing them in the moft indecent manner, to whip them with rods feverely, and fometimes till they became infenfible through pain, fhame, and lofs of blood. This was practifed in all quarters of Paris, and moft provinces of France. It was thus that laws were obeyed, perfons protected, and *liberty* eftablifhed. M. Necker's indignation broke forth at this, and at a decree that had been made to condemn minifters who had acted unfaithfully to the pillory and the gallies. But the indecent and barbarous cuftom of whipping ladies had begun on Necker's account, and when he was in full power in Paris, and then he fhewed no difpleafure, which would have been more ufeful and honourable than a letter from Switzerland, after he was no longer of any fort of importance. Whilft the rage for whipping was only exerted againft ladies who prophaned Necker's plaifter buft, all was well; but when it went any further, then the philofopher muft take up the cudgels in favour of modefty and liberty of opinions.

Another

Another danger menaced the Jacobin faction also. Though we have already seen, the constituted authorities were all placed by Jacobins, and rendered almost independent of each other, and of the executive power; yet the position in which they were placed put them, if it were only for self-defence, under the necessity of supporting some degree of order and obedience to the laws; they, therefore, became suspected persons, or aristocrats, and considerable danger was to be apprehended from a general union of effort in the cause of order, arising from a general union of interest; for, although Petion was mayor of Paris, and Manuel and Danton were officers under him, yet the spirit of the common council was by no means such, as enabled them to count upon the co-operation even of the municipality of Paris, much less upon those of the other cities in the kingdom.

Petion Manuel Danton

The disorder in which every thing was, did not permit delay, for it was evident that the present state of affairs could not continue long; it was, therefore, probable that the victory would remain to the most enterprising and active.

The Jacobin club now counted amongst its members all the leading men of the assembly and the ministers, and it was was now they adopted the red cap of liberty, with an intention to try their force; but as it did not muster so strong as it was expected, the mayor Petion, under pretext of preventing disorder, represented to the club that it was imprudent to count their friends in this manner, for that the aristocrats would probably adopt the new head-dress, and so screen them-

red cap of liberty.

themfelves from their juft anger. Red bonnets were then lefs generally worn, and the wifdom and moderation of the mayor were applauded by thofe who did not know that if his party had appeared more numerous, fuch an harangue would never have been pronounced.

During the fame period the affembly decreed that the non-juring priefts, whom they now called refractory priefts, fhould be banifhed from *refractory Priests.* the kingdom, and that the lands and effects of all perfons who had emigrated fhould belong to the nation.

As both of thefe decrees were not only in themfelves unjuft, but were contrary to the conflitution which the king and the affembly had fworn to execute and obey, his majefty was juftified in a double manner, in refufing his fanction ; but this did not fcreen him from the reproach of the Jacobins, and the difpleafure of the affembly.

At the fame time that all thefe caufes for internal difputes were ftarting up day after day, the new minifters procured a declaration of war *War vs Emperor* againft the Emperor and the King of Pruffia, on account of the treaty of Pilnitz,* and the permiffion

* This treaty of Pilnitz was an agreement, in cafe of neceffity, to maintain the liberty of Louis XVI. and the independence of other kingdoms.

The Emperor was treated in the difcourfes from the tribune with all manner of contempt and indignity. He is a droll fellow, that Emperor, faid M. Ifnard (the Barnave of the new affembly—*un plaifant garçon)* and the titles of defpot, permiffion granted to the emigants at Coblentz to enrol themfelves in a military manner.

It would require a very long difcuffion to enter minutely and completely into the origin of the war, but that is the lefs neceffary, as the affembly by its daily conduct had plainly fhewn that war was what they wanted, and the death of the Emperor Leopold feemed an excellent occafion for beginning, when his fucceffor was only King of Hungary and Bohemia, and Duke of Brabant by hereditary poffeffion, but could not, until the ufual flow ceremony of election fhould be over, act with the united forces of the empire.

Dumourier was minifter at war when the decree was paffed, and, by virtue of the new fyftem of honour and of liberty which France had adopted, the meffenger of the Imperial ambaffador was detained in Paris till the fourth day after ; and it is a fact, that the frontiers of Auftrian Flanders were attacked before the letters containing a declaration of war had been difpatched from Paris.

It is not at all our province or intention to enter into any military details. The little fuccefs which attended this firft expedition is well known,

defpot, &c. were applied without any fort of ceremony to all the crowned heads of Europe.

The rabble had made a proceffion with a head, which they called the Emperor's, through the gardens of the Thuilleries, and had carried it under the windows of the queen. This was juft a few days before the Emperor's death.

as

as is alfo the cruel and unfortunate end of General Dillon, who, not having been fuccefsful,   *Dillon*
was fufpected by his foldiers, and cut in pieces
with that fame favage fury which the Parifian
cannibals had been accuftomed to difplay.

The declaration of war was followed with a
decree to order off fome troops of the line from
Paris, who were fufpected of civifm, that is to
fay, of attachment to the royal caufe.

The Jacobins were now without any regular
opponents ; but, as they could not be certain how
the Parifian guards might act, moft of whom
were attached to the conftitution, they wifhed to
have a regular army at their command, and,
therefore, decreed a camp of twenty thoufand men   *camp of 20, 000*
which fhould be collected from the whole of the
kingdom,* and affembled under the walls of
Paris ; and as the manner in which this camp
was to be compofed of fans culottes from the different departments was no fecret, it was confidered as the total overthrow of kingly power.

One of the Jacobin minifters had, without the
king's orders, demanded this camp, and all his
minifters had been privy to the demand ; there
was only one mode of refiftance confidered as

---

* It had always been the practice of the Jacobins to hurry
through fuch decrees as they thought likely to meet with oppofition ; fo that the weightieft fubjects were always determined
with the flighteft difcuffion ; the abolition of feudal rights and
of nobility had been done without a moments reflection or difcuffion. The arreft of one of the minifters had been demanded and executed in a few hours; and this camp was decreed in the fame manner without previous notice or any difcuffion.

poffible

poffible for his majefty. confiftent with the conftitution,* this was to refufe the fanction, and
to difmifs the minifters by whom he had been
betrayed.

Thus did part of the plan of the Jacobins receive a momentary check, but it was only momentary.

It is impoffible to conceive how the different
governments of Europe, who had ambaffadors at
Paris, fhould have remained ignorant of thofe
preparations for deftroying the French monarchy;
or if they were not ignorant, how they remained
inactive, and thereby let flip the laft opportunity
of making an effort to prevent the cataftrophe
that was fo evidently preparing, and which, when
once brought on, it would be fo difficult to
remedy.

From the beginning of the revolution till this
prefent hour the nations of Europe have been
too flow in all their efforts againft the levelling
fyftem. Before they have been warned of the
danger and prepared for defence, the manner
of attack has been changed by their able and vi-
able & vigorous. gorous adverfaries, who have thereby triumphed
over fuperior force, and far fuperior means, by
addrefs, activity, and energy.

If that energy on their fide continues, and we
continue our flow and calm pace, the conteft

---

* The king alone was perfectly faithful to this code, and
kept always in his apartments a copy of it, which he made
his rule of conduct on all occafions.

will

will certainly be decided againſt us, and before many years paſs over, kings and proprietors will ſink under the attacks of audacious and active indigence.

Dumourier, turned out of the miniſtry, went *Dumourier* off immediately to the frontiers, and ſoon obtained that ſuperiority over La Fayette, Luckner, and Dillon,* which a man of genius ſo eaſily acquires over men who have none, and which an audacious Jacobin acquires ſtill more eaſily over a ſilly ſupporter of the French conſtitution.

Roland, ſurnamed the virtuous by the Jacobin *Roland* faction, and who, ſince then, ſigned the death warrant of the king his maſter, and finiſhed his worthy career by cutting his own throat, publiſhed a letter to the king on being diſmiſſed, which is a model for its inſolence, and the contents of which were in total oppoſition to the conſtitution.

Claviere, another of the miniſters, retired in *Claviere* ſilence, but not to ſit idle ; things were too far advanced to remain long without an open rupture ; and ſince the camp of twenty thouſand men could not be had, it was reſolved by the diſmiſſed miniſters and the mayor to have twenty thouſand men without a camp.

A petition to the aſſembly ſerved as the pretext for collecting all the rabble from the different

* There were two generals of the name of Dillon ; the one as we have ſeen, had already been maſſacred, and this other Dillon was reſerved for the guillotine, having been ſince included in one of the imaginary plots againſt Robeſpierre.

quarters

quarters of Paris, who, in place of coming peaceably as petitioners ought to do, came armed, and
defiled through the hall of the affembly with
pikes, pitchforks, fcythes, axes, and clubs. The
affembly, which in fact was acceffary to this
breach of the conftitutional laws, applauded the
lawlefs and unruly proceffion, which paffed to
the king's palace, before which there were more
than fix thoufand of the national guards in arms.

Petion

Petion, the virtuous mayor of Paris, was abfent,* fo that no orders could be given for oppofing force to force, and the national guards
ftood lookers on, while this multitude affailed
the palace, and entered by violence into the
apartments of his majefty.

The avowed intention of the populace was
to oblige the king, through fear, to fanction
the decrees for the banifhment of ecclefiaftics and
the camp of twenty thoufand men. The firmnefs
of his majefty, who had, without fear or delay,
prefented himfelf to the enraged multitude, defeated the Jacobin projects once more. The decrees were not fanctioned, the king acquired the
efteem of all men who love courage and virtue,
and the leaders of the mob were covered with
eternal difgrace.†

* This mob was expected, and the object was known,
therefore Petion's abfence was intended. He, as well as
Roland, was called always the virtuous.

† Petion arrived *calmly* in his carriage from Verfailles,
(where he had been, nobody knows for what) after the bufinefs was nearly over, and when nothing more could be
gained by remaining, he and Santerre, the brewer, difmiffed
their ragged auxiliaries till another occafion.

The

The conftitution, which all the nation had fo often fworn to maintain, was thus openly violated, and every one plainly faw, that whether the king were confidered as a public functionary or a private man, the attack upon his houfe and perfon were equally illegal and unjuft.

The members of the common council, and of the department, difapproved of what had happened; and as the part which Petion, as mayor, had acted, was too vifible to be vindicated, the department fufpended him from his functions. All the conftituted authorities feemed to have gained courage and fortitude from the firmnefs of the king, and there was once more fome reafon to hope, that he would meet with fupport and protection.

La Fayette, at that time general of one of the armies on the frontiers, and attached to the conftitution, but, above all, enraged to fee the king, his former prifoner, ill treated by any mob where he himfelf was not prefent, left his army without afking leave of abfence, and unexpectedly prefented himfelf at the bar of the affembly, to complain, in the name of his army, of the infult offered to the conftitutional head of the nation.*

This ftep of La Fayette announced a determination that gave the royalift party fome hopes; but the leaders of the Jacobins knew what fort

* Thefe conftitutionalifts are undefinable men; Was this 20th of June, when the king was attacked in his palace, any worfe than the 5th of October, or than the mob that prevented the royal family from going to St. Cloud, at both of which M. de la Fayette affifted?

of

of a man they had to deal with, and La Fayette was glad to quit Paris next day, without any farther effort than that of empty declamation and menace, after having left his army without leave, and fhewn a difpofition to defend the conftitution and his want of force and of means to do it.

This feeble and imprudent ftep of La Fayette ferved to fhew the factions at Paris, that they had nothing to fear from the armies; and the Jacobin club, and all the papers that were devoted to its caufe, were let loofe upon La Fayette and the defenders of the conftitution with double vigour.

During the fufpenfion of Petion from the office of mayor * he had been employed in writing a fhort pamphlet, entitled, *General Rules of my Conduct towards the People.* In this production he declared, it had always been his determination never to let the blood of the people be fhed, and he fhewed, that the peaceable and factious were confidered by him in the fame light; and that any extravagances or violation of juftice which they might commit would be confidered as errors only and not as crimes.

Such a declaration was a fufficient motive for the difturbers of public repofe to redouble their efforts in order to have him re-inftated, and in

* The king was obliged, according to the conftitution, to confirm or reject this, and all fuch depofitions of municipal officers by the departments. He wifhed, through delicacy, not to exercife his power in this cafe, where he was in reality a party concerned, but being obliged to decide he confirmed the fufpenfion.

every

every quarter of Paris the Jacobins cried out, Pe- *Petion ou la mort.*
tion ou la mort.

Though the camp of twenty thousand men
could not at prefent be eftablifhed, yet, as the
third anniverfary of the revolution approached,
and as it was neceffary to recruit the armies, the
Jacobin leaders found a pretext for inviting to
Paris fœderates from all parts of France, and
amongft others from Marfeilles, from whence
came a number of robbers and murderers by
profeffion, who had been particularly active in
the maffacres at Avignon; but thefe latter arrived too late for the fœderation, and thofe who
came were not fufficiently ripe in mifchief to execute any great or bold exploit; fo that the fœderation paffed over quietly, only with this point
gained, that to infure peace and tranquillity the
king and the department had tamely fubmitted
to the re-inftatement of Petion as mayor of Paris.

This fœderation was the triumph of the enemies of the conftitution, as the two former ones
had been of the conftitution itfelf, the cries of
vive la conftitution were changed for *vive Petion.*
and many cried VIVE LA MORT.

As the war now began to take a ferious turn,
and as the ftate of the interior was fo worked up,
that it was impoffible long to prevent an open
war between the two parties, in which it was
pretty clear, that all well-minded and peaceable
citizens would fupport the king, the ruling party
in the affembly hit upon a plan towards the end
of July of infuring themfelves fuccefs.

S s   A decree

Le Country in danger A decree was paſſed, declaring the *country in danger*, and rendering permanent all the aſſemblies of ſections, municipalities, and departments; by which means any number of members who choſe to make an appointment at an uncommon hour for deliberating, might paſs what reſolutions they pleaſed, and overturn every thing. This was ſo abſurd a thing, and ſo diametrically oppoſite to common ſenſe, that if it had not ſoon after been employed to overturn the whole order of things, we could ſcarcely expect that it could meet with credit, but the extraordinary proceedings of the night that preceded the 10th of Auguſt are a too *10 Aug.* certain evidence of the fact.

The arrival of the Marſellois, who were not in number above 400, put the bravery of the gallant national guards of Paris to the proof; 32,000 brave burgeſſes, armed and equipped, and who boaſted for their firſt exploit the taking of the Baſtile, trembled before this handful of determined ruffians.

Marsaillois The Marſellois entered Paris at the Bariere du trone,* and traverſed the city till they came to the aſſembly. Though this banditti were fatigued with a long journey, and with very bad treatment from the national guards of ſome of the towns through which they had paſſed, they began by obliging every perſon they met in Paris to change their cockades made of ſilk for others made of worſted. They overturned in their way all the ſtalls where ſilk cockades were ſold, and the

* This was as if a body of men were to enter London by Whitechapel, and to paſs to St. James's or Hyde Park.

32,000

32,000 guards complained, that it was very hard that ſtrangers ſhould come from a diſtance, and oblige them to wear a cockade they did not chuſe, and when the conſtitution made no difference between ſilk and worſted, provided the colours were national.

It was a ſcene that afforded great matter for reflection, to ſee the armed Pariſians, who had made all Europe refound with their democratic bravery for three years, collect themſelves into groups, and ſeriouſly complain of the cavalier treatment of a ſmall party of banditti.*

After having paid their homage to the aſſembly, where they were received with applauſe,† the Marſellois went to a tavern in the Elyſian-fields, where Santerre, the intended commander of the *Santerre* Pariſian guards entertained them, and where near an hundred of the officers of the Pariſian guards were alſo dining. A quarrel was ſuddenly ſtirred up, and the effeminate Pariſians were put to flight, with the loſs of one killed, five wounded, and two taken priſoners. Chance might account

---

* Notwithſtanding all theſe murmurs and complaints, the vain Pariſians adopted the worſted cockade before the evening of that day.

† This band of Marſellois waited on M. Petion before they went to the aſſembly, and were well received by him, whoſe duty would have been to chaſe them out of the city, as had been done at Lyons and ſeveral other places, and even at Melun, which is but a very ſmall place. The brave brigands confoled themſelves for the ill-treatment they received in the towns by pillaging and oppreſſing the country peaſants, and raviſhing ſuch defenceleſs women as fell in their way.

for

for the dead and wounded, but that 400 men fhould carry off prifoners in the face of 32,000 of their companions, is a novelty that cannot be fo eafily accounted for. The whole of the Parifians were in arms directly, they paraded and prepared for action, but durft do no more. Thus did audacity and four hundred fabres gain a victory over pufillanimity with an hundred and twenty cannons and thirty-two thoufand bayonets; and on the very fpot where the Prince de Lambefc three years ago had let fticks and ftones triumph over a regular army. It was on this fpot that the Parifian burgefs triumphed over the regular army of the fovereign; and it was here that a handful of the loweft clafs of the people triumph-ed over the Parifian burgefs. The triumph was complete in the latter cafe, the moment that au-dacious indigence found that the defenders of law and property were feeble and undecided.

Audacious indigence.

The Jacobin club was the next that received the homage and fraternal vifit of the banditti of Marfeilles, who became a part of the club itfelf, and, like the affembly of the nation, were by this means both a deliberating and executive body.*

Paffive citizens

The paffive citizens, thofe who had not beds to lay upon nor breeches to wear, and who paid no taxes, had now a point of rallyment, and did not want inftigators; fo that the complaints againft the conftitution multiplied and became loud, and its deftruction became eafy.

* After the tenth of Auguft, as the affembly was merely a paffive inftrument, it could not be looked upon as an affem-bly deliberating.

As

As we already approach the laſt moments of the legiſlative aſſembly, it is neceſſary to give ſome attention to its compoſition. The firſt aſſembly had, as we have ſeen, been divided into three parties, this was divided into four. The partiſans of the conſtitution were now called the mo *Moderates* derates, and occupied the ſame end of the hall, on the right hand of the preſident, where the ariſtocrats uſed to ſit. On the left extremity, formerly occupied by thoſe who raiſed the conſtitution, ſat thoſe republicans who were determined to pull it down; this end was called the moun *Mountain* tain; immediately under which, and near the middle of the hall, were Briſſot, Condorcet, and *Briſſot* the Girond party, who were the conductors of the aſſembly, who combined, aſſorted, and balanced the different intereſts, ſo as to undermine the conſtitution, for which they had a moſt ſovereign contempt. The fourth diviſion of the aſſembly was alſo ſeated near the middle; theſe laſt called themſelves independents, and, without having *Independent* any particular views of change, were not much attached to the conſtitution.

The members of the Jacobin club aſſociated with none but the men of the mountain, or the Girondiſts,* who were all of them members of *Club* the club, in which the meaſures to be adopted by the aſſembly were firſt debated; ſo that the club was now actually become the legiſlating bo

---

* This party called Girondiſts was compoſed of the deputies from Bourdeaux and the borders of the Garron; that is to ſay, they were Gaſcons, a name better underſtood, and by no means miſapplied in the preſent caſe. It was Briſſot and that party who wanted to conquer the whole world, and eſtabliſh a central aſſembly at Paris.

dy for the whole of France, and this under the
name of liberty.

Though the affembly was divided into four
parts capable of dividing or uniting, yet we fhall
hereafter fee that, when under the influence of
fear the whole affembly became as one, and that
when fear ceafed to operate, they divided again ;
but that at all times the parties bore that hatred
for each other, which oppofes fo invincible a barrier to the peace and happinefs of France.

Before we quit the *firft* revolution of France
which gained fo many admirers all over Europe,
which is ftill with fome an object of admiration,
let us take a view of the ftate to which it had reduced the country ; let us examine the evils it
had produced, and the bleffings it had procured.

Infubordination

The firft of the evils was the principle of infubordination, which, foon becoming general, rendered order and government impracticable ; and,
inftead of leading to freedom, led directly to
anarchy. The fubftituting a vain and illufive
Philofophy for expe-
riences
philofophy for the maxims of common fenfe and
experience, opened a door for error and for
crimes which are its natural confequences, and
which muft pervert feveral generations, and pro-
long the miferies of the country. Sophifms put
into the mouths of working men, who are not
capable of feeing the danger to which they conduct,* give a wrong turn to the mind, which
ceafes

* As for example, the people were at firft told that the nobility and privileged people were *fo numerous*, that they de-
voured every thing. Under this idea, they revolted, and
when

ceafes to be capable of diftinguifhing moral truths from moral deceptions, and right from wrong ; and thus the confcience of man, and that preference given by our nature to what is juft, over what is unjuft, deprives us of the moft folid foundation which our Creator has laid for our prefervation and happinefs.

The fubftitution of reafon for religion was another fund of mifchief. Reafon fhould purify, but not deftroy religion, which is the only check upon the paffions of men, by holding up to all, the hope of reward and fear of punifhment ; by giving fupport in adverfity, and moderation in profperity.* The man who hopes for a future reward, or fears a future punifhment, is as attentive to his conduct in a defert, and without witneffes, as when furrounded with the officers of juftice of a great city. Thofe who confider death as an eternal fleep have nothing to confult but their appetites and their will ; for, as their lot is to be like that of the brutes that perifh, fo, alfo will their conduct naturally be. Public in-

reafon for Religion (handwritten marginal note)

when the ci-devant privileged perfons demanded juftice, or at leaft compaffion, they faid, that *fo fmall a portion* of the nation did not merit attention.

* The manner in which the favage philofophers of the revolution have acted with regard to each other and to themfelves, is a ftriking example of this. Never was there lefs moderation nor lefs humanity fhewn by the chiefs of factions to each other. Men who had acted together as friends became fuddenly the moft implacable enemies ; and fo fenfible were thofe who funk in the ftruggle that no mercy was to be expected, that many of them have put an end to their own miferable exiftence. Such is the conduct of men when mercy and hope are banifhed from the human breaft.

fubor-

fubordination and private injuftice are the natural confequences of the derangement of mind which took place with the French revolution, and with which the world will always have to reproach the framers of the French conftitution.

We have feen the evils of their principles ; let us now review the confequences of, their adminiftration.

The people had become poorer and more miferable fince they paid no more feudal rents, nor any more tythes to the clergy ; and the nation had become greatly more indebted than ever fince it had feized the lands of the church.* The nobility had been humiliated to gratify the vanity of bankers and burgeffes, and the bankers and burgeffes were more humiliated than ever by being obliged to cringe to the off-fcourings of the nation.†

Bankers deſtroy the nobility and Bankers deſtroyed by the off-ſcourings of the Nation.

Commercial men had been pillaged that the poor might have plenty, and the poor were in greater want than ever of every neceffary of life. The duty on the entrance of towns had been taken off commodities to render them cheap, and

Merchants pillaged by the poor, who thereby became poorer.

* The affignats already iffued amounted to more than the whole value of the church lands ; and the annual fum which the nation was bound to pay as falaries to the clergy, was about five millions fterling, or rather more.

† In private tranfactions the bold and violent reduced the refpectable citizen to filence ; and in every public affembly the advantage in point of numbers was fo great in favour of the former, that the latter were fain to conceal their inferiority by keeping themfelves away.

they

they had become dearer than before.* The power of arbitrary imprisonment had been snatched from the hands of *one* monarch, and it was now exercised by *forty-seven thousand municipal officers.* The liberty of the press had been granted to all by a decree, but every word written or spoken against the general will† was a crime of the deepest dye, and never was liberty of opinion less enjoyed.

[handwritten margin note: 47,000 Bastilles for one liberty of opinion destroyed]

All religions had been permitted by a decree, but the religious of all sorts were insulted and oppressed; and, to conclude with all in one sentence, liberty had been decreed, but men were neither free to speak nor dress, except in the way that pleased the rulers of the Jacobins. Suspicion was as dangerous as conviction; denunciation was amongst the number of the patriotic duties of a citizen; it was become dangerous to be obnoxious, but not dangerous to be guilty.‡ Rags had become honourable and ragamuffins powerful, and industry and arrangement were banished

[handwritten margin note: Ragamuffins in Power.]

* In Paris the articles of life were dearer than ever; wine that used only to cost ten sols cost now fourteen or fifteen; and according to the expectation before the duties were taken off, it ought to have been reduced to five or six sols; other articles were in the same proportion. The reason was, that assignats and anarchy were so great enemies to industry, that the consumption of every necessary of life exceeded the produce.

† This was a very ingenious contrivance to correct the principle of insurrection and sedition, which were protected and encouraged under their former names, but were repressed as disobedience *à la volonté générale.*

‡ The criminal and civil codes were to be altered, and juries had been instituted, but justice had never taken its course. In party matters every thing went by the spirit of the times.

from

from the face of that miserable country. Poverty, discontent, and misery, had come to such a pitch under this complication of evils, that the still voice of reason could no longer be heard, nor the mighty promises of the saviours of the nation be believed; it was, therefore, necessary and natural to have recourse to the remedy of insurrection; the miseries of the people had began with one, and they were taught to think, that another might bring them to an end.

The general practice of the revolutionists has been to ask a little in order to take a great deal, and to promise a great deal and perform very little; by this double deception the moderate party was then made dupes, and constrained often to assist in doing what they did not approve of, but which they found themselves forced to do by necessity.

We have already seen the rapidity of that progress which men make in crimes, as soon as they have thrown off a regard for those rules which have, in civilised nations, been considered as the foundation of order and happiness; whoever will take the trouble to consider the consequences to which the declaration of rights led, and the impossibility which the legislative power experienced of reconciling their general principles to practice, will be convinced, that men should be very careful how they adopt such general principles; and that if modifications are necessary, it should be in the declaration of rights itself, and not in the application of them to practice.

The

The rights of savages is one thing, and the rights of men in civilised society another. Unluckily for the first promoters of insurrection, they mistook the one for the other, and promulgated the code in France, which might have done amongst some of the inhabitants of the forests of America, but which was totally unfit for any nation where regular government is established, and wealth accumulated by the industry of our ancestors;* and after once ostentatiously promulgated that code, they had the vanity and folly to think, that it would be possible to set bounds to its application.

This folly was most conspicuous in the law respecting the rights of voters in the primary assemblies for elections; and at the time we are speaking, the clamour of the passive citizens, who had no votes, became daily more and more serious, so that it was very evident, that the constitution would not long exist.

The friends of the constitution were now treated something in the same way that the friends of the ancient government had been treated three

* Far as the levelling principles have been attempted to be carried, their ultimate extent is not yet known, or, at least, has not been applied. If posterity are not bound by what their predecessors have done, why are the creditors of the state paid interest or reimbursed their capitals? What right has one man to exact rent from another for a house, which he himself neither built nor purchased, but which came to him by inheritance? According to the principles of the revolutionists applied in a pure manner, property would no more descend than personal virtue or vice; and no man would have a right to any thing which he had not made, or purchased with the fruits of his own labours.

*This has been pre-
cisely the Courst
of Things in all
ages.*

years before; the attachment which they professed to order and principle was called ariftocracy;
the rich merchants were all accufed of monopoly;
and to be a proprietor of a great magazine of
fugar or coffee, was as great crime in 1792 as to
be lord of a caftle was in 1789.

A ragged coat was now become more honourable than the embroidered epaulet, which the
citizens of Paris honoured and refpected fo much
in the firft days of the revolution. The citizens
now began to feel what it was to flatter the rabble,
and to accuftom and encourage them to attack
property; even Petion had complained, that he
had been placed between the people and his duty;* and thofe who had applauded the deftruction of feudal rights and gentlemen's caftles,
murmured and complained when the grocer's
fhops were pillaged.

*Even Petion com-
plained of popular
Tyranny.*

Things were in this ftate of diforder when the
Jacobin party finding that La Fayette had not
ventured to attempt any thing vigorous, and
that, therefore, the armies on the frontiers were
not to be confidered as likely to offer any ferious
oppofition to their defigns, determined to pufh
on boldly, to either fink under their enemies, or
to crufh the conftitution and the royal family.

The king had been induced to fhut up the
garden of the Thuilleries, on account of the perpetual mobs of people who affembled there, and
who infulted every perfon belonging to the royal
family who appeared in it. The queen had been

* Entre fon devoir et le bon peuple.

infulted

infulted in one of the walks, and the audacious and ungenerous populace were perpetually under the windows of the king's apartments, loading him with infults and injuries ;* and none of thofe perfons who were attached to his majefty's perfon or family could vifit the palace in peace and fafety.

The affembly, contrary to every principle of right, determined, that though the garden belonged to his majefty, yet the terrace on the fide next the affembly belonged to the nation. The confequence of this was, that the doors were opened and the nation occupied its terrace ; and the populace were ftirred up to diflike the king more than ever by an invidious and unmeaning diftinction,† to excite which was the real end in view, as the fimple poffeffion of a terrace was not in itfelf any object, particularly when the conftitution and the contract between the nation and the king was to be violated in order to obtain it. This fucceeded as the Jacobins could wifh ; the king attracted the fury which indivi-

* One of the methods of infult confifted in accufing the queen of every abominable crime ; another, in finging fongs where the king was treated with infolence and ridicule : the chorus of one of thefe will ferve as a fpecimen,

Nous te traiterons, gros Louis
Biribi,
A la façon de Barbari
Mon ami

† This decree was fo ridiculous, that though the affembly defired nothing more fincerely than to pafs it, yet one or two members oppofed it with fuch folid arguments, that the motion was on the point of being thrown out, when the mob in the galleries, by menaces and noife, filenced the oppofers, and obliged them to pafs the decree.

dual

dual mifery and difappointment occafioned, and which fhould have been directed againft the affembly.

The country having been declared in danger, and all the fections and other affemblies permament, the moment for explofion was ready, it only became neceffary to affign a motive and to give a fignal.*

Collot D'Herbois

The comedian, Collot d'Herbois, fince then become more famous, and a poet of the name of Chenier, put themfelves at the head of the paffive citizens on the fections, and demanded the depofition of the king. The active citizens protefted againft the legality of fuch petitions, and a week was fpent in hearing petitions and protefts, in that affembly, which, as guardian of the conftitution, ought to have punifhed feverely, or at leaft, refufed to liften to the petitioners, who, in propofing the depofition of the king, propofed the deftruction of the conftitution.

Petions Petition

When a week had been paft in this manner, to fave time the *infurgent commiffaries* of the fections employed Petion to prefent a general petition in the name of all the fections, and the infolent mayor of Paris revenged himfelf againft his fovereign by formally demanding his *fufpen-*

---

* When the country was declared in danger, a decree was made to arm the whole mafs of the people, but as mufkets could not be procured for fo many, it was decreed that they fhould be armed *with pikes.*

fion.

*n.** This petition, for which Petion certainly merited the severest punishment, was applauded, ordered to be printed, and sent to the eighty-three departments.

A committee of twelve members, composed of the Girondist party, was named to examine into the important but illegal question. The danger of pronouncing was thought so great, that the report was retarded from day to day, and, in fact, never given, as the question was decided soon after by the insurrection of the 10th of August.

12 Girondists

10. August

La Fayette had been accused in the assembly, for his journey to Paris; the double charge of deserting his post as commander, and of aiming at becoming protector in France, was brought against him, and contrary to the expectations of every one who knew any thing of the disposition of the assembly, he was absolved by a considerable majority. Those deputies who had spoken in his favour, were beat by the populace and dragged in the kennel. The insurrection was once more employed against the man who had first given it a sanction,† and the constitution

* Jacobins never call things by their true names. Suspension seemed to imply a momentary cessation of those functions which it was, however, firmly determined the unfortunate monarch should never again exercise.

† Æsop, perhaps, had a view to La Fayette when he wrote the fable of the boy who bit off his mother's ear when he was going to be hanged. If you had corrected me for the first offence, said he, I should not now have been here.

violated

violated in attacking the members of the assembly for their opinions in favour of its author.

Various attempts were made to render victory more secure, by obliging the king to send off the only troops that now remained to protect his person. The regiment of Swiss guards, composed originally of twenty-two hundred men, was reduced to between fifteen and sixteen hundred : The king refused, or at least delayed sending them all away, and only sent three hundred into Normandy ; a few remained in their barracks, at seven or eight miles distance from town, some were sick, and some absent, so that officers and men included, there remained about nine hundred at the palace of the Thuilleries.

During this regular operation of preparing the people for attack, and rendering the king incapable of defence, which in point of manœuvre yields to no military tactics whatever, the approach of the Duke of Brunswick and the Prussian army added a stimulus to the attacking party.

The brigands from Marseilles had been transferred from their first barracks, which were in one of the suburbs, to the section of the Cordeliers ; there they were near the center of the city, and positively in the most revolutionary quarter of Paris : as this change took place during the night, its object could not be considered as a very legitimate one.

On the 7th of August regular plans began to be laid for attacking the palace. It is not our
                                        intention

intention nor our bufinefs to enter into all the details which are pretty generally and well known; we fhall be contented with fhewing, as hitherto, the perfidious manœuvres of the revolutionary party to obtain victory, and their crimes and cruelties when it has been obtained.

We have already feen that the revolution has totally changed both men and meafures. That what we alledged to be true concerning the danger of its firft principles, is confirmed by experience; that the gradual fteps from infurrection to fettle their firft rights, and then to overturn them, has been not only a natural but neceffary confequence of the fetting out on falfe grounds at firft. What we have now to fee, is rather the crimes than the manœuvres of the revolution; the firft are nearly over, becaufe there will fhortly remain no enemy againft whom they can manœuvre. All principle, all plan of government, and all law being from the 10th of Auguft at an end, it became a perpetual conflict of parties at war with each other for power, but not for principles.

With the phantom of a conftitution, every thing capable of captivating opinion in neighbouring nations was at an end; but the rulers got poffeffion of riches, and the hireling tribe were all at their fervice. Till this fecond means of troubling the repofe of Europe fhall be wrefted from them alfo, they will ftill be formidable.*

Never

* Thofe who calculate on the duration of the revolution, fhould attentively confider, that while they can create affignats

Never had the approaches of a befieged city been carried with more art and fkill than the attack upon the king in the palace of the Thuillerics. We have feen that his guards have been difmiffed, his confidential fervants imprifoned, or frightened away ; royalty had been already degraded in the eyes of a turbulent populace, and the armed force of Paris, which might have made fome effort in his favour, had been diforganifed, and to crown all, was under the command of Petion, the moft cruel and revengeful of all the king's fervants.

It was well known at the palace and in the affembly, that an attack was meditated, but no effort was made by his Majefty [*Note* K.] to do any thing more than what felf-defence entitles every man to do, and what as firft magiftrate of the nation the conftitution made it his duty to do. The calumnies upon that head are all long fince done away, if to have confulted perfonal fafety, by all the means in his power, could be any foundation for accufation.

Infurrection, holy infurrection, was the only way to get rid of the king and the conftitution, and on the 9th of Auguft the procureur fyndic of the department of Paris, M. Rædever, announced to the affembly that it was preparing. Petion appeared at the bar, and was interrogated

nats in France, and with a ream of paper pay for the building of a hundred gun fhip ; and with another ream fend ten thoufand men into the field, that country muft be formidable ; but by degrees the impoffibility of fuch exertions approaches, and we may from that moment expect the return of fomething like order, for crimes will then coft money.

as

as to the state of the people ; he declared that
they were very discontented, and mutinously dis-
posed. The project of firing the cannon of
alarm, and founding the tocsin were announced,
yet the mayor, who had the whole national
guards at his command, and the cannon of alarm,
as well as the tocsin, in his power, spoke as if he
could not find any means to prevent what he
pretended to fear.

Never was a more complete imposition attempted to be practised upon mankind, than to
examine the mayor about his means of preventing what it was well known he was occupied in
preparing ;* nor never did any people let themselves in so dastardly a manner be juggled out
of a constitution, which with all its faults they

Imposition

---

* Besides all the other proofs, the petition for suspending
the king presented by Petion, and sent to the eighty-three
departments by a decree of the assembly, was a plain and well
authenticated proof of his and their wishes, particularly, as
of forty-eight sections, twenty-two had protested against the
petition, and no notice had been taken of their protest ? besides, the sending to the eighty-three departments was either
to influence their opinion, or to know their will ; if it had
been this latter, the assembly should have addressed the people of Paris to demand peace and a suspension of their plans,
until the views of the departments should be known ; but
this would not have answered their purpose, for a great majority throughout France was for the king and the constitution.
The reveries about the republics of Condorcet and Brissot
had not made great progress in the provinces. They were
not so well adapted for seducing the opinion of the lower
class as the principles of the first assembly ; and it was only
by decorating the name of republic with the word equality,
that it went down at all. It is to be presumed, when the
discovery shall have penetrated into France, that men are not
more equal under a republic than under monarchy, their illu-
sion will vanish and they will see things in their true colours.

*Condorcet
Brissot
Equality.*

R R

ftill wifhed to maintain. The difpofitions, as
well as the conduct of Petion were well known,
and the national guards ought to have chofen
a chief who would give them permiffion to act.
If it was lawful to rebel, *they fhould have rebelled
againft the mayor* when he refufed to let them
carry arms without particular orders, except in
their own fections, while the rabble, fuperior to
all orders, were preparing to attack the palace.

Here is a good and awful leffon for thofe men
who are foolifh enough to oppofe law to revolt
and rebellion, when they fhould only oppofe
force. The conftitution which all France had
repeatedly fworn to maintain, was going to be
openly attacked by an armed rabble, and the
foldiers of that conftitution, attached to it by
duty, by principle, and by oaths, in obedience
to one of its regulations, which faid that the
mayor was to give command to the military,
without which it could never act, ftood peaceably by, and let the whole be overturned.

For men fo ftupid or fo pufillanimous it was
not worth while to make laws, nor eftablifh principles, for they were incapable of applying
them when made, or of protecting them from
deftruction.

It has already been faid that the council-gene-
ral of the Hotel de Ville was difpofed to fupport
the conftitution and the king; and as Petion was
obliged to obey this council, he began by deceiving it till the hour fhould arrive when he might
act for himfelf. The mayor in order to prevent
the council and the department, both of which
                                                        were

were superior to him, from penetrating his defigns, or at least from having any pretext for
superseding him in his authority, stationed some
troops to defend the palace, and gave an order
in writing to M. Mandat, the commander of
that guard, to oppose force to force, should the
palace be attacked.*

Mandat

The council at the Hotel de Ville was permanent, like all the other assemblies, but in the
present crisis was better attended than the others.
The assemblies of the forty-eight sections were
permanent by law, but could not be said to be so
in fact, for most of the citizens were, as national
guards, occupied at different posts in their respective quarters of the city.† At twelve o'clock
at night a body of those men who were determined to destroy the constitution, separated from a
meeting which they had held; a few of them
went to each of the forty-eight sections, and in-
stantly taking possession of the books and papers,
suspended their deputies in the general council at
the Hotel de Ville, and named some of themselves in their place: those new deputies set off

Revolution in the Hotel de Ville.

* This order has been considered by some as a proof that
Petion really meant to exert himself against the people. But
it is evident that it was only given as a blind to the opposite
party, as the first thing done was to get possession of that
order, and to destroy it. Petion was apparently under the
greatest anxiety till he knew that this order was destroyed.

† The king's ministers had applied to the national assembly for a decree that would permit the national guards to rally
themselves wherever danger might require; but Petion opposed this proposition, so that this measure so necessary for
public security was stifled at the very moment it was most necessary.

immediately,

immediately, and by violence expelled such members of the council as were there. Petion the mayor, Manuel, and Danton alone, were not suspended.*

Petion Manuel Danton not suspended

By this sudden, violent, and illegal step, all opposition from the common council was prevented; and the virtuous Petion had colleagues with whom he could act, and from whom he was certain of assistance.

The first use made of their new power by those intruders, was to send for M. Mandat, the commander of the guards stationed at the palace. The unfortunate Mandat, undecisive between his duty to his sovereign and his obedience to the town council, hesitated to obey, although totally ignorant of the change that had taken place. He was sent for a second time, and with reluctance obeyed. When arrived at the Hotel de Ville, he was interrogated, treated like a criminal, and ordered to prison; on descending the stairs, under a guard, his brains were blown out, and his body thrown into the river.† By this murder

Mandat

assassinated

---

* The suspended deputies were ordered to return quietly to their respective homes, and to say nothing. This is the mode that highwaymen dismiss those whom they have robbed. Perhaps, without this injunction, enforced by threats, some of the members might have gone to the palace and disclosed what had happened, which, if they had done, Mandat would not have obeyed; and, perhaps, the department might have taken some violent measures, for there was yet an interval of six hours to be dreaded by the new magistrates, before their forces, the rabble, should be fairly on the march.

† The order of Petion was searched for, was found, and destroyed. This is a clear proof, if any were wanting, that the

murder the order of Petion, to oppose force to force, was suppressed, and the few guards who were at the palace were left without any com-mander, and without knowing what was become of him, or who to obey.

Let thofe who cry out perpetually for affem-blies of the people think of this, and confider with what facility a very few, and thofe the moft worthlefs of the people, by affuming the name of the whole at the hour of midnight, overturned the conftitution by depriving its anointed king of the only means of protection which he had left; never after this let the fignal given by the infam-ous Charles IX. from the tocfin of the Louvre, be cited as an example of kingly government, with-out joining to it the fignal which at this hour was heard from the cathedral of Notre Dame,* as an example of what the leaders of the people are capable of doing.

During all this time, the audacious Marfellois were affembling and leading on the infurgents,

the whole was concerted between the new municipality and the mayor, otherwife they could not have known that fuch an order exifted. It proves alfo, that to deftroy that order was one of the chief motives for killing the unfortunate com-mander.

* It is not pretended that the carnage of the 10th of Au-guft was equal to that of the St. Barthelemew for the number of its victims, but it was fully equal for the cruelties exercifed, and was brought about by an abufe of power (unwarrantably feized upon by men who called themfelves reprefentatives of the people) full as flagrant as that of Charles IX. the one is an example of the crimes of monarchical, and the other of po-pular goverment, but they are equally odious.

collected

collected from all quarters of Paris, and compofed of the loweft of the people, but chiefly from the Fauxbourgs St. Antoine,* and St. Marceau.

A part of this banditti, armed with pikes, arrived at the Place de Caroufelle, behind the palace, at about feven in the morning, and obtained admiffion into the court, by pretending to come for the protection of the king; but this army of pikemen was no fooner admitted, than it manifefted a very different intention, and began to pervert the fpirit of the national guards, who had been there during the night.

With fo many precautions and manœuvres to enfeeble the defence of the palace, and deliver the king and his family into the hands of his enemies their fuccefs could not be very problematical; but the democratic tyrants wifhed to make " affurance doubly fure," and M. Rœderer, the procureur fyndic of the department, at the head of a deputation of its members, put the finifhing ftroke to the work by deceiving the king, and thereby prevailing upon him to go to the national affembly.†

In

* Thefe were always the quarters of the city famous for *petit peuple*, fomething like St. Giles's and Seven Dials in London. St. Antoine is by much the moft extenfive, and furnifhed three times as many as the other; the whole amounted to about twenty thoufand. The democrats of the firft affembly had flattered the St. Antoine heroes by calling it the Fauxbourg de Gloire.

† The attachment of the directors of the department to royalty and the conftitution was known, but it was compofed of timid men, and all of them a little tinctured with democracy.

In following the council of Rœderer, the king is more to be blamed than, perhaps, in any action of his life; firm in refifting the friends who coun- felled him to quit his palace, and truft himfelf into the hands of the friends of the conftitution, he yielded to the advice of an enemy,* and de- livered himfelf into the hands of that affembly, which had applauded the petition prefented but a few days before for his fufpenfion.

Since the king had accepted the conftitution, and fworn to maintain it, he had fhewn the moft determined refolution to keep his word, and had refifted every offer,† and every tempation to the contrary; there can, therefore, remain little doubt, but that he embraced this fatal determina- tion from a belief, that it was the only method of preventing bloodfhed; that the term of kingly

cracy. We have always feen, that fuch men are incapable, upon any ferious crifis, of taking the meafures they ought to take, and that the lovers of anarchy have an immenfe advan- tage over them.

* Roederer himfelf could never be miftaken as a friend to the king. He was in fact, a man who, acting only from per- fonal motives, made court to all parties, and took care not to offend any openly. Even in the prefent cafe, when he led the monarch and his family captive, he might and did boaft of having faved their lives. The queen oppofed herfelf ftrong- ly to this meafure.

† For the offers made to the king by the royalifts and con- ftitutional parties, who had coalized in order to oppofe the anarchifts, fee *Note* L. at the end; as none of thefe were at- tempted to be put in execution, we fhould not have noticed them, were it not to prove, that the party of moderate re- volutionifts could confpire as well as others, as foon as they could no longer rule.

X x dominion

dominion in France was near approaching, he had long had reafon to fuppofe, and ever fince the 20th of June muft have been certain. But though he muft have conceived, that his enemies wanted his throne, he had, probably, no idea, that they wanted his life, nor that of his family. Royalty had long been a burthen, and ceafing to act as a king, he determined to fubmit in the manner that was the leaft likely to be fatal to his people, to his family, and to himfelf.

We have already obferved, that the details of this terrible day are foreign to the prefent work; befides, this day alone would require a volume: we muft, therefore, only look to the conduct of the leaders of the people, and ftill follow them out in their villany and in their cruelty.

On the arrival of the royal family at the affembly, they were not received with any ftudied marks of difrefpect, for the queftion of which party was the ftrongeft was not yet decided.

The king, on quitting the palace, had given orders, that no refiftance fhould be made,* he

* The words of the king were, " *Allons, Meffieurs, il n'y a plus rien a faire ici.*" This was a direct order to abandon all idea of refiftance, and even to abandon the palace itfelf; and had it been tranfmitted to the guards and gentlemen who were in the apartments, would have prevented the battle, and thereby greatly diminifhed the horrors of that bloody day; but in the midft of the confufion it was forgotten, and this made the guards in the palace think that the king had bafely abandoned them. M. Bertrand in his letter to the prefident of the national convention, fays, that there were fo many witneffes to the truth of this fact, that it is impoffible to doubt its reality.

had

had even ordered that it fhould be evacuated; but, through the confufion which reigned at the time, his orders were not communicated to the Swifs guards, nor to the other foldiers who were in the palace; and it is probable, that if the king had remained in the palace, or if the order which he left had been attended to, that day would not have been fo fatal to his party.

Though the Swifs, and all the guards and other perfons in the palace, loft courage when they found themfelves abandoned, and thought that they were betrayed, yet the victory was at firft on their fide, and it is aftonifhing how they made head againft fuch a numerous enemy. There were not above 1000 perfons in all who defended the palace, and who were difperfed in different courts and apartments; their affailants had cannon, while thofe in the palace had none; yet above 4000 of the affailants were killed, and the victory would, in all human probability, have been decidedly in favour of royalty, had its brave defenders not thought they were abandoned by his majefty, and left to be facrificed.* There are, therefore, many reafons for thinking, that without the infiduous advice of Rœderer, the Jacobin

---

* If they had not thought this, their firft outfet having been victorious, the national guards would have joined them, as thofe brave fellows always prefer the ftrongeft fide, and it would have ended like the fufillade of the Champ de Mars, the caufe of order would have triumphed, and, perhaps, time might have operated gradual changes on the conftitution, that would have rendered it capable of maintaining itfelf.

faction

faction would not have fucceeded, notwithftand-
ing all its precautions.*

10 Aug.

The 10th of Auguft is, no doubt, the day on
which the anarchifts prevailed completely ; but
there is not a day in which they were either more
contemptible or more horrible. The cowardice
of the morning was equalled only by the cruelties
of the afternoon ; cowardly combatants they became mercilefs conquerors, and the affembly fet
the feal upon its infignificance and its perfidy
to the nation, by becoming the paffive inftrument of the faction which ruled.

No fooner had victory declared on the fide of
the people, than the fanguinary meffengers of
the mob and the affembly vied with each other
in humbling his majefty and exalting the leader
of the factious, the mayor of Paris. The decrees
of that memorable day are too defcriptive of the
abject and mean fpirit of the affembly,† but that
of

* The contraft between the 14th of July, 1789, and the
10th of Auguft, 1792, is very ftriking. At the period firft
mentioned, the peaceable and quiet inhabitants of a large city
rife in a mafs, and put to flight, without bloodfhed or refiftance, a very numerous military force ; on the 10th of Auguft,
a very confiderable military power is oppofed, and at the firft
with great fuccefs, to a mafs of people, bred up to infurrection and plunder, and well fupplied with arms and ammunition, which laft the guards of the palace wanted. The Marfellois and their companions were commanded by General
Wefterman, a Pruffian, and had abundance of ammunition,
each man having 100 cartridges, while the guards fent to protect the palace had only three charges.

† During the whole of the day the mob fent addreffes and
propofitions to the affembly, fome of which were ridiculoufly
extra-

of their hatred to royalty, not to be preserved as
specimens of their manner of acting.

It was decreed first, that his majesty should be
sent to the palace of the Luxemburg, with his
family. The decree of suspension was only pro-
visional, the civil list was suspended, but a revenue for the king was to be assigned. There
appeared in all this *some remains* of a regard for
royalty, but no—These decrees were to deceive
the eighty-three departments of France, seventy-
three of which were known to be in favour of
royalty, and a miserable prison, hard treatment,
and the bare necessaries of nature, were for
Louis XVI. and his unfortunate and amiable family. This more than Machiavilian duplicity and
savage cruelty was planned in presence of that
interesting assemblage of suffering goodness, in-
nocence, and beauty, that would have disarmed
any *other* band of savages and robbers, except a
French national assembly.*

All men are not obliged to be brave, for bravery is a natural quality, and not an acquired
accomplishment; the assembly might, therefore,
be excused for the conduct it pursued while
under the immediate influence of personal fear,
were it not that, in proportion as that fear wore

extravagant, and all were received with enthusiasm, and
whatever was proposed was decreed by acclamation and unanimity. [*See the Appendix Note* M.]

* As it is esteemed a republican virtue to call things by
their true names, besides, as brigandage and murder have
become honourable in France, it is to be presumed that the
calm representatives of the French people will have no ob-
jection to their own rules being applied to themselves.

off,

off, its decrees became more cruel and unjuſt.
At the end of the fourth day the king and his family found the proviſional ſuſpenſion converted
into impriſonment, in which all the comforts, and
many of the neceſſaries of life, were denied them;
while the aſſembly added to the mockery of the
injuſtice by aſſigning them a fixed ſum of money*
for ſupplying their wants, which was never intended to be paid.

The aſſembly was afraid to ſhow their intentions till all the faithful attendants of the monarch had been diſperſed; and it was not till after
the few gentlemen were diſperſed who had followed him to the national aſſembly, that the
royal family was put under the care of its moſt
cruel enemies, Petion and Manuel.

Petion & Manuel

The monarchy of France had ceaſed morally
to exiſt ever ſince the 14th of July 1789, and
an end was put even to the ſhadow of kingly
power by this laſt inſurrection. Hitherto a jumble of principles ill-combined had been the occaſion of much miſery, misfortune, and crime; but
what follows was reſtrained by no principles
whatever, by no government, nor even by the
appearance of one; and, if what is paſt is a ſpe-
cimen of the conduct of men under the combined
influence of miſtaken principles and violent paſſions, what follows is a ſtill more terrible one of
what men do when under the influence of paſ-

* Half a million annually was propoſed, or about twenty
thouſand pounds; but decrees were now no more than the
words of an intoxicated man—never thought of after.

ſion

Passion only

fion only, without the controul of any principle at all. In the firft part of the revolution people talked of right and juftice, though they do not feem to have been underftood ; but, in the latter part of their career, the democratic leaders have only talked of neceffity, expediency, and feverity.

END OF VOL. I.